LEGENDS, MONSTERS, OR
SERIAL MURDERERS?

LEGENDS, MONSTERS, OR SERIAL MURDERERS?

THE REAL STORY BEHIND AN ANCIENT CRIME

DIRK C. GIBSON

PRAEGER

AN IMPRINT OF ABC-CLIO, LLC
Santa Barbara, California • Denver, Colorado • Oxford, England

Copyright 2012 by ABC-CLIO, LLC

Library of Congress Cataloging-in-Publication Data

Gibson, Dirk Cameron, 1953–
  Legends, monsters, or serial murderers? : the real story behind an ancient crime / Dirk C. Gibson.
    p. cm.
  Includes bibliographical references and index.
  ISBN 978–0–313–39758–5 (hard copy : alk. paper) — ISBN 978–0–313–39759–2 (ebook)
  1. Serial murderers—History. 2. Serial murders—History. I. Title.
  HV6505.G53 2012
  364.152′3209—dc23   2011043413

ISBN: 978–0–313–39758–5
EISBN: 978–0–313–39759–2

16 15 14 13 12   1 2 3 4 5

This book is also available on the World Wide Web as an eBook.
Visit www.abc-clio.com for details.

Praeger
An Imprint of ABC-CLIO, LLC

ABC-CLIO, LLC
130 Cremona Drive, P.O. Box 1911
Santa Barbara, California 93116-1911

This book is printed on acid-free paper ∞

Manufactured in the United States of America

This book is respectfully dedicated to a few of the significant others in my life.

Mark S. Agness was an exceptionally nice man and a talented poker player and Uno fiend. His widow Laura, daughter Emily, and Cooper, and I will always miss him but enjoy the wonderful memories.

My brother Dennis has always been incredibly generous and caring and supportive. Same with Si Ming. Without Aunt Noo-Noo (Lauria Garcia) and my main man Lionel Beatwood (aka Dean), this book would have been impossible.

Mitchell and Erica inspire and motivate me. Remember, kids, just do well in school. And look out for the clown and the roadrunner. I suppose that depends on what you mean by clown.

CONTENTS

INTRODUCTION

This is a very different type of book about serial murder. It is about the early days of serial murder, before the modern era. Ancient civilizations suffered from serial killers just as contemporary societies do. But that fact has largely escaped the attention of the serial murder literature.

In times past, people did not believe that other humans could mistreat their fellow man as some serial slayers do, so it is my belief that they created a variety of supernatural phenomena to explain away premodern serial murder. Cultures all around the world have accepted the reality of a series of mythic entities since ancient times. But is it likely that mankind really was visited by werewolves, vampires, and their supernatural kin? I think not.

This introduction sets the stage for my study of historic serial murder. My purpose here is to briefly introduce you to the main concepts documented in this book. Four main sections are presented, beginning with the recognition that serial murder is widely perceived to be a relatively recent phenomenon. But this is not the case, I suggest in my second introductory point. The third subject discussed is the misidentification of serial murder victims as prey of the supernatural, and we conclude with a brief identification of the main types of premodern serial killers.

SERIAL MURDER IS PERCEIVED AS A RECENT PHENOMENON

An examination of the serial murder literature strongly suggests that this is a relatively recent recidivist offense, a modern crime. There were substantial increases in the incidence of serial killing in the 1950s and again two decades later that some observers have mistaken as the genesis of this crime. Others have pointed to the age of industrialization as the origin of this offense. And it may not be a coincidence that the development of newspapers and substantial improvement in literacy occurred at about the same time.

A survey of serial murder authorities has documented the prevalent perception that serial murder is exclusively a contemporary concern. For instance, Colin Wilson asserted that Eusebius Pieydagnelle, who killed in 1871, "has a claim to be the first serial killer."[1] Another authority asserted that it is commonly believed that serial killing is a contemporary phenomenon.[2]

Multiple books and articles have reported that serial murder is an unprecedented type of crime.[3] A study of serial slayings in Spokane, Washington, observed that in the 1960s and 1970s the notion of serial murder came into existence.[4] But the recency of serial murder is questionable.

SERIAL MURDER IS NOT A RECENT PHENOMENON

It seems that there is a widespread perception that serial murder is a relatively contemporary crime. But that does not appear to be true, and this book documents my belief with 14 cases of premodern serial killers. This contention of mine is not entirely new, of course. Serial murder expert Katherine Ramsland correctly noted, "Contrary to what many people believe, serial killing did not begin with Jack the Ripper in 1888."[5]

Serial slayers, like mass murderers, are not truly a novel criminal and social phenomenon, according to serial murder authorities Ronald M. Holmes and James De Burger.[6] Another recent analysis corroborated Holmes and De Burger: "Serial killers have been with us for longer than some might think. While there is a general impression that serial murder has emerged only in the last few years, this perception cannot be supported."[7] I agree with these serial murder authorities that this crime is not merely a modern malady but an ancient human activity.

SERIAL MURDER MISTAKEN FOR SUPERNATURAL ENTITIES

If there has always been serial murder, why has that fact escaped widespread public and expert recognition? The answer to that question takes us out of the realm of criminology and law enforcement and into the sphere of the supernatural. Premodern people ascribed the crimes committed by serial slayers to sinister supernatural species.

Chapter 1 develops the argument that virtually every ancient and premodern culture accepted the reality of these supernatural entities. In Africa, Asia, Europe, the Middle East, and the Americas, there was widespread public acceptance of and belief in vampires, werewolves, and the rest of these mythic creatures. I would suggest that the empirical evidence of the existence of these evil entities was the human carnage produced by premodern serial killers.

Supernatural subjects have enormous public appeal. Even today in contemporary industrialized nations, there is substantial popular belief in these nonexistent organisms. People believe that they are vampires, werewolves, or witches, and some believe that they are tormented by demons. Dragons are similarly real for many.

I intend no disrespect to those who accept the reality of these mythic creatures. But there is no credible evidence to the best of my knowledge that substantial numbers of ancient people were victimized by vampires, werewolves, or any of the other purported supernatural killers. Yet someone or something was killing premodern men and women in sufficient numbers to create the social need to invent explanations to understand the phenomenon.

The criminals in the first three sections of the book engaged in serial murders reminiscent of supernatural entities. Some were mistaken for werewolves, like Gilles Garnier, the Werewolf of Chalons, and Peter Stubbe, while others were thought to be vampires (Erzsebet Bathory, Vincenzo Verzini, and Joseph Vacher) or witches like Catherine Monvoison and Gilles de Rais. In several cases, the same serial slayer was considered to be both a werewolf and a vampire or thought of as being a witch, a vampire, and a werewolf. What the historic public record reveals is that when people believe in and expect to be victimized by vampires, werewolves, or witches, that is precisely what they believe happens.

TYPES OF PREMODERN SERIAL MURDER

The types of serial murderers probably have not changed appreciably over time. Some crimes were sexual in nature, while others seemed more motivated by cannibal or religious inclinations. In addition to the serial murderers mistaken for supernatural monsters, there were two main types of premodern serial murder: aristocratic and commercial.

Vampiric serial killers are discussed in Part I of this book, and those who appeared to be werewolves are included in Part II. Part III introduces witch-like serial slayers.

Aristocratic serial slayers abounded in ancient times. In Part IV, a trio of premodern rulers will be explored for their serial murder activity, Queen Nzinga of Ndongo (Angola), Vlad the Impaler, and the dowager empress Cixi. Each of these individuals took advantage of their aristocratic status to murder with seeming impunity for relatively lengthy periods of time.

The other main type of premodern serial killer was the killer motivated by money. Commercial serial killers have been a historic reality as long as there have been people. Locusta, La Tofania, and Andreas Bichel typified this variety of serial slayer in Part V. Those especially interested in serial murder for profit might also examine my 2010 Praeger publication *Serial Killing for Profit*, which documented the reality of commercial serial killing through a dozen cases.

1

INVISIBLE SERIAL MURDER

The majority of serial murder studies identify the United States as the home of most serial slayers. However, that strikes me as counterintuitive because the United States has existed for less than 250 years, while other nations have far longer histories. If Americans invented and/or developed serial murder, why has there always been a smattering of acknowledged cases?

Is it possible that there is a terrible dimension of the American psyche making us relatively more inclined to commit serial homicide? The difference cannot be attributable to the greater availability of firearms in the United States because serial killers are not limited to that particular type of weapon. Why is it that America has suffered a disproportionate number of serial slayers? Perhaps it hasn't.

The serial murder rate has most likely corresponded closely to the growth in world population. It is my opinion that a substantial percentage of serial murders throughout ancient times, the medieval era, and the Dark Ages were simply not recognized for what they were. Instead, they were attributed to one of a half dozen mythic enemies of mankind.

Is it a coincidence that the number of vampire and werewolf reports began to decline at the same time that serial murder reports began to increase? The same is true of witchcraft accusations, demon infestations, and other types of monsters, although dragons admittedly disappeared a bit earlier. The increasing recognition by police and the media of the serial murder phenomenon led to replacement of supernatural human killers with a distinctive breed of humans: the serial murderer.

There are those who cling to belief in the existence of vampires, werewolves, other monsters, and even dragons. Nevertheless, substantial numbers of our ancestors most likely were not killed by any of these mythic monsters. So what terrible force was killing and abducting enough people on a regular basis to give rise to public belief in our assortment of supernatural slayers? Serial murderers are the only reasonable alternative.

Table 1.1
Serial Murder Incidence by Decade, 40 BCE to 2000

Number of Decade	Decade	Number of Cases	Percentage of Total
1	41–50	1	.1%
2	500	1	.1%
3	1400	2	.2%
4	1500	2	.2%
5	1520	2	.2%
6	1540	2	.2%
7	1570	2	.2%
8	1590	2	.2%
9	1600	2	.2%
10	1660	1	.1%
11	1670	1	.1%
12	1700	5	.5%
13	1710	1	.1%
14	1720	2	.2%
15	1780	2	.2%
16	1790	2	.2%
17	1800	10	1%
18	1810	4	.4%
19	1820	9	.9%
20	1830	6	.6%
21	1840	6	.6%
22	1850	5	.5%
23	1860	7	.7%
24	1870	12	1.2%
25	1880	12	1.2%
26	1890	17	1.7%
27	1900	17	1.7%
28	1910	47	4.7%
29	1920	46	4.6%
30	1930	57	5.7%
31	1940	45	4.5%
32	1950	49	4.9%
33	1960	122	12.2%
34	1970	208	20.8%
35	1980	286	28.6%
36	1990	240	24.%
37	2000	51	5.1%

Serial murder seems to have occurred on a very limited but relatively consistent basis throughout history or at least for the last 2,000 years. Then came a slight but very meaningful bump in the early years of the twentieth century followed by a half decade at a stable rate. In the 1950s, a quantum change of some sort seems to have occurred, as reflected in Table 1.1.

CAUSES OF HISTORIC SERIAL KILLER UNDERSTATEMENT

It is easy for observers in the twenty-first century to appreciate the relatively thorough contemporary documentation and record keeping of serial murder. This criminal phenomenon has been studied for more than 100 years, and it is certainly not a new or mysterious act anymore. But that was not the case previously in world history, when people faced an entire set of frightening problems popularly accepted during those ancient times. This section examines six historically accepted lethal entities: (1) dragons, (2) demons, (3) witchcraft, (4) werewolves, (5) vampires, and (6) other monsters.

Dragons

Throughout history, there have been reports of deaths caused by dragons, necessitating knights to vanquish the beasts. It is likely that dragons never killed anyone but that public opinion at the time felt that such creatures existed and killed people. Even today, the existence of dragons remains a debatable issue in some circles. "The dragon is a large lizard-like reptile of which there are a number of different species. In order to identify all the different types of dragons that the student may encounter, it is useful to compare them with a standard type. The most obvious candidate for comparison is the common European dragon, *Draco occidentalis magnus*," Drake contended.[1] The issue of whether dragons have existed and are real is vexing for some, complicated by the lack of an acceptable working definition for the term "dragon."[2]

The existence of dragons has been accepted by some since ancient times. Although the precise date when dragons initially appeared in myth is not known, they can be traced back as far as 4000 BCE.[3] Dragons assumed special salience in China, where a typology included nine different types: Tianlong, Shenlong, Fucanglong, Dilong, Yinglong, Qiulong, Panlong, Huanglong, and Long Wang.[4]

People unaware of the existence of serial murder might well explain inexplicable deaths involving broken and burned bodies as being the work of supernatural creatures like dragons. Western dragons traditionally have been considered to be a symbol of evil. They could reportedly fly and breathe fire and were popularly perceived as monsters to be destroyed.[5]

According to prevailing European folklore, dragons ate maidens and then were slain by knights in retaliation. Some Native American tribes passed on tales about fire-breathing dragons capable of burning crops and carrying away animals as large as dogs, cows, and even buffalo. The nasty nature of Western dragons was frequently reported; their razor-like teeth, sharp claws, and ability to breathe fire made them dangerous beasts that heroes must vanquish.[6]

Demons

Demons were considered decidedly dangerous and unpleasant phenomenon. One might expect that in an entity directly the opposite of an angel. It was believed that the abduction of men's souls resulted from the diabolical deeds of demons.

Sixteenth-century demonologist Alphonsus de Spina categorized demons in 10 ways; fates, poltergeists, incubi and succubi, marching hosts, familiar demons, nightmare demons, sexually created demons, deceptive demons, clean demons, and demons who deceive women.[7] In 1589, Peter Binsfeld correlated seven demons to their devilish domain: Lucifer with pride, Mammon with avarice, Asmodeus with lechery, Satan with anger, Beelzebub with gluttony, Leviathan with envy, and Belphegor with sloth. A three-tiered demonic hierarchy was proposed by Father Sebastien Michaelis in his 1612 book *Admirable History*. The First Hierarchy included Beelzebub, Leviathan, Asmodeus, Balbwerith, Astaroth, Verrine, Gressil, and Sonnellion. Carreau, Carnivean, Oeillet, Rosier, and Verrier made up the middle tier. The Third Hierarchy included Belias, Olivier, and Invart.[8]

The Christian Broadcasting Network discussed them in a 2009 message by James N. Watkins titled "Are Demons, Exorcisms Real?"[9] This interest in demons has not recently developed. Demons have, on the contrary, been a historic concern.

Demons were believed to have existed to torment humans. According to Merrill F. Unger, demons are pervasive enemies of man dedicated to the often tragic damage they inflict on human beings. Even more frightening is this assessment of demonic prowess: "Their superhuman intellect is accompanied by superphysical strength. . . . Perverted power and strength are thus conspicuous attributes of fallen angels."[10] Wilson Miles Van Dusen hypothesized that there were two types of demons: those of a "higher" or a "lower" nature. These lower demons have been termed "stupid and malicious," and their purpose involves teasing and tormenting humans for their enjoyment. Nevertheless, they frequently have caused disaster and death.[11]

Witchcraft

Witchcraft involved sorcery, the casting of spells with the assistance of the Devil. Some claim that the belief in witchcraft began in Europe toward the end of the Middle Ages. The witchcraft phenomenon did not progress rapidly at first. It is believed that the European witchcraft movement began slowly in the Pyrenees and the Alps.[12]

Popular belief in witches has characterized nearly every culture in all lands from ancient times until the present day. One extended witchcraft "craze" lasted longer than 400 years, from the fourteenth through the seventeenth centuries, and resulted in the death of millions in Europe between the Middle Ages and the end of the age of reason.[13] By the end of the sixteenth century, many Europeans were convinced that their continent was rife with witches.[14]

Perhaps the best evidence of public belief in witches was witch burning. It took 200 years for European countries to burn an estimated 100,000 witches. Other accounts suggested much higher totals. A figure of 9,000,000 burned witches was widely accepted as the total of executions from witch trials. But more recent analyses have substantially reduced this amount, and now most estimates range between 50,000 and 100,000.[15]

Witches were believed to injure people in a variety of ways; they ate their victims while they were still alive or killed and buried them before digging up and consuming the corpses. In ancient Greece, Diana and Hecate were believed to be able to "harm the living with nightmares and madness." Witches had the power to kill people through magic spells, as it was commonly believed. King James of Scotland mentioned in his book *Demonologie* that "witches can cause death by burning a person's picture."[16]

Fourteen women were accused of murder by bewitching and acts of malice at St. Osyth, Essex, England, in 1582. Trials such as these occurred for more than 400 years throughout Europe, revealing great public fear concerning the ability of witches to kill. Witchcraft was routinely blamed for damage to people, crops, or livestock that was actually caused by nature, poison, or other causes.[17]

Werewolves

It is believed by some that there are three main types of werewolf cases: "false," or lycanthropic disorder cases; legitimate werewolf cases; and theriomorphism. Werewolves have been observed since ancient times. One of the oldest known werewolf tales involved the Greek mythological figure Zeus, who became furious when Lykaon gave him human flesh to eat, so he turned Lykaon into a wolf.[18]

In 500 BCE, Scythians recorded their belief that the Neuri were werewolves, and in 400 BCE, Damarchus, an Arcadian "werewolf," won the top award in boxing at the Olympics. Petronius, a Roman official in the court of Emperor Nero, wrote about a werewolf case in 60 CE.[19]

We might consider a final fact about the nature of werewolves. There is a medical syndrome known as hypertrichosis, which produces excessive hair growth all over the human body. It is a rare condition, but abcnews .com reported on a case in 2007.[20]

Stories about werewolves were commonly believed by Europeans in the Middle Ages. During the medieval era, European and Baltic countries were characterized by widespread public belief in werewolves. In Russia, people believed in werewolves and werebears, and Scotland was preyed on by werecats. The Eskimos feared wereseals, and in Japan there were reports of werefoxes. And Africa was victimized by wereleopards, werehyenas, and the werehippopotamus. In ancient China, one might encounter a werecat, weretiger, or even a werecrocodile.[21]

France was particularly thought to be infested with werewolves during the sixteenth century. It was suggested that France was afflicted with "an epidemic of werewolves." The years between 1520 and 1630 constituted a peak period for werewolf sightings with 30,000 recorded cases in France.[22]

"There is another deadly creature roaming parts of the United Kingdom which has also killed people, and that is the Welsh Werewolf," a 2009 BBC report asserted.[23] A study of French werewolves noted that numerous werewolf cases were heard in the courts involving murder and cannibalism. Several were convicted of murdering small children and ingesting some of their flesh. According to the "Werewolf Timeline," werewolves were believed responsible for several attacks on monks in 617 CE.[24]

The following public proclamation was posted in the town square of Dole, France, in 1573:

> According to the advertisement made to the sovereign Court of Parliament at Dole, that, in the territory of Espagny, Salvange, Courchapon and the neighboring villages, has often been seen and met, for some time past, a werewolf, who, it is said, has already seized and carried off several little children, so that they have not been seen since, and since he has attacked and done injury in the country to some horsemen, who kept him off only with great difficulty and danger to their persons; the said Court, desiring to prevent any greater danger, has permitted, and does permit, those who are abiding or dwelling in the said places and others, notwithstanding all edicts concerning the chase, to assemble with pikes, halberds, arquebuses, and sticks to chase and to pursue said werewolf in every place where they may find or seize him; to tie and kill, without incurring any pain or penalties. Given at the meeting of the said Court, on the thirteenth day of the month of September 1573.[25]

The definitive history of Scandinavian werewolves was written by Olaus Magnus. This sixteenth-century church official was also a historian of some reputation. He vividly described a werewolf Christmas Eve holiday tradition: "When a human habitation has been detected by the werewolves, they besiege it with ferocity, trying to break in the doors, and if they do so, they devour all the human beings."[26]

Vampires

Vampires have been noted in most cultures and countries of the world at one time or another. They may have drawn attention away from serial murderers. Terrible tragedies and mysterious mishaps, such as unsolved murders, were frequently attributed to vampires.

One authority asserted that 500 CE was when the initial public mention of a vampire occurred. Others have placed the initial vampires much earlier. The first vampiric figures and legends may well date back approximately 4,000 years to the time of Mesopotamia. The ancient Greek civilization also feared vampires.[27]

Dom Augustin Calmet wrote *Traite Sur Les Apparitions* in 1751 and claimed that vampires were a phenomenon of the last half century; he specified Hungary, Moravia, Silesia, Poland, Greece, and Albania as the worst-hit nations. One account offered a much later initiation for vampire activity, pointing to a 1721 outbreak of so-called vampire attacks in East Prussia and another in the Halsburg Mountains between 1725 and 1734.[28] Southeastern Europe was reportedly "ravaged" by both vampires and epidemics of various diseases in the late seventeenth century and early eighteenth centuries.[29]

People across the globe have believed in vampires since ancient times. Wilson called vampires "an epidemic." McNally identified belief in vampires in ancient civilizations like the Babylonians, Assyrians, Greeks, Chaldeans, Balkans, and Armenians and more recently in Europe, Ireland, Serbia, Greece, Normandy, Dalmatia, the Philippines, Japan, China, and Transylvania.[30]

Even the Roman Catholic Church conceded the existence of vampires. It was during the Middle Ages that the Catholic Church accepted the existence of vampires. This altered the status of vampirism from a matter of pagan folklore to being a spiritual phenomenon and the work of the Devil.

Early vampires included the Sumerian Akhkharu and Lilu from Babylonia as well as the Indian version, Brahmarak-Shasa.[31] The Egyptian goddess Sekhmet also was a vampire.[32] In cultural terms, vampires have been a universal global phenomenon.

We might consider the 1733 work of John Heinrich Zopft, *Dissertatio de Vampiris Serviensibus*: "Vampires issue forth from their graves in the night, attack people sleeping quietly in their beds, suck out all the blood from their bodies and destroy them. They beset men, women and children alike, sparing neither age nor sex. Those who are under the fatal malignity of their influence complain of suffocation and a total deficiency of spirits, after which they soon expire."[33]

In ancient Babylonia, it was thought that the Lilu roamed during the hours of darkness, hunting and murdering newborn infants and pregnant women. According to vampire believers, all vampires were once human beings who were bitten by a vampire, then died and later arose from their grave as a vampire. Kaplan attempted to mathematically disprove the lethality of vampires based on the length of time it would take to kill the entire global population.[34]

Other Monsters

In addition to werewolves and vampires, there have been other types of monsters believed to be residing on our planet. Sea monsters are indicated on ancient navigation charts, and variations of the Abominable Snowman and Bigfoot abound.

Monster myths in various cultures may not pertain to the same cultural phenomenon, but monsters have virtually always represented evil. In ancient Persia during the times of Zoroaster, the monsters mentioned in their myths typically took the form of evil demons. The White Demon (also known as Div-e-Sepid) "was especially ugly, mean and formidable."[35]

American Indian mythology mentioned multiple monsters. They included man-like beasts, giants, dwarfs, cannibals, and hermaphrodites. There were animal monsters, bird monsters, and water monsters as well as malformed creatures, harpies, serpents, giant birds, and forest monsters.[36]

Sea monsters have been reported since men took to the oceans centuries ago. Aristotle noted sea animals capable of wrestling a large ship to an underwater grave. Hans Egde, a Norwegian missionary sailing near Greenland in July 1734, saw a sea creature, "a very terrible sea-animal, which raised itself so high above the water, that its head reached above our maintop [sail]." In 1775, Erik Pontoppidian, the bishop of Bergen, saw a kraken that spread itself out over a length of a mile and a half.[37] The bishop was not known to exaggerate.

A Greek monster named Sphinx was thought to have terrorized Thebes, a Greek city-state. One specific type of monster inhabited the myths of most indigenous native African cultures, humans who could transform themselves into animals. The Norwegians believed that monsters were either giants or dragons. Shape-shifting beings and giants were thought of as the most popular native North American monsters from ancient times.[38]

The Inuit people feared shape-shifting monsters. Olaus Magnus estimated the size of a Scandinavian sea serpent as 200 feet in length and 20 feet thick. Belgian zoologist Bernard Heuvelmans collected a total of 587 sea monster sightings covering the 1639 to 1966 time period and, after removing debatable stories, wound up with 358 "convincing cases."[39] Tibetans have long acknowledged the existence of *yeh teh* in the Sherpa dialect; one study referred to "the Tibetans' profound belief in a hairy man of the snow."[40]

It was thought that ancient monsters were capable of killing people. In India, the *asuras* were originally gods who were demoted to the infernal underground regions or beneath the sea who took out their anger on unwary humans. The *rakshasas* were believed to be Indian monsters with an absolutely grotesque appearance, often looking like a gorilla. In Africa, the "beast-man" was usually described as a tricky and cunning creature who preyed on humans by deceiving them somehow and then eating them.[41]

CONCLUSION

This chapter has explored two issues: the apparent recency of serial murder and the existence of historical alternatives to serial murder. It has been noted that there have been reported cases of serial murder for more than 2,000 years although relatively few compared to the modern era. My data support most other published studies in this respect.

While the records of ancient times reveal few serial murders, there were consistent reports from around the world of other threats to humans from supernatural forces. A variety of mythic monsters were believed to have caused considerable carnage. However, in all likelihood, these were imagined and not real dangers.

I contend that serial murder was prevalent in ancient civilizations but largely unknown and unrecognized. Our ancestors could not comprehend that their fellow citizens were capable of such crimes. Instead, they invented supernatural explanations like dragons and vampires to explain the victimage caused by serial murderers. "Few records of serial killings from mere centuries ago still exist today," Perry suggested. Examination of early crime records shows that crime detection depended on the police locating some connection between the victim, the crime, and the criminal.[42]

We know today that serial murders typically lack such linkages, making this crime essentially invisible to ancient people. As a result, we have underestimated the past incidence of serial murder. This may account for Schechter's salient summary of the situation: "So its impossible to say how many serial sex-murders were committed five hundred years ago, when newspapers didn't exist and crimes among the peasantry went largely unrecorded."[43]

This chapter has surveyed a half dozen mythic entities accepted as lethal and frighteningly real in the past. It is not likely, however, that such supernatural specters actually preyed on ancient people, but that is what was documented in a wide variety of historic accounts. There exists substantial persuasive anecdotal evidence in numerous historic sources alleging the existence of vampires and their supernatural kin.

But sometimes history is wrong. And while it is very difficult to perform revisionist historiographical analysis on topics from the distant past, we can be certain of a few things. Something was killing substantial numbers of ancient people, enough so that the deaths were noticed and explanations sought. The thesis of this work suggests that the work of premodern serial killers was attributed to supernatural entities.

The alternative to my theory is to accept as real the dangers allegedly posed by mythic monsters of the past. Unless a more convincing and parsimonious explanation for mysterious murders of ancient times can be produced, it is reasonable to assume that serial slayers were at work. This is a bold notion, but the remainder of this book documents the reality of historic serial murder.

PART I

VAMPIRE SERIAL KILLERS

COUNTESS ERZSEBET BATHORY

Scholars from King's College referred to Countess Erzsebet Bathory as "one of the most infamous figures in history."[1] She was called a distant relative of Vlad the Impaler, and it was speculated that he was related to Bathory among the Hungarian members of his family. Historic parallels have been drawn between Bathory and Vlad.[2]

She wanted to be the queen of Poland. And she was next in line to be named the reigning Polish monarch. Yet she was publicly forgotten in her homeland after the king of Hungary, King Matthias II, banned the mere mention of her name.[3]

First and foremost, she was a torturer. Torture was her thing. Bathory tortured because she derived pleasure from it.[4]

THE SERIAL MURDERESS

She is often referred to as Countess Elizabeth Bathory. Her first name was Erzebet according to one version. The most commonly used name is Erzsebet. It has been reported that her married name was Countess Elizabeth Bathory Nadasdy. However, she did not take her husband's last name; because her family outranked his considerably, he took her name becoming Count Ferencz Bathory Nadasdy.[5] Bathory's birthday was August 7. The year was either 1560 or 1561. She was most likely born at Ecsed Castle in 1560 near the border between Romania and Hungary.[6]

She was the daughter of George and Anna Bathory. Her father hailed from the Ecsed branch of the family, while her mother was a Somlyo. George or Gyorgy was a soldier, and her mother was the sister of the king of Poland. Royal inbreeding was not unusual for sixteenth-century eastern European aristocrats concerned with the purity of their noble bloodline.[7]

Her childhood was spent at the family estate at Ecsed. Childhood did not last long then, even for daughters of the aristocracy. She was engaged at the age of 10, the result of an arranged marriage.[8]

She was kin to princes of Transylvania, and her cousin Gyorgy Thurzo served as a Hungarian prime minister. Another relative was a Catholic cardinal. Her Uncle Stephen was a Transylvanian prince who became the king of Poland.[9]

Not all of Bathory's family and ancestors were famous. On the contrary, several were decidedly infamous. Bathory's lesbian aunt was also thought of as a witch, her uncle was a Devil-worshipping alchemist, and her brother was considered a danger to women and children.[10]

She was the "Countess of Transylvania." That term has frequently been used to characterize her nationality. Yet there is disagreement on this point. One version of her background maintained that Bathory has been mistakenly described as living in Transylvania when she actually resided in Vishine (present-day Bratislava), where Austria, Hungary, and the Slovak Republic met.[11]

Other authorities described her Hungarian citizenship. Her nationality was Hungarian, concluded one analysis. She was referred to as an Hungarian countess and "Hungary's Elizabeth Bathory."[12]

One additional possibility might be considered: the Slovakian identity. Bathory was often associated with the Slovak Republic.[13] She was, in fact, claimed by many nations.

May 8, 1575, was her wedding day. The groom was Ferencz Nadasdy. Nadasdy was a famous Hungarian war hero, and Bathory was a 15-year-old bride.[14]

The wedding itself was a gala affair. The Roman emperor Maximilian II was invited but could not attend because of security concerns, so he sent a lavish gift and a delegation to represent him. The nuptials ceremony was performed in Varanno Castle.[15]

Bathory hated her mother-in-law. She sought to rid herself of her husband's mother, Ursula. When her husband died, she promptly expelled the despised woman from the castle.[16]

One final aspect of the marriage is significant. It was above all a politically ordained marriage. And despite the fact that she did not particularly care for her husband, Bathory was reportedly a good wife in his presence.[17]

Most sources praised Bathory's maternal behavior. She was typically depicted as a dedicated and doting mother. She was often described as a loving and caring mother.[18]

Does it seem improbable that a sadistic torturer and murderer would be an ideal mother? There is some disagreement about Bathory's maternal excellence. It was recalled that "when, in 1600, the Black Hero died she shipped her four children off to relatives and devoted herself wholly to her macabre pleasures."[19]

Elizabeth and Ferencz were apart most of the early years of their marriage because of his military career. In fact, during their first 10 years of marriage, they rarely saw each other. Then she gave birth to four children, three daughters, and a son, delivered one after another starting in 1585.[20]

Two of her four children failed to survive infancy. The four Bathory children included Anastasia Bathory (1574), Anna Nadasdy (1585), Katalin (Katherina) Nadasdy (1594), and Paul Nadasdy (1598). Other versions indicate that Nadasdy and Bathory had Anna in 1585, then two more daughters named Ursula and Katherina and a son named Paul.[21]

Bathory was considered an intelligent and highly cultured woman. Her level of intellect surpassed most of the men of that time. Bathory possessed a good mind, but unfortunately she applied that intellect to the pursuit of additional victims.[22]

Not only was she naturally intelligent, but she was educated as well. Bathory was a good student and was fluent in Hungarian, Latin, and Greek. Unlike most women of her time, she was exceptionally well educated.[23]

"A most attractive woman" is a typical description. Bathory was beautiful or very beautiful, most accounts agree. When she was young, Bathory was said to have been quite lovely with delicate features and a slender build. One biographer observed that she was very beautiful with long raven hair that stood out against her milky complexion. Her large amber eyes were cat-like, and her figure was voluptuous.[24]

But was she beautiful? It is possible that her great beauty resulted from fear of her status and power. Although she is typically described as having been very attractive, it is possible that no one would have dared say otherwise about a member of an important family.[25]

Bathory suffered from severe epilepsy since infancy. What some perceived as madness may actually have been epileptic fits. Numerous authorities have suggested the possibility of epilepsy.

Was Bathory epileptic, or was there another cause of those painful symptoms? There is another possibility: a brain disorder. It is uncertain whether her headaches were causal or symptomatic of a specific neurological or physical malady.[26]

There is evidence that Bathory was insane since her childhood. It is believed that she was psychotic and that the psychosis accelerated as she aged. Some sources claimed that she was more mentally ill than intentionally evil.[27]

Her first sexual sin may have been the most benign: promiscuity. She did not save herself for marriage and had sexual relations with other men after she was betrothed to be married. A brief romantic affair with a local peasant resulted in her pregnancy.[28]

For much of her marriage, she indulged herself with numerous affairs while her husband was gone.[29] Bathory had several young lovers and ran away with one of them before returning to her husband. He forgave her, and they reconciled.[30]

It is frequently contended that Bathory was a lesbian. In light of her overall sexual conduct, that label may be restrictive. She did manifest a preference for young girls.[31]

When her husband was gone, she would visit her Aunt Karla. There she participated in incestuous sexual orgies.[32] Karla was a lesbian, bisexual, or both.

Bathory was a sadist who enjoyed inflicting pain on others. "Sado-eroticism" was Bathory's sexual system.[33] She combined causing pain with creating pleasure during sex. One witness at Bathory's trial told an incredible tale. This servant saw the Devil himself frolicking in Countess Bathory's lap before they had sexual relations, with her being completely spellbound. The witness attributed Bathory's submissiveness to his impressive male organ. Perhaps this diabolical encounter caused Bathory's "sexual ambivalence."[34]

Bathory reportedly was vindictive.[35] She engaged in sadistic crimes and reveled in acts of depravity. Contemporary accounts referred to her as a vain beauty. She was described as being ruthless, conceited, and cruel.[36]

"Countess Dracula" is what she was sometimes called. A similar nickname, "Lady Dracula," was also used but was somewhat less popular. "The Hungarian Whore" was the most mean-spirited of the nicknames. By far, the nickname most frequently encountered is the "Blood Countess."[37]

Her husband was also a person of renown. Many called him the "Black Hero of Hungary." The other popular nickname was the "Black Knight of Hungary."[38]

OTHER CRIMES

A flesh eater is what Bathory was. She reportedly committed numerous acts of cannibalism. Cannibalistic appetites were frequently attributed to Bathory.[39]

But Bathory was not the only flesh eater. On occasion during torture, she compelled her victims to eat pieces of their own flesh. And Bathory sometimes tricked her soldiers into eating human flesh, making them unknowing cannibals.[40]

Witchcraft, sorcery, and diabolism were her primary interests. At Bathory's 1610 arrest, the grounds for arrest involved her alleged witchcraft. She practiced sorcery, alchemy, and the black arts.[41]

She made incantations. These were equivalent to spells; some were meant to protect her, and others were intended to harm other people. After her incarceration, she was deeply upset about the loss of her favorite magic incantation.[42]

It has been suggested that Bathory killed her husband. One version of events identified poison as the cause of death.[43] Although he may have been poisoned, his death was attributed at the time to witchcraft.[44]

She was fascinated with torture. It was her hobby. She liked to inflict torture from the front of the victims so that she could observe the reactions on their face. Her style was termed "extreme torture." She preferred lengthy, protracted torture sessions.[45]

Torture was all around her. As a little girl, she watched her father torture prisoners, including a case where a peasant was sewn into a horse. She watched her husband torture with a special pair of silver-bladed pincers in his dungeon.[46] She tortured at times with her husband, according to some accounts. It is believed that the Black Hero taught his wife about torture in the basement dungeon of the family castle.[47] Numerous torture techniques were used. Victims were bitten; beaten; frozen to death outside in winter; covered in honey and chained outside in the spring or summer; had burning rags held between their upper thighs or between their toes; were slashed with scissors, knives, or razors; and had pins placed under their skin and through their lips. Other methods were being tightly bound; having fingers and toes cut off; having mouths sewn shut; being burned with molten wax, a candle, scalding-hot water, or oil; being forced to hold burning coins in their hands; being assaulted with a red-hot poker; having a heated branding iron placed against the face; and being placed in the Iron Maiden, also known as the Iron Virgin.

Victims were punctured, whipped, partly dismembered, and defleshed. Some girls were forced to stand naked in front of men. Eyes were gouged out, and red-hot pokers were thrust up noses and into mouths and down throats.

The instruments used to inflict torture varied greatly. They included barbed wire, silver pincers, branding irons, molten wax, razors, and torches. Manacles, needles, scissors, clubs, rags, pokers, honey, chains, whips, candles, and knives were also used.

The importance of torture to Bathory cannot be overstated. Her personal torture chamber was referred to as "Her Ladyship's Torture Chamber." She took a portable torture chamber with her when she traveled.[48]

THE SERIAL MURDERS

Modus Operandi

Victims were lured in a variety of ways. In 1609, Bathory opened a school in the castle to educate 25 girls of nobility. She offered instruction in social graces.[49] Promised jobs as servants was how Bathory acquired a number of her victims. The lure of employment was persuasive. Her servants obtained additional virgins from local villages by pretending to hire them as servants.[50]

There was a third way of procuring victims. Some were purchased. Unscrupulous individuals in some villages provided girls in return for money.[51] Who obtained the constant supply of virgins for Bathory's needs? Sometimes it was her accomplices. At other times she roamed the countryside at night searching for suitable girls.[52] Victims were taken to the castle to be fattened up prior to their bloodletting experience. They were held in large jail-like cells in the lower recesses of the castle dungeon. And many were eventually buried in the castle and on the castle grounds.[53]

Number of Victims

The precise number of her victims is unknown. And there is a relatively wide range of death count estimates. Dozens to several hundred women were victimized.[54] There were between 30 and 60 victims according to a relatively conservative conclusion. Bathory's victimage total has also been quantified at forty. One version noted her conviction of 80 murders.[55]

The remainder of the estimates are higher. It was said that the Bathory crimes may have resulted in the murder of more than 100 victims. There were, in fact, between 300 and 650 victims, contended a pair of authorities independently. A quartet of studies decided that there was a total of 600 victims.[56]

Six hundred serial murders is a large amount, but Bathory's total may have been even greater. A trio of sources suggested in excess of 600 victims. And the single most common estimate was 650 victims, which was mentioned in nine published reports.[57]

Time Frame

The duration of the serial slayings was five years, according to one account. Yet others recalled a 10-year period of serial murders. A slightly longer 11-year time period has also been specified. The crimes occurred over a 30-year time frame, according to three studies. We might consider a final estimate: 35 years.[58]

When did the crimes occur? The dates of death were between 1580 and 1610, according to most reports. One account noted a time frame between 1610 and 1614.[59]

Victimology

Bathory was consistent in her choice of victims. Four victimology variables were at work: (1) Slovak servants, (2) buxom women, (3) youth, and

(4) soft skin and beauty. She lived at a time of warfare when the Ottoman Empire fought Hungary and other eastern European nations. There was considerable ethnic and religious animosity. Slovak servants dominated her victimage selections.[60]

Her victims were well-endowed and buxom women. The girls Bathory chose to punish were usually those with the largest breasts. Most of the victims were teens, and a few were as young as 12.[61]

It is said that she preferred beautiful victims. Her servant Ficzko confessed this fact. "They had been chosen for the softness of their skin—even of their tongues—and for their youth and beauty."[62]

Motives

It has been frequently speculated that Bathory began her serial torture and murder career during her husband's lengthy military campaigns. She was bored and missed him. Later, after his death, she feared her own mortality and began torturing her servants.[63]

She wanted to be young and beautiful forever. Bathory was motivated by her belief that she could remain youthful through vampirism. Her servants kidnapped young virgins, tortured and slashed them, and collected the blood, which she used for bathing.[64]

Sixteenth-century Europe was a fractured place. There was political, ethnic, and religious disharmony. In an area divided by religious differences, her family supported Protestantism and opposed Roman Catholicism.[65] Most of her victims were Catholic. She did not act alone. Bathory was assisted by a number of helpers over the years. Her lover Darvulia was an initial main helper, followed by Erszi Majorova.[66]

The roster of accomplices varied over time. It was said that Helena Jo, Dorothea Szentes (aka Dorka), and Johannes Ujvary (aka Ficzko) were her crew. She was assisted in these crimes by Dorka Szentes, Iloona Joo, Johannes Ujuvary, Anna Darvulia, and Damien Thorko, according to another account. The assistants were Thorko, Ilona Joo, Dorottya Szentes, Darvulia, and Johannes Ujvary, it was claimed.[67]

VAMPIRISM

Bathory was considered one of the most infamous vampires in history and listed among the most notorious historical vampires. However, she was not a vampire, most authorities now contend. But it was alleged by some that she drank blood and bathed in it, and she certainly spilled enough of it during her lengthy and frequent torture sessions.

The first allegations that Bathory drank or bathed in blood were contained in a book written a century after the crimes. The records of her trials reportedly failed to mention Bathory ingesting or bathing in blood. But since her cousin was conducting them, it is possible that those gory details were not communicated or recorded at the trials.[68]

SERIAL KILLER COMMUNICATION

Bathory corresponded with her soldier husband away on the battlefield. One dispatch advised, "Thurko has taught me a lovely new one. Catch a black hen and beat it to death with a white cane. Keep the blood and smear some on your enemy. If you get no chance to smear it on his body, obtain one of his garments and smear it."[69]

She believed deeply in the power of her incantations. These documents were dedicated to her diety Isten. She had one "parchment (Penrose says the shriveled caul of a newborn child) on which was prescribed an incantation for protection."[70]

A notebook-like document called a register was discovered in Bathory's private rooms. It was submitted into evidence at her second trial. Most accounts called the item a register, but this document has also been referred to as a ledger.[71]

The register was very incriminating because it was said to have been written entirely in Bathory's handwriting. In addition, the register was discovered in her personal quarters. It included the names and details about the torture and murder of 650 victims.[72]

It came to light through the efforts of a servant named Zusanna. She claimed that she found the register in Bathory's bedroom. It is curious that the register was not found before the first trial; could its discovery be the reason for the second trial?[73]

One final word about the register. All we have is Zusanna's word on it. This evidence is questionable because the register was never produced in court.[74]

THE INVESTIGATION

The official investigation into Bathory's crimes started in 1610. It was reported that Hungarian King Matthias II ordered the inquiry. It is believed that the Hungarian Parliament commissioned a full investigation in the winter of 1610.[75]

Bathory was arrested on December 19, 1610, it was claimed, while another source mentioned that the date was December 29. Another version denied that she was arrested before or at the raid. Bathory was instead confined under regal house arrest. Sixteen members of her household servant staff were arrested.[76]

Four battered and bloodless corpses were found beneath the castle ramparts, setting off a public outcry that eventually reached the king. Locals reported hearing screams coming from the castle. But despite countless rumors, Bathory's murderous tendencies were undetected or ignored until 1609.[77]

The big change was the killing of girls from noble families. Darvulia had strictly forbidden the practice, but Majorova reversed the policy and encouraged Bathory to initiate the murder of aristocratic girls. But she decided on her own to start killing noble girls, according to other research.[78]

A raid was conducted on the Bathory castle. What motivated this bold act against a reigning monarch? Numerous possible reasons for the raid are examined here.

The first motive was an eyewitness report. A young woman barely escaped from Bathory and told local police about her experience. A second factor was that the king had heard about dark deeds at the Bathory castle. There were rumors about torture.[79]

A great many complaints about the countess were made, so many that King Matthias felt compelled to act. Another factor motivating the raid was the intervention of local priests. They had begun refusing to accommodate Bathory's frequent requests for burials of her victims, and they informed police of their suspicions.[80]

But by far the major crime-related motive for the raid was the death of a girl from a noble family. After the murder of a young lady of minor nobility (or four deaths), the authorities finally realized that they had to act. Bathory tried unsuccessfully to disguise the death(s) as suicide.[81]

The raid was not ordered to prevent peasant deaths or preclude further torture. Bathory's cousin Gyorgy Thurzo acted to prevent Bathory from selling away any more of the family property. She had been reduced to selling off parts of her estate to finance her lifestyle. And the king wanted to avoid repaying a considerable amount of money he had borrowed from her husband while simultaneously appropriating her land and other possessions.[82]

The raid was conducted by her cousin Gyorgy. He is called Prime Minister Thurzo by some. His title is Lord Palatine in other versions.[83]

The raid reportedly occurred on December 30, 1610. According to another account, it took place during the Christmas holidays in 1609 or 1610. It is said that the raid was timed to avoid interference by the Hungarian Parliament, which had adjourned over the holidays. King Matthias II played a role since both he and church officials ordered an investigation.[84]

THE TRIALS

The first trial was administered by Count Thurzo acting on behalf of the king. A panel of 21 judges made up the special tribunal, which was headed by Theodosious de Sulzo of the Hungarian Royal Supreme Court. The judges who heard the testimony in this case were appalled.[85]

There were actually two trials. One study claimed that they occurred two weeks apart, but most sources find a one-week separation in time. They began on January 7 and January 21, 1611, and each lasted a week.[86]

Considerable uncertainty concerning major aspects of the trials should be mentioned. Bathory was on trial, according to one version. Others deny that she ever stood trial. It has been documented that her family prevented her from being tried. She was allowed to attend the trials, in the opinion of some authorities. Yet some claimed that she was prevented from attending. She was convicted, some experts suggested. An alternative view maintained that she was not convicted of any charges. She was found criminally insane, in the opinion of one study. "Two hurried show trials" were criticized. But another version concluded that her trial was secretly conducted in a remote Slovakian village.[87]

Her accomplices were thought by some to provide the most persuasive evidence against her, but it was recognized that they had been tortured, and their testimony was accordingly devalued. The tortured human remains, along with the personal effects of the victims, were also very incriminating. Testimony from traumatized survivors was compelling, as they recounted their stories of being pierced, beaten, and burned.[88]

Family played a role in her trials. Her son Paul wrote to the special tribunal on her behalf, although daughter Anna refused to have anything to do with her mother. Thanks to Bathory's family's intervention, her role in the crimes was concealed. And before the raid, Count Thurzo began plans to ensconce her in a convent.[89]

Hungarian law prevented her prosecution because of her royal status. Then there was a bad break for Bathory. The Hungarian Parliament adopted new legislation to eliminate this protection.[90]

The accomplices were tortured and then beheaded, dismembered, and burned to death. Each accomplice's specific torture was selected in an individualized but quite appropriate way. The method of their execution matched their roles in the torture.[91]

Bathory was also sentenced to death, but her penalty was commuted to life imprisonment. She was essentially "walled in"; her bedchamber was shortened to the size of a closet. Bathory was literally walled up in her bedroom.[92]

CONCLUSION

Bathory was a witch, sexual sadist, cannibal, and, above all, devotee of extreme torture. Her sexual style included affairs, lesbianism, bisexuality, incest, sadism, and sex with the Devil. She was depraved and evil. She was also a serious serial slayer.

Bathory may have killed more people than any other serial killer in history. It is believed that 650 victims were killed in her vain campaign to stay young forever. In serial killer circles, that is a relatively large number of murders.

3

VINCENZO VERZINI

He is seldom mentioned today, but Vincenzo Verzini was a terrifying criminal in Italy in the late 1800s. Verzini was singled out by one authority on serial murder as the first well-known sexual serial killer.[1] He was called one of the very earliest Italian serial killers about whom anything is known today.[2]

He was considered a precursor to Jack the Ripper. A Mexican newspaper, *El Universal*, provided a contemporary account in 1889. Verzini's crimes were described as "a whole series of frightful deeds which resemble the work of his imitator on the banks of the Thames."[3]

Verzini was indeed a model for later serial killers. According to a 1920 study, *Medicolegal Aspects of Moral Offenses*, "Verzini may well be called the prototype of the criminal sadist."[4] He has been characterized as quite similar to modern serial slayers.[5]

THE SERIAL MURDERER

It is not unusual for there to be inconsistency in factual information in serial murder cases. This is especially true in older cases where the passage of time and failure to properly document information resulted in diversity of specific facts. The spelling of Verzini's name is one of these disputed items.

His name was Vincenzo Verzini, according to several authorities. But there are other popular versions of his name. The name was Vincenz Verzini, according to a trio of serial murder experts.[6] Vincent Verzini was the actual name, in the estimation of several others, and one report gave the last name as Verzeni.[7]

He was born in a small Italian village in 1849. The village was named Bottanaucco, according to several sources.[8] His exact date of birth is unknown.

It is difficult to discuss Verzini's family life because of the considerable differences in historic reports and available information. It is frequently reported that he came from a good family. Yet another depiction of his family portrayed a vastly different and darker domestic life.

He was a child in a seemingly respectable family, declared a contemporary newspaper story on this case. Verzini enjoyed an irreproachable background. As the child of loving and Christian parents, he seemed to benefit from an idyllic family life.[9]

The rest of the family reflected decidedly suboptimal characteristics. Disturbing signs of physical degeneracy in his ancestry were reported. Two of his uncles were called cretins, and another was a convicted thief. One was missing a testicle, and others manifested numerous abnormalities.[10]

He was apparently a bit of a loner. Verzini was considered slightly peculiar and somewhat inclined toward solitary pursuits. It was said that he was relatively calm and quiet and kept to himself. He was usually very friendly but with quiet ways.[11]

Other aspects of his personality were problematic. He was unable to create any meaningful interpersonal relationships because of his significant fear of his father. Verzini also did not later display any remorse or guilt in connection with any of his crimes.[12]

There is not much information about his intelligence. The fact that he could repeatedly assault women and escape reveals some mental ability. He was said to have been a person of average intelligence.[13]

We know something about his appearance. The famed Italian criminologist Cesare Lombroso interviewed Verzini and provided this firsthand depiction. The killer's head was determined to be asymmetrical, and it was bigger than average. His ears were defective, and the right one was smaller. His penis was "greatly developed," and the right frontal bone of his skull revealed evidence of degeneracy.[14]

There was at the time and still remains considerable speculation about Verzini's mental health. No evidence of mental disease was observed, according to one authority. At the time, the court failed to find any evidence of mental illness.[15]

Despite these opinions there is a greater likelihood that this serial killer faced severe mental issues. His vampirism was a manifestation of derangement, it was suggested. His cranial asymmetry was reportedly responsible for "overdevelopment of the left frontal lobe and the bony crest which is found in the large apes and in primitive savages." A pretrial clinical assessment observed "nothing in his past that points to mental disease but his character is peculiar."[16]

Lombroso's assessment was an expert analysis of the killer. He concluded that Verzini was partly insane. Verzini was diagnosed as having necrophilomania by Lombroso, and we will learn later that he also presented symptoms of anthropoghagy (blood drinking).[17]

His sexuality seems central to the serial slayings. The murders and assaults were caused by his need for sexual satisfaction. It is perhaps unnecessary to point out that he failed to possess normal sexual instincts.[18]

The 12-year-old Verzini discovered that he could achieve an orgasm by strangling chickens. Later he progressed to strangling women, again with a sexual motivation; he strangled women, leading to orgasm.[19] Verzini admitted that "I had an unspeakable delight in strangling women, experiencing during the act erections and sexual pleasure."[20]

The aberrant nature of his sex drive and release mechanism eluded some observers who decided that Verzini's crimes lacked a sexual aspect. He never assaulted the victims sexually or raped them, declared one account of the crimes.[21] This conclusion certainly assumed conventional sexual behavior and overlooked the decidedly unconventional nature of Verzini's sexual preferences and practices.

He claimed that choking a woman was sexually more exciting for him than masturbating. He admitted that murder and mutilation excited him sexually. When he put his hands around the throat of a woman, he got an erection, he confessed. The clinical assessment noted that he masturbated regularly.[22]

Most if not all serial killers are bestowed with nicknames. Verzini was no exception. He was called the "Strangler of Women."[23]

OTHER CRIMES

The mutilations were frightful. According to a contemporary account, the victims "were found completely naked and so horribly mutilated. . . . The abdomen had been cut along its whole length, the intestines pulled out, the limbs smashed to pieces and the entrails, scattered on the road with bloody clothing or carefully hidden in the basements or beneath piles of straw in the vicinity."[24]

Johanna Motta was killed and disemboweled. Her intestines and genitals were found nearby. A victim known only as Frigeni was similarly mistreated, with her intestines ripped from her body and placed next to it.[25]

Was Verzini a cannibal? That belief has been asserted. It was contended that Verzini ripped open the bodies of victims and chewed on the flesh.[26]

But the facts might be somewhat more complicated. Verzini told the police that he took pieces of Motta's calf and intestines to cook and eat at home. But he changed his mind because he feared that his mother would find out.[27]

Verzini cut Motta's body and took pieces, acts considered as desecration of a corpse. It seems that he especially enjoyed one aspect of the experience. He later said that he found the feel of intestines very pleasant.[28] The tactile sensation excited him.

THE SERIAL MURDERS

Modus Operandi

These were not complex or complicated crimes. Victims were tied up and then strangled. Both Motta and Frigeni were strangled and disemboweled, and their mouths were filled with dirt.[29]

Verzini's killing method developed over time, and his initial attempts were unsuccessful. It is known that he attacked his initial victim when he was an 18-year-old, but he let her go. He would similarly spare a pair of other potential victims before his first murder.[30]

Number of Victims

How many women did Verzini victimize? There were two murder victims according to most accounts.[31] Much of the disagreement in this case involved the number of nonlethal assaults.

There were two deaths and three assaults, it was contended. Other sources reported two deaths and four assaults or five assaults and two murders. Another account mentioned two dead and a half dozen unsuccessful attempts.[32]

Not all versions of the Verzini victimage quantified the total at two deaths. There were 12 murders, one analysis decided. And it is believed that Verzini was suspected in several other similar slayings.[33]

Motive

A number of different factors might be cited to explain these crimes. It is quite possible that there was more than one cause involved in this case. Five motives might be considered: (1) epilepsy and moral insanity, (2) family retardation, (3) sexual pleasure, (4) anger, and (5) enjoyment.

Psychiatry was in an embryonic state in the nineteenth century. Lombroso was an acknowledged expert and pioneer criminologist whose knowledge was state of the art at the time. Lombroso attributed Verzini's criminality in part to "epileptic and moral insanity."[34]

Lombroso cited another factor in this case that may have been a causal element. He contended that the Verzini family was afflicted by severe mental retardation. The clinical assessment agreed and asserted, "Verzini's family is bigoted and low-minded."[35]

Sex might have been the primary and most influential motive behind these murders. The sexual dimension of these crimes has already been documented and the primacy of sexual behavior noted. Verzini reportedly told Lombroso that strangling, mutilating, and drinking blood caused "a paroxysm of sexual pleasures."[36]

Could anger have motivated these murders and mutilations? That was the perspective provided by one report. Verzini's anger, fed by frustration and resentment, was suggested as the cause behind these crimes.[37]

A final possible motive might be examined: enjoyment. Some serial slayers derive pleasure from the act of murder. In this case, Verzini said that he found the experience a pleasant one.[38]

Time Frame

There is relatively little variation in the reported time frames of the Verzini crimes. Nevertheless, there is a lack of agreement on the specifics. Some sources asserted that the crimes took place between 1867 and 1871. It was also claimed that the crimes began in 1870 and lasted until 1874. A relatively narrow time frame estimate of 1871 to 1872 has also been offered. The most precise time frame suggestion was December 1870 through August 1871. We might also consider one estimate of the duration of the serial murders: less than two years.[39]

Victimology

There was considerable variance among Verzini's victims. It is believed that all were women. Beyond that, however, he was not particularly picky. The victims were "old, young, ugly or beautiful."[40]

One specific victimology variable might be examined. It was alleged that Verzini's victims were frequently family members. A contemporary newspaper story reported the fact that most of the women he attacked were members of his family.[41]

In another sense, there was a random element in his victimology selections. Verzini sought his victims in remote, lonely country locations. His were victims of opportunity whose presence in a particular place placed them in peril.[42]

Not all the women he assaulted were killed. In fact, the majority of his victims survived the experience. Verzini told the police that if he climaxed sexually before the woman died from strangulation, she was allowed to live.[43]

Victims

Her name was Johanna or Giovanna Motta. She was a 14-year-old girl at the time of her death. When she encountered Verzini, she was reportedly on her way to reunite with her family. Another version suggested that she disappeared on her way to the village on an errand.[44]

Her body was discovered four days later. It was claimed that her mother found her body hidden under some straw in a field. Her body was discovered by her master, according to an alternate perspective.[45]

She was choked to death, and her body was left naked and mutilated. This occurred in December 1870. Another version offered a December 1871 date of death.[46]

The first name of the second victim is lost to history, but we know her as Frigeni. She was twice as old as Motta, 28, when she was killed. She was strangled and mutilated in August 1871. Her husband discovered her body.[47]

VAMPIRISM

Verzini was called a vampire. He reportedly sucked the blood of his victims. According to another account, he sucked the blood from the thigh of a victim.[48]

His modus operandi was direct as it pertained to the blood. Verzini would seize his victim's throat, bite it, and drink the blood directly from the wound. One authority contended that he was afflicted with a mental disease known as anthropoghagy, as "he sucked and drank the blood from cadavers."[49]

Verzini himself repeatedly expressed his enjoyment derived from blood. He confessed excitement from drinking Motta's blood.[50] Verzini was also quoted as testifying, "I have really butchered some of the women, and I have tried to strangle a few more, because I take immense pleasure in these acts. The scratches found on the thighs weren't the product of my nails, but of my teeth, because after the strangulation I bit her and sucked the blood that dripped out, which I enjoyed very much."[51]

THE INVESTIGATION

The task of identifying the killer was made more difficult by the fact that Verzini was able to escape from the crime scenes. A contemporary report emphasized the ease with which he escaped. Verzini fled the crime scenes without ever being recognized.[52]

Perhaps the main factor involved in his apprehension was the choice of his cousin Maria Previtali as a victim. He attacked the 19-year-old the day after the Frigeni murder. As he was attempting to kill her, he was interrupted by a passerby, and she talked him out of murdering her.[53] He let her go, and she went to the police, who immediately arrested Verzini.[54]

THE TRIAL

Although it occurred a long time ago, we know something about the trial and aftermath in this case. Verzini made some provocative statements worthy of our recollection. And his fate was a bit unusual.

There are different versions of the Verzini judicial proceedings. The Court of Justice of Bergamo reportedly adjudicated the case. Another rendition suggested the Assizes Court of Bergamo as the tribunal with jurisdiction in this trial. The trial was a relatively brief one.[55]

His conduct and communication carried weight at his trial. He was considered to be a bad person and ineffective defendant because he did not act sorry or contrite in any way for his deeds.[56] He confessed the murders, mutilations, and miscellaneous related criminal acts.[57]

His confession was explicit and extreme evidence against him:

> I had an unspeakable delight in strangling women, experiencing during the act erections and real sexual pleasure. It was even a pleasure only to smell female clothing. The feeling of pleasure while strangling them was much greater than I experienced while masturbating. . . . It also gave me the greatest pleasure to pull the hairpins out of the hair of my victims. I took the clothing and intestines, because of the pleasure it gave me to smell and touch them.[58]

He also told the court that he should never be set free because he would undoubtedly resume his murders and mutilations.[59]

Verzini was convicted of murder, corpse desecration, and vampirism. He was not sentenced to death; that would have required a unanimous verdict, which was not achieved in this case. The jury decision was actually extraordinarily close with a one-vote margin in favor of conviction.[60]

CONCLUSION

Verzini was a model or prototype of the sexually oriented serial slayer for later offenders to emulate. Verzini was motivated mainly by sexual desire. His aberrant sexuality made the satisfaction of his libidinous urges a lethal matter for his partner.

Verzini displayed classic signs of serial murder potential as a youth. Choking chickens to achieve orgasm revealed both his sexual aberration and his homicidal potential. Did his fear of his father produce this pathological personality?

Verzini was not a vampire, but he most likely did drink blood. And he was clearly a sadist who was sensuously stimulated by the suffocation of his sexual partners.

PART II

WEREWOLF SERIAL KILLERS

4

JOSEPH VACHER

This case was one of the most horrible cases in the history of serial murder.[1] A depraved monster is what Joseph Vacher was.[2] The *New York Times* reported, "The crimes of Joseph Vacher have surpassed in number and atrocity those of the Whitechapel murderer known as 'Jack-the-Ripper.' "[3]

Vacher said some strange and provocative things. For example, he told a magistrate that he was a scourge sent to Earth by Providence to punish and afflict the human race.[4]

It was reported that he suffered from a severe homicidal compulsion.[5] Vacher was thoroughly despised and infamous at the time.[6] Part of his terrifying identity was his status as a vagabond.

Nineteenth-century France was a nation with a homeless problem, then referred to as vagabondage. Vagabonds were feared throughout France at the time of Vacher's serial crimes.[7] The *Journal of Social History* provided this perspective:

> The nation was suffering from an alarming social crisis, widespread vagabondage.... There was fear and fascination with vagabonds and marginals in general that was so common in France before the war.... Indeed, here was one of France's most serious social problems. Scarcely one decade before the outbreak of the First World War, the problem of vagabondage and mendicity was so widespread in many parts of rural France that social commentators often likened the situation to the explosive one of the 1780s.[8]

Not only was he infamous, but that infamy translated into popular culture artifacts of an unusual sort: children's nursery rhymes. And there was inspiration in Vacher's deeds for cinematic enterprises as well. French filmmaker Bertrand Tavernier produced and directed *Le juge et l'assassin* (The Judge and the Murderer) in 1976.[9]

Vacher was infamous at the time, but that time has passed. He was forgotten years ago, according to one authority on serial murder.[10] The

Vacher affair was a "cause celebre in fin-de-siecle France, but one long forgotten."[11]

THE SERIAL MURDERER

Vacher was born in 1869. To be precise, his birthday was believed to be November 16, 1869. His place of birth was Beaufort, a small town in the Isere province of France.[12]

Not much is reliably known about his family. His father was said to have been an illiterate farmer. Vacher was raised in a poverty-stricken family, the last of 15 children. And it appears that he may have been a bit of a bully even though he was the youngest; one account reported him "slapping his 14 brothers and sisters around."[13]

As a general rule, little is known about the school record of serial killers from the distant past. However, we do know something about Vacher's education. For instance, it is believed that he attended a strict Catholic school. And he was expelled from school for a rather serious offense: instructing his classmates in "mutual masturbation."[14]

He enlisted in the army at the age of 21, possibly to escape the poverty of his home life.[15] When he failed to receive an expected promotion to colonel, he attempted suicide by slashing his throat. The resulting scars disfigured him but impressed his military superiors, who promptly promoted the pouting Vacher to the post he prized.[16]

On one occasion, he reportedly shot at members of his own army. He frequently assailed fellow soldiers with paranoid threats. He was discharged from the military in 1893 because of confused speech, persecution mania, and violently threatening language.[17]

One girl rebuffed his advances, hurt his feelings, and nearly paid with her life. In 1893, he met a young maidservant named Louise. There is some disagreement over the circumstances of their meeting because some contend that Vacher met her while on sick leave from the military. Yet other authorities are certain that he was discharged from the army prior to meeting Louise.[18]

There is little disagreement about what happened next. Vacher shot Louise three or four times (after she rejected and mocked him) before turning the gun on himself. He fired directly into his face. One version maintained that Vacher managed to shoot himself twice.[19]

He was treated in an asylum after killing a woman and having sexual relations with her corpse. Vacher had twice been committed to asylums, it was said. He was entrusted to the monastery at Saint-Genis-Laval as a "postulant." But he was expelled after teaching fellow novices about masturbation and sodomy.[20]

After nearly murdering Louise and almost killing himself, he was committed to the Asylum of Saint Ylle. However, because of outrageous behavior, he was soon transferred to the Asylum of Saint Robert. He was released from the Saint Robert institution "cured" on April 1, 1894.[21]

But there were alternate perspectives on these events. One version suggested that Vacher was committed to the Dole Asylum. He was initially sent to the Asylum of Saint Robert according to another tale.[22]

A few facts about his institutionalization seem to be a matter of consensus. The reason for the mental health confinement was persecution complex. And Vacher made several unsuccessful attempts at escaping from the asylum.[23]

Vacher had a history of confused talk, spells of delirium, persecution mania, and extreme irritability.[24] His aberrant behavior began early in life. It was alleged that he received considerable pleasure from torturing animals when he was a child.[25]

He was called an insane misfit. His specific mental maladies included paranoia and a persecution complex. Vacher also experienced delusional episodes, and it was reported that the incidence of delusional incidents increased during the investigation and trial.[26]

Vacher admitted one fact that might be indicative of mental health motives in the crimes. He confessed to feeling a sense of relief after the murders. His mental issues began after the romantic rejection from Louise.[27]

His face was partly paralyzed, one eye "exuded a constant flow of pus," and his lips were scarred. His speech was made difficult by the facial injuries. The net effect of suicide attempts by knife and gun was a decidedly unpleasant countenance.[28]

It is believed that he contracted a sexually transmitted disease from a prostitute and lost part of a testicle as a result. A sexually sadistic serial killer is how one authority described him. Vacher was one of the first known bisexual serial slayers. He masturbated frequently and instructed others in masturbation techniques.[29]

His personality has been described in critical ways. "This desperate criminal was notoriously vain," a contemporary newspaper account claimed. He was known for a bad temper; not just occasionally but throughout his life, Vacher manifested demonstrative tantrums.[30]

He was a tramp, according to several authorities. Others referred to him as a drifter. He was frequently called a vagrant. A few reports described him as a nomadic vagabond.[31]

The accordion set Vacher apart from most serial slayers. It was something he typically carried with him. It is said that he played his accordion for his captors after he was apprehended.[32]

He is usually known as the "French Ripper." That nickname was given because of these crimes' similarity to the Jack the Ripper murders. An alternate perspective asserted that the nature of the mutilations inspired the nickname.[33]

The "French Disemboweler" was another nickname. Yet another pseudo-
nym was the "Disemboweler of the Southeast." The French version of his
nickname was *"L' eventreur du Sud-Est."* He was also called the "Ripper of
the Southeast."[34]

OTHER CRIMES

Vacher had sex with the corpse of his first victim, Eugenie Delhomme, a factory girl. He engaged in acts of necrophilia with four victims, it was reported.
There were three such depraved acts, according to another version.[35]

Vacher disemboweled his victims after he killed them. On their death, he
often engaged in this criminal behavior.[36]

Serial slayers not infrequently take parts of their victims. These body parts
are eaten, touched, and/or sent to the police or media. In this case, the vulva
and breast of a victim were retained by the murderer.[37]

The Vacher victims were violated sexually. These vicious murders were
characterized by the killer "sexually mutilating" the victims. The sexual
organs of his victims were desecrated and purloined on several occasions.[38]

Most of Vacher's sexual contact with his victims was postmortem. But his
first crime was an exception. It is known that he raped but did not attempt to
murder a 19-year-old boy.[39]

Vacher engaged in extensive mutilation of a couple of his victims. In all, he
violated the corpses of 11 children. These victims were mutilated after death.[40]

One final crime might be mentioned. It has already been established that
Vacher symbolized the serious French vagabondage problem. He reportedly
was incarcerated for six months for this offense.[41]

THE SERIAL MURDERS

Modus Operandi

Vacher's crimes began with him loudly knocking on the doors of farm-
houses and demanding food. The victims were then stabbed repeatedly.
The modus operandi involved strangling, stabbing, mutilating, and disemboweling, one authority claimed. Another version suggested that victims
were stabbed, strangled, mutilated, and bitten. Male victims were stabbed,
sodomized, bitten, and castrated, it was alleged, while females were stabbed,
raped, bitten, and disemboweled.[42]

His weapons included a set of knives and a cudgel. Vacher named his
cudgel Mary of Lourdes, and inscribed on the weapon was "Who does good
finds good." The killer's other weapons included scissors, a cleaver, and
knives.[43]

His murder area was southeastern France, although others believed that the crimes occurred in southwestern France. The country around Belley, in the southeastern part of France, was a specific identification of the place where killings took place. The murders were committed within 40 miles of Lyons. It was also contended that Vacher was a migratory serial killer.[44]

Number of Victims

There is disagreement concerning the volume of Vacher's victimage. At the time of the crimes, the *New York Times* claimed that the true number of victims would forever remain unknown. A rather vague estimate was nearly a dozen victims.[45]

One authority asserted that there were 10 victims. The consensus of opinion accepted a total of 11 deaths. Vacher confessed to 11 murders. There were 14 deaths, according to one version. A contemporary newspaper account reported at least 23 victims, while 26 victims were attributed to Vacher by another authority.[46]

Other estimates were expressed as ranges or were conditional in nature. There were between 10 and 20 deaths, it was contended. Eleven to 14 victims were observed in one account. Another analysis asserted that there were from 11 to 23 murders. There were 11 definite murders and an additional 15 possibilities, it was concluded. He was suspected in 15 unsolved murders.[47]

Victimology

Shepherds and farmhands made up Vacher's primary victimology cohort. Some accounts described shepherds and shepherdesses as the victims. "Farmhands" were identified as the main victimology group.[48]

Gender was not a variable. The victims included seven females and four males. The women ranged in age from 16 to 58, while the males were between 14 and 16 years old. There were eight females and three males, according to one report. Another account described the victims as being one woman, five female teens, and five male teens.[49]

Two more factors might be cited. The victims were for the most part teenagers. And there was a potential geographic factor as well. Vacher attacked victims in isolated spots.[50]

Time Frame

One account placed these crimes in the 1890s. More precise was an estimate of 1894 to 1897. Even more specific was a time frame of March 20, 1894, to June 18, 1897.[51]

The duration of the crimes was similarly uncertain. The murders occurred within three years, it was said. They happened within three and one-third years, according to other authorities. The duration was actually three and a half years, one version maintained. We might consider a fourth estimate of four years.[52]

Motive

At his trial, Vacher claimed that he was motivated by the desire to make people think about the importance of religious faith. He said that he was sent by God just as Joan of Arc had been. Or he may have killed because of general resentment at his lot in life.[53]

The real motive most likely involved his severe facial disfigurement. It is believed that he looked so hideous that people would flinch and visibly react on seeing him. Vacher blamed his murders on this negative public reaction to him.[54]

A final potential motive might be considered: a political one. At his trial, Vacher described himself as an anarchist who was opposed to all societies and governments.[55] Later, we examine the defendant's statement to this effect in court.

The Murders

Eugenie Delhomme was a 21year-old factory worker. She was killed on March 20, 1984. He cut her throat, sliced off and took part of her right breast, disemboweled her, and raped the corpse.[56]

A 13-year-old girl was murdered and mutilated on November 10, 1894. About a half year later, Vacher murdered and mutilated a girl who was 17 at the time. Later in 1895, on August 24, he killed a 58-year-old woman and committed necrophilia.[57]

Four days later, he murdered and disemboweled a 16-year-old girl. Three days after that, on August 31, 1895, Vacher killed, castrated, and raped a 17-year-old shepherd boy. Victor Portalia, a 15-year-old shepherd boy, was killed and castrated about a month later, on September 29, 1895.[58]

Almost a year passed before the next crime, on September 10, 1896. Vacher murdered and raped a 19-year-old newlywed woman. On October 1 of the same year, a 14-old shepherd girl was slain, and Vacher cut out and took her vulva with him. A shepherd boy of the same age was raped, killed, and thrown down a well on May 27, 1897. The final murder took place on June 18, 1897, when a 13-year-old shepherd boy was murdered and sodomized.[59]

VAMPIRISM

At the time of his crimes, Vacher was believed to be a vampire. He consumed the blood of his victims, according to numerous reports. He confessed before and during his trial that he ingested blood from his victims. A contemporary media account reported that he demonstrated a passionate desire for human blood. He claimed that he cut the throat or bit the neck of victims and lapped at the blood directly from the wound.[60]

MASS COMMUNICATION

There were two mass communication dimensions of this case. Initially, it appears that the substantial popular interest in Vacher resulted from the media coverage. Public interest in the case was rooted in the sensationalistic manner in which newspapers and tabloids (both respectable and not-so-respectable ones) reported the story.[61]

The criminal himself took notice of his press and sought to manipulate the media reporting the crimes. Vacher set two conditions for his confession. The *New York Times* reported that one condition was publication of the complete story of the murders in leading French newspapers.[62]

INVESTIGATION

Vacher was arrested on August 4, 1897, but there is considerable controversy over the location. It is variously reported that he was caught in Bois de Pelleries, Ardeche and Tournon. The intended victim was gathering pinecones when Vacher attacked her, and her cries alerted her husband and children to run to her assistance.[63]

After being caught in the unsuccessful assault, he was convicted of violating public decency laws and incarcerated for six months. While in jail on this charge, he wrote to the judge confessing his role in the murders and related crimes. Vacher was not under suspicion for the serial slayings until he confessed.[64]

It is generally believed that his confession initiated police interest in him as a serial killer suspect. However, there are alternate perspectives on this fact. Vacher confessed only after being implicated in the murders, according to another version of events.[65]

Perhaps his confession was not the groundbreaking revelation some believed that it was. The authorities had already begun to suspect him in the serial slayings, it has been contended. Some suggested that he was apprehended after the body of a murdered 17-year-old teen was discovered. It was also noted that French authorities had discerned a pattern in the descriptions of their suspect and started to close in on the killer.[66]

This serial murder investigation was beset with a variety of problems and barriers. French police were totally unaccustomed to such crimes, and the murders and related deviant deeds were completely outside their professional experience. Nevertheless, they were criticized for their inability to catch the killer, a typical factor in these crimes. Vacher killed with impunity for nearly three years, although an accurate description of his appearance (a vagrant with a superurrating right eye and paralyzed right cheek) was circulated to every police station in southeastern France.[67]

How did this distinctive criminal avoid capture? Although gendarmes received numerous reports about Vacher, he kept moving and did not stay in one place for long. And it must be borne in mind that there were hundreds if not thousands of similar vagrants roaming around France at the time. A considerable amount of investigative effort was required before French law enforcement officials finally apprehended their man.[68]

TRIAL

Vacher was tried in the Court of Assizes in Ain, France. One version suggested the location as "Bourg-en-Bresse, capital of the Department of Ain." The trial was held in October 1897, and the presiding judge was Emile Fourquet.[69]

Vacher was tried for one count of murder. That was the 1985 murder of Portalia, a young shepherd. Other estimates indicated that he was tried for between 11 and 14 murders.[70]

This trial attracted state-of-the-art psychiatric and medical experts. They included Dr. Alexandre Berard and Dr. Alexandre Lacassagne, who provided the court-commissioned psychiatric assessment of the defendant:

> Vacher is not an epileptic nor is he an impulsif [sic]. He is a violent, immoral man who was temporarily overcome by delirious melancholy with ideas of persecution and suicide. . . . Vacher, cured, was responsible when he left the Saint-Robert asylum. His crimes are those of an antisocial, a bloody sadist, who believes in his invincibility. . . . At the present time, Vacher is not insane; he fakes madness. Vacher is therefore a criminal and should be considered responsible, this responsibility being scarcely attenuated by his previous psychological problems.[71]

Prolonged examination by these psychiatrists determined him to be sane and fit for trial.[72]

His behavior was an important factor in court. He reportedly acted crazy during his trial,[73] and his courthouse communication certainly disserved his cause.

His comments during the trial were noteworthy. He declared on one occasion, "My victims never suffered, for while I throttled them with one hand I simply took their lives with a sharp instrument in the other. I am an Anarchist, and I am opposed to society, no matter what the form of government might be." Vacher also testified, "Glory to Jesus! Long live Joan of Arc! Glory to the great martyrs of our time! Glory to the great savior!"[74]

We have already considered the Vacher confession made while incarcerated that resulted in his apprehension for the serial slayings. But there was a second, subsequent confession made during the trial. He initially denied his crimes in court, then confessed.[75] When he decided to confess, he admitted everything. This subsequent confession was also written out for Judge Fourquet. The document was described as a "sickeningly detailed confession." Vacher's pride motivated his confession; he wanted public awareness of his atrocious accomplishments.[76] Vacher's defense anticipated contemporary serial murder strategies by asserting that diminished mental capacity made the defendant not responsible for his actions. He protested that he was innocent and acted insane, according to a contemporary media report. One authority called it a temporary insanity defense.[77] He testified that a rabid dog had bitten him when he was eight years of age. The dog merely licked him, according to one version. Vacher claimed to have suffered from rabies after this incident that progressed to madness. He was given a strong herbal medicine by the village herbalist, and after drinking, it he became irritable, violent, and brutal, whereas before he was relatively quiet and inoffensive.[78]

He was convicted and sentenced to death on October 28, 1897. But it was contended that Vacher was really convicted because he was a vagrant who symbolized the national vagrancy problem.[79] This symbolic conviction was intended to publicly demonstrate the French government's resolve and response to the vagrancy problem.

He refused to cooperate with his executioners and made them half drag and half carry him to the guillotine platform. He was executed at dawn on New Year's Eve in 1897.[80] A sizable audience outside the prison walls celebrated the execution.

CONCLUSION

These were complicated and multidimensional crimes. In addition to the murders, a number of concurrent crimes were committed, not the least of which was vampirism.

Vacher was a cold-blooded serial slayer; of this there is no doubt. He looked frightening and acted aggressively. He was a premodern panhandler and a homeless person who terrorized France along with thousands of fellow vagabonds.

5

GILLES GARNIER

Gilles Garnier outdid Jack the Ripper in the ferocity of attack on his victims more than three centuries before the Whitechapel murders. One serial murder authority declared him as "the most notorious French werewolf." A comparative historic honorific held that Garnier was one of the two most infamous French werewolves.[1]

Garnier was a suspect in local property crime, which was rampant in rural France in the mid-1500s. And Frenchmen and Frenchwomen attributed much of this crime to the predations of werewolves. Werewolves were considered one of France's most serious social problems. Europe experienced an estimated 30,000 instances of werewolf allegations between 1520 and 1630.[2]

At the time, werewolves were believed to be the world's worst danger. Public belief in werewolves was a pervasive European superstition.[3]

THE SERIAL MURDERER

Garnier lived in France. We first consider the respected opinion of Sabine Baring-Gould, as recorded in *The Book of Werewolves*. She provided this description:

> In a retired spot near Amanges, half shrouded in trees, stood a small hovel of the rudest construction; its roof was of turf, and the walls were blotched with lichen. The garden to this cottage was run to waste, and the fence round it broken through. As the hovel was far from any road, and was only reached by a path over moorland and forest, it was seldom visited.[4]

Garnier lived near Dole, France,[5] which was described as a small French village. The largest nearby town was Lyons.[6] On the map, both Dole and Lyons were situated in Franche-Comte province.[7]

Garnier was commonly described as a hermit. That might be unusual when a married man with children is involved. The other frequently employed term used in explaining his general demeanor and behavior was "recluse."[8]

We are told that Garnier had a wife and children. That is not typical behavior for a hermit. He surrendered the solitary life of a recluse to begin a family.[9] According to another account, after years of living in solitude, he eventually married.[10]

Serial killers are often fearsome in appearance. Garnier was described as odd looking.[11] An extended description might be considered: he was "a somber, ill-looking fellow, who walked in a stooping attitude, and whose pale face, livid complexion and deep-set eyes under a pair of coarse and bushy brows, which met across the forehead, were sufficient to repel anyone from seeking his acquaintance."[12]

He certainly presented symptoms of mental illness. But a panel of experts decided that he was sane enough to stand trial. It was reported that he was conscious and aware of the crimes he had committed. Besides believing that he was a werewolf, Garnier seemed reasonable and rational on all other issues.[13]

His life changed considerably after an eerie incident in the woods one day. While the precise details of the event differ between versions, there is consistency in the overall historic record. This incident placed the Garnier crimes in a sociohistorical context in an era when the Devil was greatly feared.

As the story was told, a "spectral man" met Garnier one afternoon in the woods as the Frenchman sought something to feed to his family.[14] According to another analysis, a phantom or demon tempted him.[15] An apparition or demon visited him, according to Werewolves.com.[16]

This unidentified but spooky individual gave Garnier something: a substance to enable him to hunt prey and feed his family. Some described this gift as an "ointment."[17] It was also referred to as an "unguent."[18] When he rubbed it on his body, Garnier claimed that he was able to transform into a wolf. Garnier had a nickname. It was not bestowed on the serial killer but was given to him before he committed the crimes. Some called him the "Hermit of St. Bonnot," while others used the term "Hermit of Dole (St. Bonnot)."[19]

OTHER CRIMES

Garnier was a cannibal.[20] There were numerous reports of Garnier eating his victims.[21] Garnier was thought to have made a deal with the Devil, an overt act of witchcraft. The werewolf hysteria throughout Europe was linked to the epidemic of witchcraft activity prevalent in the same places during the same period.[22]

His victims were discovered mutilated. Some reports sounded like the mutilations were methodical in nature. Badly mutilated and dismembered bodies were described by one account.[23]

THE SERIAL MURDERS

Modus Operandi

The modus operandi in this case can be discerned from the reports of the discovery of the bodies. It was thought that local youth were being attacked by wolves.[24] Children from town started to disappear, and there were reports of ferocious attacks on small children.[25]

Garnier strangled, ripped apart, and ate his victims.[26] Strangulation was the specific means of murder.[27] Some murders were committed while he was in wolf form, but he was a human during other murders. In one case, he tried to kill a young boy without transforming into a werewolf. We might conclude this analysis of the modus operandi in this case by considering a letter sent by Daniel D'Ange to the dean of the Church of Sens:

> Gilles Garnier, lycophile, as I may call him, lived the life of a hermit, but has since taken a wife, and having no means of support for his family fell into the way, as is natural to defiant and desperate people of rude habits, of wandering into the woods and wild places. In this state he was met by a phantom in the shape of a man, who told him that he could perform miracles, among other things declaring that he would teach him how to change at will into wolf, lion or leopard, and because the wolf is more familiar in this country than the other kinds of wild beasts he chose to disguise himself in that shape, which he did, using a salve with which he rubbed himself for this purpose, as he has since confessed before dying, after recognizing the evil of his ways.[28]

Number of Victims

There was a relatively small number of victims in this case, and several rather vague estimates and indications of victimage can be considered. There were at least two victims, according to common knowledge.

Other, more specific victimage measurements can be examined. There were four victims, according to most observers.[29] One authority quantified the death toll at five.[30]

Time Frame

These murders occurred in the sixteenth century.[31] More specifically, they took place in the late 1560s and early 1570s.[32] An October 1572 series of crimes was also asserted.[33] The autumn of 1573 was suggested as the appropriate time frame.[34]

Victimology

The victimology selections made by Garnier were simple and few. It is known that all his victims were children.[35] And gender was not an apparent variable, as the victims included two boys and two girls.[36]

The Murders

The initial murder took place on the first day of Michaelmas, according to some reports, while others placed it after the Feast of St. Michael. It happened a mile from Dole on the farm of Gorge in the vineyard of Chastenoy, adjacent to the Le Serre Woods. Garnier killed a 10- or 12-year-old girl and took her body into the woods. He stripped the body and ate much of the flesh, enjoying it so much that he took some home for his wife to eat.[37]

Eight days later, he seized another young girl "near the meadowland of Le Pouppe, in the territory of Athume and Chastenoy." On All Saints' Day, he killed the girl and was about to eat her when a trio of peasants came along and spoiled his plans. She was reportedly rescued by "country people." The girl died of her injuries after being seized by Garnier's teeth.[38]

A 10-year-old boy was strangled two weeks after All Saints' Day. This crime took place about a mile from Dole between Gredisans and Menote. Garnier ate the victim's arms, legs, and stomach. He also tore off a leg and took it with him.[39]

A week later, Garnier claimed another victim on the Friday before the last Feast of St. Michael. A boy (12 or 13 years of age) was seized on the road and taken into a thicket under a pear tree and murdered near the village of Perrouze. He was unable to consume this victim because some villagers happened to pass by the crime scene. This crime was considered particularly egregious and even sacrilegious because the killer dared to eat meat on Friday in contravention of common Catholic custom.[40]

The final Garnier murder was committed on November 8, 1573. Peasants of Chastenoy returning to the village after work heard a child screaming and a wolf-like baying in the woods. They followed the sounds to a frightening sight: a terrified young girl trying to fend off what appeared to be a monstrous animal. Some accounts reported a male victim. Startled by the villagers, attacker managed to escape in the darkness, but some of the peasants claimed to recognize Garnier's face because he attacked in human form. The girl died.[41]

Motive

What caused these horrible crimes? In this case, the answer might be indicative of the horror of the homicides. The reasons behind Garnier's crimes were possibly as shocking as the murders themselves.[42]

It may have been a simple matter of poverty. Garnier was unable to provide enough food for his family. After his marriage and the addition of children, the number of mouths increased. Believing himself invested with werewolf powers, Garnier most likely rationalized his hunting of his fellow humans.[43]

LYCANTHROPY

Garnier was believed to be a werewolf at the time of the crimes. Local authorities strongly suspected that a werewolf was responsible for these ghastly crimes.[44] The fact that the wounds on several children revealed bite marks also tended to incriminate a werewolf in the minds of the public and gendarmes.[45]

A girl's arm and leg were eaten on the first day of Michaelmas in 1573.[46] Garnier confessed that he brought human flesh home for his wife to eat as well.[47] In 1573 on the fourteenth day after All Saints' Day, the legs, arms, and stomach of a young boy were ingested.[48] He brought some meat from this murder home for his wife to cook for both of them.[49]

MASS COMMUNICATION

The Garnier case was characterized by a solitary mass communication dimension, but it was an important one. A brochure or pamphlet was published at Sens, France, in 1574. This document vividly described his crimes, conviction, and punishment in great detail. The purpose of the brochure was to warn the public about the dangers posed by werewolves. This pamphlet is also important because it is the basis for much of what we know about the case today. As a result of this pamphlet, this case was called the "widely publicized and often cited trial of Gilles Garnier."[50]

INVESTIGATION

Initially, the culprit went undetected and unsuspected. Baring-Gould's classic account noted that "the hermit does not seem to have been suspected for some time."[51] A number of slightly different accounts have been offered to explain the unraveling of the case.

The most commonly accepted tale of Garnier's apprehension involved the November 5, 1573, encounter with a little girl in the woods where some peasants interrupted a cannibal act but could not prevent the murder of the child. It is believed by some that Garnier was apprehended and forced to confess in the aftermath of this incident.[52] A similar tale asserted that a group of villagers saw Garnier bending over a victim's body. Another version alleged that Garnier was seen dragging a young boy into the woods and was apprehended at that time.[53]

Other, very different versions of the apprehension have been reported. He was seen during the commission of two of the attacks and tracked down afterward, according to one analysis of the case.[54] Several villagers claimed to have seen a wolf-like creature with Garnier's face, it was reported.[55]

TRIAL

The trial began with the reading of the indictment by Dr. Henri Camus, doctor of laws and counselor to the king. It read,

> He, Gilles Garnier, had seized upon a little girl, twelve years of age, whom he drew into a vineyard and there killed, partly with his teeth and partly with his hands, seeming like a wolf's paws; that from thence he trailed her bleeding body along the ground with his teeth into the wood of *Le Serre*, where he ate the greatest portion of her at one meal, and carried the remainder home to his wife; that upon another occasion, eight days before the Feast of All Saints, he was seen to seize another child in his teeth, and would have devoured her had she not been rescued by the country people, and that the said child died a few days afterwards of the injuries he had inflicted; that fifteen days after the same festival of All Saints, being again in the shape of a wolf, he devoured a boy thirteen years of age, having previously torn off his right leg and thigh with his teeth, and hid them away for his breakfast on the morrow. He was furthermore indicted for giving way to the same diabolical and unnatural propensities even in the shape of a man, and that he had strangled a boy in a wood with the intention of eating him, which crime he would have effected if he had not been seen by the neighbors and prevented.[56]

He was tried at Dole.[57] The precise trial schedule is unknown, but it is thought that the date was late 1573. The trial was conducted under the jurisdiction of the Parliament of Franche-Comte.[58]

Perhaps the most persuasive trial testimony was that evidence (extracted after torture) from Garnier and his wife.[59] It has been emphasized in most accounts of the case that these confessions were corroborated in detail by numerous witnesses.[60] In fact, there was eyewitness confirmation of their detailed confessions.[61]

Garnier attempted to mount a relatively unorthodox defense during his trial. He tried to shift the blame for his crimes to the Devil or demons.[62] The court acknowledged Garnier's demonic influences but turned his defense against him.

There is a belief among some observers that Garnier was an innocent man. It is believed that "wolf predations" were the real problem and produced the tangible evidence against the alleged werewolf. This theory suggested that Garnier was a perfect candidate for accusations of werewolfism because of his marginal social status, reclusive lifestyle, and unusual behavior.[63]

He was convicted of lycanthropy and witchcraft. The court held that Garnier had been corrupted by the admitted Devilish or demonic influences in his life. The sentence was to be burned at the stake.[64]

Garnier was burned alive on January 18, 1573.[65] The execution was conducted by the Dole's master executioner of high justice.[66] His meager possessions were confiscated by the state and used to pay for trial and execution expenses.[67]

CONCLUSION

Garnier was thought to be a witch, a cannibal, and a werewolf. He was definitely a premodern serial killer. The murders were merely instrumental to his main motive of obtaining food.

The children he victimized suffered a cruel and terrifying death. Especially because he simulated a werewolf scenario, the crimes were traumatic and terrible. His torture and execution were richly deserved and culturally appropriate.

Garnier said that he was a werewolf, but under the threat of torture or after the application of torture, false confessions are not unusual. It is believed that he committed his crimes to feed his family, and he did bring human flesh home on two occasions for his wife to enjoy with him. Yet there is no evidence that he shared the grisly human "meat" with his children. Perhaps that was best for the children.

PETER STUBBE

The good and gentle German people of Bedburg (near Cologne) confronted a frightening problem in the sixteenth century. "Dismembered limbs were found in fields on a regular basis," according to one report.[1] A lengthy series of inexplicable murders was observed.[2] Local residents repeatedly found bodies scattered in the fields. The entire community was terrorized by the cannibalistic monster.[3]

Stubbe was the most infamous convicted werewolf of his era, according to one source. He was called one of the two most prominent werewolves in history. Another authority referred to him as a very vicious and violent werewolf.[4]

THE SERIAL MURDERER

Even the most basic facts pertaining to serial murder cases are frequently in doubt. This offender's name is one of those facts. I chose to use the name Peter Stubbe because eight of the sources I consulted in writing this chapter chose that name. Peter Stubb was the name used in a pair of accounts of the case.[5] Multiple names were mentioned in numerous accounts of the case. Some contend that the name was Peter Stubbe or Stump. According to another source, the pair of possibilities included Peter Stubb and Peter Stump.[6] Numerous names were mentioned in multiple accounts. The killer's name might have been Peter Stumpe, Peter Stebb, Peter Stumpf, or Peter Stubbe. According to one source, the possible names included Stubb, Stubbe, Stump, and Stumpf.[7]

He was born in Bedburg, Germany, according to most accounts. Another slightly more specific version suggested that Stubbe was born in a village named Epprath near Bedburg in the electorate of Cologne. The date was sometime in 1525, but all public records of this sort were destroyed during the Thirty Years' War.[8]

We know little about Stubbe's family life. He was described as a widower with a pair of children. He had a daughter and a son, according to most authorities. His daughter was named Sybil Stubbe or, according to some, Beell.[9]

His sexuality was a personal sojourn into sadistic and aberrant intimate behavior. He reportedly had a mistress named Katherine or Katherina Trompin. Stubbe may have had numerous extramarital liaisons; one account reported the existence of his "mistresses."[10]

Not every aspect of his sexuality was conventional—or mortal for that matter. In fact, there was a pair of supernatural sexual stories in this case. Stubbe was accused of having consorted with a demon who appeared to him in the form of a woman. A pamphlet written in 1590 provided this report:

> But his lewde and inordinate lust not being with the company of many Concubines, nor his wicked fancye contented with the beauty of any woman, at length the Devil sent unto him a wicked spirit in the simillitude and likenes of a Woman, so faire of face and comelye of personage, that she resembled rather some heavenly Helfin than any mortal creature, so farre her beauty exceeded the choisest sorte of women.[11]

It was also reported that the Devil sent a succubus to him for his carnal pleasure because he was sexually insatiable. The succubus was kept in his bed, he said. And a final dimension of his sex life might be mentioned: he committed incest with his daughter.[12]

There are portraits and sketches of some serial killers from the past to give us an idea of their likely appearance. In Stubbe's case, we have a verbal description of the killer in wolf form. He had "eyes great and large, which in the night sparkled like brands of fire, mouth great and wide, with most sharp and cruel teeth; a huge body and mighty claws."[13]

Few serial killers have had praiseworthy personalities in my experience. Stubbe was no exception: he was an evil character from a young age. A contemporary description of this serial slayer might be considered:

> In the towns of Cperadt and Bedbur neer unto Collin in high Germany, there was continually brought up and nourished one Stubbe Peter, who from his youth was greatly inclined to evill, and the practicing of wicked Artes even from twelve years of age till twentye, and so forwards till his dying day, insomuch that surfeiting in the Damnable desire of magic, necromancye, and sorcery, acquainting him selfe with infernal spirites and feendes.[14]

What did he do as a child that caused others to judge him so harshly? The answer is black magic. He confessed that at the age of 12, he began to practice black magic and engage in acts of witchcraft.[15]

Almost all serial killers past and present are bestowed nicknames. Stubbe was, too. He was referred to as the "Werewolf of Bedburg."[16]

OTHER CRIMES

Stubbe was a rapist, not just a murderer. In light of the youthfulness of his victims, perhaps it should be emphasized that he raped children. He even raped his sister and daughter, it is believed by some experts. He was referred to as a sex offender.[17]

Stubbe was a cannibal. He ate two unborn infants, fetuses torn from their mothers' wombs. He confessed to tearing out the hearts of victims so he could eat the muscle while it was still pumping. No trace whatsoever was found of one female victim, and it is thought that she was entirely consumed.[18]

The killer himself proclaimed his cannibal tendencies. "Hearts panting hot and raw" was the preferred cuisine for this cannibal serial killer. He called human flesh "a most savory and dainty delicious" meal.[19]

Stubbe's precocious childhood interest in black magic has been documented. He began the wicked art (as he referred to it) when he was 12. It is widely believed that he practiced witchcraft, casting spells and invoking spirits.[20]

In the Middle Ages, the theft and destruction of livestock belonging to others was a serious offense. He caused terror among farmers by feeding on their livestock, one respected account of this case contended.[21] The next step in Stubbe's criminal career was the murder and mutilation of human beings.

The incestuous relationship with his daughter Sybil played an important role in this case. And one unfortunate consequence of this immoral and illegal intimate activity was the birth of a boy whose mother was also his sister.[22]

Acts of mutilation also characterized his crimes. Stubbe deliberately desecrated the corpses.[23] The mutilation may have resulted from his consumption of the corpses. Victims were reportedly "sexually tortured."[24]

Filicide refers to a very specific type of homicide: the murder of one's child. We know that Stubbe fathered a child by his daughter. It has been widely reported that he killed his child and ate his brains.[25]

THE SERIAL MURDERS

Modus Operandi

The modus operandi in this case was about as simple as it gets in serial murders. He would sexually assault his victims while in human form and then transform into a wolf for the murder and cannibal acts. Most of the murders were conducted by Stubbe while he was transformed into lupine shape.[26]

Victims were acquired in an unsystematic and haphazard way. He reportedly roamed the fields searching for victims. Another account mentioned his scouring the countryside, attempting to assault strangers.[27]

Where did these atrocities take place? Most histories of the case situate these crimes in and near Bedburg. The land in the vicinity of Bedburg and Cologne was also identified as the murder locale. According to another account, the Rhine River valley near Westphalia hosted these serial murders.[28]

Time Frame

These crimes took place in the middle of the sixteenth century. A bit more specific was the placement of the murders in 1573.[29] The year of the crimes was actually 1589, according to an alternate version of the case. The year 1591 was also suggested as the time frame. The longest time frame estimate was from 1564 to 1589.[30]

There is similarly a lack of consensus on the duration of these criminal events. They lasted for five years, one authority suggested. A 25-year duration was identified by about a half dozen sources.[31]

Number of Victims

How many people did Stubbe kill? While there is some disagreement about the precise victimage total, the range of suggested estimates is relatively limited. Most versions of the case accepted a total of 15 victims.[32]

There were 15 or 16 deaths, according to one authority. An alternate perspective estimated 16 victims. He reportedly confessed to 16 murders. There were instead 17 victims, some have claimed.[33]

Victimology

Stubbe's victimology system and preferences have been described in a half dozen ways. Children were said to have been his primary victimology cohort. Young children were described in another account as his most preferred prey. Young girls were reportedly his main target. The victimology variable of gender was apparent: he preyed on "women and girls."[34]

Two other factors might be considered. One involved pregnancy: two of his targets were pregnant women. And another main set of victims were people who had incurred Stubbe's wrath.[35]

Victims

Little is known about Stubbe's victims. We know that he killed his own son, and it is believed that he murdered 13 children and two pregnant women.[36]

The victims in one crime were two men and a woman, friends who were taking a walk through the woods one afternoon. He silently killed the men individually, each out of sight of the other. He then raped, murdered, and ate their female companion.[37]

Motive

What forces and factors might have motivated these terrible crimes? A trio of possible motives have been mentioned. Initially, it was claimed that Stubbe murdered for the sake of pleasure. Another motive might have been revenge. It was reported that he began to attack his enemies, whether real or imaginary, to attain revenge.[38]

Religion might have been another possible factor in this case. Germany was ground zero for clashes between the establishment Roman Catholic Church and the emerging Protestant churches. It has been suggested that Stubbe was a Protestant and therefore fair game when the German Protestant movement was defeated.[39]

LYCANTHROPY

Germany and the rest of Europe was a relatively superstitious place during the Middle Ages. The agrarian lifestyle resulted in villages being frequently located next to forests. Among the many dangers in the woods, wolves stood out as the most feared, resulting in restricted travel at times. According to histories of that time, a ferocious werewolf was terrorizing the region. "German concerns about werewolves in their midst" were recalled.[40]

This context might enable us to better understand Stubbe's role in these monstrous crimes. It was noted that whatever the circumstances of Stubbe's death, it occurred during a surge of panic over werewolves.[41] People were conditioned to believe in and fear werewolves, and they interpreted serial murder through that supernatural prism.

Stubbe reportedly made a pact with the Devil to become a werewolf. The Devil gave him a magic belt capable of transforming the farmer into a werewolf. The belt changed him into a large wolf. He obtained the belt from "the infernal powers."[42]

This magical transformational item was reportedly a wolfskin belt, which was a supernatural method of transmutation. It was also referred to as the "enchanted belt." A magic girdle was how others described the Devilish device.[43]

A final factor is suggestive that Stubbe was believed to be a werewolf at the time: he confessed to being a werewolf. Further, he was also convicted of being a werewolf.[44]

MASS COMMUNICATION

An ancient mass communication document vividly portrayed Stubbe's capture. The pamphlet is thought to have been published in 1590. The English-language version was translated from high Dutch (German) by George Bores and witnessed by Tyse Artyne, William Brewer, and Adolf Staedt.[45]

This pamphlet, "A True Discourse Declaring the Damnable Life and Death of One Stubbe Peter," has been described in a variety of alternate ways. Broadsheets were widely circulated throughout southern Germany based on the pamphlet. One report referred to a "1590 chapbook." The "Stubbe booklet" was how an alternate analysis described this print material.[46]

Why was this document so important? Simply put, there are very few print materials about the Stubbe crimes still available to us today. Our knowledge about Stubbe comes mostly from one solitary surviving account, one history of this case claimed. But that might be an overstatement. The diary of a Cologne city alderman named Hermann von Weinsberg has recently been discovered and represents an additional invaluable document on this case.[47]

INVESTIGATION

The exact details of Stubbe's apprehension are probably lost to history. Since the crimes occurred for more than two decades, the killer obviously successfully eluded law enforcement. A contemporary account of the case reported the following:

> And although they had practiced all the meanes that men could devise to take the ravenous beast yet until the Lord had determined his fall, they could not in any way prevaile: notwithstanding they daylye continued their purpose, and daylye sought to intrap him, and for that intent continually maintained great mastyes and Dogges of much strength to hunt & chase the beast whosesoever they coulde find him.[48]

A number of different versions of the detection and arrest of this criminal have been recorded. Probably the most popular of these tales was that his escapades continued for 25 years until hunters tracked him, thinking that he was a wolf. We might consider several other versions of events. Another commonly told tale had a number of villagers attacking a wolf near the village until it suddenly turned into Stubbe before their startled eyes.[49]

When a wolf was seen attacking a little boy, several men went to his aid and captured the beast, according to another perspective on this case. The werewolf eluded his pursuers until they resorted to the use of bloodhounds, contended a different version of the apprehension. Another account asserted that the gendarmes apprehended Stubbe, chasing him for a considerable distance before he took off the belt and was transformed back into a man and easily captured. A final story insisted that Stubbe's transformation back from wolf to man had been observed on more than one occasion.[50]

After his apprehension, the subsequent events are somewhat more familiar to us. Stubbe was promptly conveyed to the Bedburg magistrates. There he was immediately threatened with torture on the rack, the wheel, or possibly both.[51] He promptly confessed. He was "broken" on the wheel, according to one perspective on the case. Another account observed that he was "put on the wheel." He reportedly confessed after being tortured on the rack.[52]

Stubbe confessed to having slipped off the belt as he was being captured and hiding it. He had "cast this instrument of metamorphosis in a particular valley before he was captured." His captors didn't locate it. Searchers were designated and sent off to locate the belt, but no one was able to find it.[53]

Whether his confession occurred prior to his torture or not, it completely and comprehensively covered the crimes. He admitted to being a werewolf, sorcerer, cannibal, rapist, and adulterer. And he also implicated both his daughter and his mistress in the serial murders.[54]

TRIAL

The trial was conducted sometime in 1589. The defendants were charged with murder, rape, and cannibalism. Stubbe, his mistress, and his daughter were tried as "a pack."[55]

There was doubt about Stubbe's guilt. The classic account of Baring-Gould concluded, "Though his case was unproved, Stubb [sic] was hastily executed." Another authority asserted that it is impossible to ascertain if Stubbe actually committed the murders of which he was accused.[56]

Then there is the matter of the belt. Searchers never could locate the artifact allegedly given by the Devil to Stubbe. The court's explanation for the inability to locate the belt was that the Devil had retrieved it. The 1590 pamphlet offered this information:

> He confessed how by Sorcery he procured of the Devil a Girdle, which beeing put on, he forthwith became a Woolfe, which girdle at his apprehension he confest he cast it off on a certain Vallye and there left it, which when the Magistrates heard, they sent to the Vallye for it, but at their coming found nothing at all, for it may be supposed that it was gone to the Devil from whence it came, for that it was not to be found.[57]

The court believed that Stubbe's daughter and mistress served as accomplices in these horrible crimes. His mistress Katherina was believed to be a shape-shifter who was able to transform herself into other forms. Both women were implicated in the crimes by Stubbe, and each paid with her life.[58]

There is some disagreement over who died first. It was reported that Stubbe was tortured and killed with Sybil and Katherina in the audience prior to their execution. Stubbe was forced to watch their executions before he went to his fate, according to an alternate description of events.[59]

We know that the case against Stubbe was far from conclusive and that he may have been innocent. Nevertheless, trials of serial slayers seldom if ever end in acquittals. The trio received guilty verdicts on all the murder counts. The convictions were announced on October 25, 1589.[60]

The executions took place in late October 1589. The date may have been Halloween, October 31.[61] What is known in some detail is the manner of Stubbe's execution.

The flesh was pulled off his legs in 10 places with a pair of red-hot pincers, one source observed. His legs and arms were broken with a wooden axe, and then he was beheaded and burned. According to another version, he was stretched on the wheel, had 10 pieces of flesh ripped from his body with the pincers, had his arms and legs severed with a hatchet, and was decapitated and then burned.[62]

After being stretched on the wheel, he lost 10 pieces of flesh, we are told. His limbs were smashed with a wooden axe, and he was decapitated, with his head displayed as a public warning. His body was then burned. According to an alternate version, he was bound to the spokes of a wheel before having chunks of his flesh ripped out. An iron rod was used to pulverize his limbs, after which he was decapitated and his torso burned at the stake. Yet another version mentioned Stubbe being tortured on the wheel prior to losing 10 chunks of flesh to the heated pincers. His legs were broken with a hammer (to prevent his return from the grave), and he was beheaded and burned.[63]

A noteworthy crowd of spectators viewed the execution. Germans took the werewolf threat seriously, and those accused of lycanthropy paid the price for pervasive public superstition. No wonder these court proceedings were referred to as an especially lurid werewolf trial and the "most sensational werewolf trial with multiple murders."[64]

CONCLUSION

A public display was intended as a warning to other potential werewolves. The torture wheel used in torturing Stubbe was placed on top of a pole along with a plaque, an image of a wolf, portraits of the 15 victims, and, at the top, Stubbe's head. It was also reported that the rack on which he was tortured was broken up into 15 pieces (one for each victim) and publicly displayed.[65]

Was the Stubbe case actually about religion and politics and not serial murder and lycanthropy? It is possible that he was a victim and not the victimizer. But I doubt it. Nevertheless, the possibility must be conceded.

This trial was important in a greater sense, with implications beyond Germany. Occurrences like werewolf trials are contagious events with early events serving as precursors to later, related ones. The social psychology of public reaction to werewolf epidemics suggests as much.

We know from decades of mass communication research that once established, public fear concerning dangers like werewolves can approach panic levels relatively quickly. Public attitudes and even perceptions can be influenced and manufactured subconsciously. Publicity about this trial was extensively circulated throughout Europe, and it served as the model and motivation behind a subsequent series of werewolf trials in France, Switzerland, and Franche-Comte.[66]

WEREWOLF OF CHALONS

This chapter introduces a relatively unknown premodern serial murderer. In fact, it is impossible to identify this culprit by name, and he is known to history when remembered at all simply as the Werewolf of Chalons. But the fact that his name is unknown does not lessen the horrific nature of these serial offenses.

He is perhaps best remembered for being a werewolf in a world where people believed in the creatures. France, at the cusp between the sixteenth and seventeenth centuries, was described as a hotbed of werewolves. One authority recalled, "The year 1598 seems to have been a particularly troublesome year in France with regard to werewolves. Indeed, this year was to produce a veritable epidemic of werewolf accusations."[1]

Perhaps it goes without saying, but the Werewolf of Chalons was best known for his lycanthropy. Werewolfpage.com portrayed the Werewolf of Chalons as deserving his reputation of ranking among the "worst" werewolves of history.[2] This infamous French serial slayer was widely regarded as being a genuine lycanthrope.

THE SERIAL MURDERER

Since we do not know who this person was, this is a relatively short chapter. However, there are a few things that are known about the killer. Three dimensions of this unknown serial murderer are considered.

Initially, we might examine the place where these crimes occurred. The country involved was France. Paris was specified as the locale in several accounts. Most likely, the town was Chalons.[3]

Since the name of the killer has been unknown since the trial and execution of the offender, a number of nicknames were created and applied to the anonymous criminal. "The Werewolf of Chalons" is probably the most common such moniker.[4] Almost as popular is a second nickname: the

"Demon Tailor."[5] A third but much less common name was the "Tailor of Chalons."[6]

He was referred to as the "unnamed man."[7] French officials decided that it was preferable to keep his identity under wraps. As a result, the killer was described only as a tailor who lived in Chalons.[8]

Not much has been documented or recorded about the criminal. He was referred to as a "wretched man." According to a contemporary account, "The man was perfectly hardened."[9]

OTHER CRIMES

The Werewolf of Chalons is believed to have mistreated his victims. Reports of the savage treatment suffered by the children repeatedly mentioned their maltreatment. Their killer took pleasure from the humiliation and abuse.[10]

It was said that the victims were tortured. This was not a common claim, but it is noteworthy. According to this story, the Werewolf of Chalons did not merely murder his victims: he also subjected them to cruel and lengthy torture.[11]

Sexual perversion was another characteristic element of these crimes.[12] One source combined the notions of torture and sexual perversion. It was claimed that the killer "tortured them with sexual perversions."[13]

The final concurrent crime committed by the Werewolf of Chalons was dismemberment. He treated the bodies of his victims just like a butcher processes and dissects a piece of meat. After killing his victims, he cut up and packaged them.[14]

THE SERIAL MURDERS

These murders and related criminal conduct shocked France at the very end of the 1500s. People were unaccustomed at that time to such savagery. Five aspects of these serial murders are examined.

Modus Operandi

In some serial murder cases, the modus operandi never varies in any appreciable way. In many cases, however, there is some flexibility or evidence of alternate methods, as was the situation with the Werewolf of Chalons. The method of victim acquisition varied. The authoritative account of Sabine Baring-Gould noted this variability; the killer lured small children into his shop or attacked them "in the gloaming when they strayed in the woods."[15]

Most accounts of these crimes mentioned victim acquisition through the use of the shop. "The unnamed man was reputed to have lured children into his tailor shop in Paris," *The Crime Library* noted.[16] The tailor's shop was therefore clearly instrumental in the acquisition of new victims.[17]

Not all victims were obtained through the Paris shop. Sometimes in the twilight of the early evening, this killer stalked the woods seeking prey. According to one version, early murders were facilitated through the shop, but when he failed to find victims in that way, he roamed the woods to obtain them. There were numerous reports that the killer terrorized the woods as a wolf.[18]

There is some disagreement in the literature on the manner of murder. Some accounts reported that victims were bitten to death. It was suggested that the killer had "torn them with his teeth and killed them."[19] On those occasions when the killer obtained them in the woods, the unlucky victims were murdered when the werewolf savagely ripped their throats.[20]

The murder method varied in an alternate version of the case. Some believe that a knife was used to inflict the fatal injuries. One report described how the killer slit their throats.[21] He "sliced" their throats, according to another account.[22]

Number of Victims

The precise victimage attributable to the Werewolf of Chalons is not a matter of agreement or consensus. There were an even dozen dead, declared one authority on serial murder. Several dozen victims were also reported.[23]

The truth is that we do not really know. The classic study by Baring-Gould concluded as much. It declared pessimistically, "The number of little innocents whom he destroyed is unknown."[24]

Victimology

What was the victimology strategy of the Werewolf of Chalons? Although we don't have any statements from the killer directly addressing this issue, we can make a trio of educated guesses. We know that he lured children into his shop.[25] The victims included little children of both genders.[26]

And there was a somewhat random element in the victimology of this case as well. Victims unwittingly endangered themselves by proximity to the killer. He victimized children who wandered near his workplace.[27]

Motive

The reasons behind the crimes committed by the Werewolf of Chalons remain unknown to us today. There is no mention of motive anywhere in the extant literature on this case. But we can examine two possibilities: cannibalism and sex. The Werewolf of Chalons was a cannibal, but these murders may have been simply a matter of acquiring something to eat. Were these crimes about sex? It does seem that the little children victimized in this case were not merely murdered but sexually abused as well. The Werewolf of Chalons may have been acting on behalf of his libido to sate his sexual needs.

Time Frame

The precise time frame is unknown. There is little information about the length or duration of these crimes. The only definite information available suggests that the killer was arraigned, tried, convicted, and executed in 1598.[28]

LYCANTHROPY

Was the Werewolf of Chalons truly a lycanthrope? The consensus of opinion at the time suggested an affirmative answer to that query. Baring-Gould reported that the killer was executed for lycanthropy.[29]

Clear and convincing evidence of cannibalism was reported by numerous authorities. After the Werewolf of Chalons murdered the little children, he consumed their bodies.[30] It was suggested that he "dressed the flesh" as a butcher might and ate it.[31] A historically accepted document contended that he prepared the flesh as ordinary meat and excitedly ate it.[32]

Children were consumed in the shop and eaten in the woods. Victims were dismembered and consumed.[33] The victims in the woods were apparently ingested on the spot.[34]

A considerable number of cannibalistic crimes were committed by the Werewolf of Chalons. He found human meat to be "most succulent," it was contended by one account.[35] It seems beyond doubt that the Werewolf of Chalons was considered a cannibal.

INVESTIGATION

The investigation into the Werewolf of Chalons murders and related crimes took place a long time ago, and the particulars are mostly long gone. There are nevertheless a few dimensions of this police probe in the public record. Four specific aspects of the investigation are documented.

According to some sources, the apprehension of the Werewolf of Chalons resulted from a police investigation. Local police discovered the evidence in a search. One report suggested that officials raided his home and shop.[36]

There is an alternate version of how the Werewolf of Chalons came to the attention of the authorities. The police were not credited with the arrest of the killer in this scenario. Instead, some authorities believe that the killer's downfall resulted from the entirely fortunate discovery of the place where he stored the victims' bones. He kept the bones instead of disposing of them, so their discovery incriminated the tailor.[37]

Serial killers not infrequently retain something from their victims as a memento or trophy. In this case, it was the bones of the little children he victimized. A variety of descriptions have been rendered of the containers used to safeguard his souvenirs.

An entire "cask" completely full of bones was discovered in his house, according to Baring-Gould.[38] The police discovered "barrels of bleached bones" in the cellar of the suspect's home. It is not known if the bones were officially identified as being human or if it was simply assumed under the circumstances that they represented evidence of murder.[39]

More than bones was found by the authorities searching the property of the Werewolf of Chalons. It is unfortunate that we do not know what that was. The historic record is almost silent on this point.

When police searched the killer's property, not only bones were discovered; other unidentified things also turned up.[40] It was asserted that bones, "along with other foul items," were found.[41] The police searchers discovered "other foul and hideous things," according to an alternate analysis.[42]

TRIAL

There seems to be more information available about the trial of the Werewolf of Chalons and his sentence than any other particular dimension of this case. It is uncertain what that means, but perhaps punishment has been emphasized in several accounts. A half dozen aspects of this trial and the posttrial stages are considered.

In contemporary legal cases, arraignment is typically an important but not memorable or newsworthy dimension of the overall justice system proceedings. Yet we know with some degree of certainty when the Werewolf of Chalons was arraigned. This legal process took place on December 14, 1598.[43]

It has been believed by historians of this case that it was completely resolved in 1598. So we know that the trial followed the arraignment relatively closely. One more thing is known about the trial of the Werewolf of Chalons: it was brief. He was quickly convicted, it seems. According to one account, "On the 14th of December at Paris, a tailor of Chalons was sentenced to be burned quick for his horrible crimes."[44]

The courtroom demeanor and displays of the defendant in serial murder trials are always noteworthy and frequently very revealing. The case of the

Werewolf of Chalons was certainly no different, and the accused played the part of the evil villain to perfection. He reportedly never manifested any sincere remorse for his victims at any time during the proceedings and refused to confess to the murders and related offenses.[45]

"The details of his trial were so full of horrors or abominations of all kinds, that the judges ordered the documents to be burned," Baring-Gould contended.[46] There were reports of murder details so revolting that all the court documents were destroyed.[47] Authorities wanted no evidence in writing about what the Werewolf of Chalons had done.[48]

The Parliament of Paris mandated the destruction of all documents about the case. Despite this blanket of official secrecy, rumors emerged and served as the basis for the information available to us today.[49] So even though the findings and documents of the court were destroyed, it was possible to write this chapter. Reverend Summers's account concluded, "So scabrous were the details of the case that the Court ordered the documents to be burned."[50]

Convicted serial killers typically die in custody, are executed, or spend the rest of their life institutionalized in prison or psychiatric facilities. The Werewolf of Chalons did not escape these normal fates.[51] His sentence was execution by being burned at the stake.[52] Reverend Summers reported that the Parliament of Paris sentenced a man from Chalons to be executed as a werewolf.[53] The Werewolf of Chalons was executed in Paris. It is assumed that the public spectacle was held toward the end of December 1598. He was burned at the stake.[54] A relatively large crowd of spectators watched the execution ceremony.[55] Observers noted that he died without any remorse or sorrow for his deeds.[56] The killer was heard cursing and loudly blaspheming until his death.[57]

CONCLUSION

The Werewolf of Chalons case is perhaps more subtle and complex than we typically believe. It was not simply a case of lycanthropy. Werewolves do not necessarily or ordinarily sexually abuse their victims, who are not invariably small children.

And then there was the official and extensive censorship of his case. That is not a frequent occurrence. We are fortunate to have been able to piece together what took place from the few remaining reports. There may have been multiple motives behind case of the Werewolf of Chalons. Cannibalism, sexual perversion, torture, and lycanthropy all characterized these crimes.

PART III

WITCH SERIAL KILLERS

CATHERINE DESHAYES MONVOISON

Catherine Deshayes Monvoison is known by several names and a nickname, but there is no mistaking who she was or her deadly deeds. She has been called "an infamous poisoner."[1] She was the most prominent poisoner convicted by the Chambre Ardent.[2] We must understand this court and the Affaire des Poisons to better comprehend the Monvoison multiple murders.

France was a hotbed of poisoning during the "age of arsenic." "Inheritance powder" was a term that elicited knowing glances and suppressed smiles. Succession powders was another derisive contemporary term for economically motivated poisons.[3]

The Affaire des Poisons constituted a crisis for French King Louis XIV, the Sun King. "The Poison Affair was rooted in a spate of (suspected) poisonings in France during the later part of the 17th century," it was noted. Several prominent persons in the French aristocracy were convicted of poisoning and witchcraft.[4]

The black stain on French honor known as the Affaire des Poisons was recalled by a biography of women serial slayers.[5] Nigel Cawthorne quantified the carnage: more than 100 men and women were executed, enslaved in French galleys, and banned or exiled. The French government reported that the Chambre Ardente officially considered 442 cases leading to 367 arrests, resulting in 36 executions and 246 people either imprisoned or banished.[6]

THE SERIAL MURDERESS

Monvoison has been known by more than one name. In many serial murder cases, the killer's name is rendered in different ways, and the Monvoison case was no exception. She was often called Catherine Deshayes. That was reportedly her maiden name. After her marriage, her name was Catherine Monvoison. The name was Montvoison, according to a couple of authorities.

Catherine Deshayes Monvoison is how some named her. One source thought her name was La Voison.[7]

Monvoison was born in 1638 in France. She lived between 1640 and 1680, according to one source. Little information about her early life has been recorded except that she was born into a poor family.[8] She was sent out to supplement the family income through telling fortunes at the age of nine.[9]

She married a man named Antoine Monvoison. She was 20 years of age at the time of her wedding. He was an unsuccessful haberdasher.[10]

Her husband next tried his hand as a jeweler, although he reportedly was not very successful at that trade. He never contributed any money to the maintenance of the household. Monvoison supported herself, her husband, and his daughter Marguerite from a previous marriage. She is believed to have unsuccessfully tried to kill Antoine on several occasions, but no details have been preserved.[11]

Her sexual needs were apparently not fulfilled within her marriage. Monvoison was promiscuous throughout the duration of that union. One of her lovers reportedly bit Antoine on his nose, nearly severing the olfactory organ from his face.[12]

Later in life, Monvoison ran a fortune-telling business. She practiced chiromancy, which is another term for palm reading. Face reading (somewhat like palm reading) was another of her divination methods. Astrology was her preferred fortune-telling method.[13]

She was also a beautician. Arsenic-based skin-cleansing treatments were a very profitable commercial enterprise. Clients came to her because of her fame as a hairdresser, barber, and beauty expert.[14]

Monvoison earned repute as an herbalist, skilled in the use of herbs as medicine. She also practiced medicine, specializing in midwifery. Another relatively lucrative service involved performing abortions.[15]

She was perhaps most famous for her potions. Love powders and death potions were her most popular products. Monvoison's main money source was potion making. The ingredients of her potions included toad bones, mole teeth, iron filings, cantharides, human blood, and dried flesh.[16]

As newlyweds, Monvoison and her husband lived in "abject poverty."[17] Antoine's business failures reduced the family income and necessitated her employment in the plethora of previously discussed jobs. Her businesses were so lucrative that she achieved financial success, especially after it seemed that her astrology services were acceptable to the Roman Catholic Church.[18]

We can glean something about her personality from the accounts of her crimes and some related sources. Those close to her declared that she loved her parents and children deeply. She supported her mother financially.[19] Monvoison was inherently resourceful. That makes sense in light of her ability to reinvent herself as a breadwinner. Among her constituency, she was considered influential. One last personality factor: she seems to have had an addictive personality because she was reportedly "usually drunk."[20]

Religion played a part in her life. It also had an important effect on her career. She attended mass regularly at the church of the Abbe Saint-Amour, rector of the University of Paris. It was reported that she even dined privately with the noted theologian.[21]

The Roman Catholic Church had the opportunity to derail her criminal career early, but fate decreed otherwise. Monvoison ran afoul of the Church when word of her astrology business reached priestly ears. She was called before a special tribunal when she incurred the holy suspicion of the Church.

Most defendants subjected to such inquiry "were flayed alive by a Grand Inquisitor," but Monvoison had other plans. She persuaded a Catholic tribunal including the vicars general and doctors of theology from the Sorbonne that astrology was within accepted Church doctrine. The result of her release and apparent vindication was the widespread popular belief that her activities were sanctioned by the Church, and she experienced a substantial increase in her clientele.[22]

We can describe the Monvoison residence in some detail. It was a secluded edifice in a seedy section of Paris. The house was located in Villaneuve, adjacent to the St. Denis section of the French capital. The property was protected by a very high fence and tall trees. Residing within the abode were Monvoison, her husband, Marguerite, and a lodger named Nicholas Lavesseur, an executioner by trade.[23]

One incident from her life might be examined, as it illuminated Monvoison's character and discussed her criminal tendencies as well. Her stepdaughter Marguerite became pregnant after an affair with a married neighbor. Monvoison was constantly searching for infants to be sacrificed in black masses. Marguerite was horrified when she noticed her stepmother carefully monitoring her pregnancy. After the birth, Marguerite sent the child away to protect the baby from the potential predations of its grandmother.[24]

OTHER CRIMES

Monvoison murdered infants. Babies were used as living sacrifices at black masses, and their blood was used in a variety of witchcraft ceremonies. The babies were used in Satanic rituals; their throats were slit, the blood was drained, and then the bodies were tossed into a furnace. Infant blood was considered an unusually pure and therefore desirable catalytic substance in witchcraft ceremonies.[25]

Babies were sometimes purchased to provide the appropriate sacrificial material. It may seem difficult to believe, but there were plenty of French parents with too many mouths to feed and an inclination to part with some children to feed others and themselves. Her Satanic ceremonial accomplice Etienne Guibourg sold the illegitimate babies resulting from his numerous affairs to Monvoison.[26]

She opened a facility ostensibly to care for women in problematic pregnancies. Monvoison's home for unwed mothers provided her with a substantial number of infants. This shelter for mothers with unwanted pregnancies became a virtual baby factory.[27]

THE SERIAL MURDERS

Modus Operandi

There were essentially dual modi operandi in this case. That is because Monvoison murdered using multiple methods. Her killing techniques included stabbing and poisoning.[28]

She was responsible for numerous murders resulting from the poison she routinely sold to women wanting to be rid of their husbands or men seeking to expedite the demise of wealthy relatives. And infants were held aloft over an altar, their throats slit with a knife. The blood was subsequently collected for ritual use.[29]

There was an accomplice. She had a lover, a magician known as Lesage, who was really named Adam Coeuret. It was suggested that he became her accomplice after the two became lovers.[30]

Number of Victims

Monvoison admitted murdering hundreds of children in the course of Satanic rituals.[31] The death toll was more than 1,500, according to another authority. There were approximately 2,000 deaths, in the estimation of one source. As many as 2,500 Monvoison victims were identified by several studies.[32] A final estimate might be entertained and even enhanced. She confessed to killing more than 2,500 children and murdering more adults than all the other poisoners of Paris combined.[33] If there was a conservative total of 250 adult victims, her death total was about 2,750. But if she murdered an additional 500 adults, her victimage would have amounted to approximately 3,000.

Time Frame

When did these crimes occur? They took place in the seventeenth century, according to one rather imprecise estimate. A similar perspective on the case offered a mid-seventeenth-century time frame.[34] The 1660s was also indicated as the time when the crimes occurred. The most specific time frame advanced was from 1669 to 1679. The sole published estimate of the duration of the crimes specified 13 years.[35]

Victimology

We know something about Monvoison's victimology choices. Two kinds of victims were targeted by this serial slayer. Monvoison catered to women who wanted to have their husbands killed[36] as well as male clients who sought to have spouses or wealthy relatives killed. The second type of victim: babies.

Victims

The identity of only one of Monvoison's victims is known to us today. His name was Judge Leferon. Leferon's wife Marguerite complained to Monvoison that he was "insufficient in bed" and wanted him killed. He died an agonizing death on September 8, 1669.[37]

Motive

Monvoison might have been primarily a commercially motivated serial killer. She certainly had an impressive and aristocratic clientele. Olympe or Olympia Mancini held the title of Italian Comtesse de Soissons and was the mother of Prince Eugene of Savoy and niece of Cardinal Mazarin. Her sister Maria Ann Mancini was also a client.[38]

Mademoiselle de Gramont (la belle Hamilton) sought her services. So did Francoise Athenais de Rochechouart, the marchessa of Montespan. Duke Marshall Luxembourg was a French military hero and client whose full name was Francois Henri de Montmorency-Bouteville. The duchess of Bouillion, the duke of Buckingham, and the duchess of Vivonne also patronized La Voison.[39]

WITCHCRAFT

Monvoison was believed to have been a witch at the time of her crimes. She was called "a self-styled witch."[40] She began her questionable career as a fortune-teller and purveyor of potions and then over time began to practice witchcraft. And she was convicted of witchcraft.[41]

She led a Devil-worshipping ring, according to contemporary reports. Monvoison organized and officiated at black masses.[42] She and Guibourg were said to have worked as a team in leading the Satanic ceremonies. Monvoison received her visitors in a darkened chamber wearing an ermine-lined cloak and hood festooned with 200 eagles stitched in gold thread on purple velvet. For the right price, Monvoison herself would officiate at a personal black mass.[43]

A French sorcerer is what one authority called her. She was also referred to as "an alleged sorcerer" and an accused sorcerer. Finally, she was burned alive as a sorcerer.[44]

She maintained a list of Roman Catholic priests who assisted her in the Satanic ceremonies. There were approximately 50 such individuals, but her favorite seems to have been Guibourg, sometimes called Abbe instead of Etienne. Guibourg held the position of sacristan of St. Marcel at the Saint-Denis Cathedral. He was critically described as a bloated and disgusting old man.[45]

Guibourg also had training and expertise in chemistry, which was an advantage because he could assist Monvoison in the concoction of potions. He has been described as a defrocked priest and a renegade priest. And although he held several public and private ecclesiastical offices, Guibourg always needed money to maintain mistresses housed throughout Paris.[46]

INVESTIGATION

As usual, there are several versions of exactly how Monvoison came to the attention of the authorities. There existed a clandestine network of police informants at various levels of Parisian society who tipped police off. An alternate version of the case suggested that Paris Chief of Police Nicholas or Gabriel Nicholas de la Reynie received information from a couple of Roman Catholic priests who had taken confessions concerning the serial killings.[47]

We might consider a third explanation for the unraveling of these crimes. It is believed that King Louis became aware of her activities in 1679. That is because she was involved in the unsuccessful assassination attempt on his life by his mistress, the marquise or marchessa of Montespan. The BBC reported that Monvoison was apprehended after she assisted in the failed attempt to assassinate Louis.[48]

One of de la Reynie's subordinates, a detective known only as Desgrez, was assigned to conduct surveillance on suspicious activities at the Monvoison residence. His officers staked out the subterranean caverns used by the Satanists and the Monvoison abode and reported on the numerous members of the French aristocracy seen frequenting the occult ceremonies. The crest of the king's mistress was seen on a carriage door.[49]

The influential nature of the black mass participants naturally concerned Desgrez, who brought the issue to the attention of his superior. De la Reynie received the potentially explosive information and contemplated the appropriate course of action to take in this politically volatile and dangerous situation. He chose to do nothing at the time but intensify the Monvoison surveillance.[50]

King Louis appointed a commission to investigate poisoners. During the age of arsenic, poisoning had become a popular means of enhancing one's income, eliminating a romantic rival, or exacting revenge upon an enemy. The French aristocracy already had a considerable fear of poisoners that led to the king's action.[51]

It was actually de la Reynie who convinced King Louis to set up the tribunal, some have claimed. The commission investigated and arrested fortune-tellers, alchemists, and those dealing in potions and magical charms. The tribunal met in April 1679. Chambre Ardente sessions were held in a plain room enveloped entirely in black drapes and illuminated only by candlelight.[52]

Monvoison had influential friends at the highest echelons of the French monarchy. The king's mistress reportedly repeatedly participated in black masses and even sought Monvoison's assistance in the foiled assassination attempt. It was therefore shocking when both Monvoison and Guibourg were taken into custody by Paris gendarmes on December 27, 1679.[53]

The scandal implicated numerous prominent persons. A great deal of the evidence was censored. There were persistent rumors that a number of suspects were allowed to flee after Monvoison's arrest.[54]

King Louis was in a very difficult position. His mistress had just tried to kill him, and he had discovered that she and a number of others at the court were Satanists who practiced witchcraft. So the king ordered the dissolution of the Chambre Ardente in early 1681.[55]

King Louis reversed himself before long. He reinstituted the special court on May 19, 1681, and it remained convened until the final dissolution on July 21, 1682.[56] The court was conducted by de la Reynie, it was reported.[57]

Not much has been recorded or preserved about Monvoison's interrogation. We do know that she was tortured, enduring a total of four sessions lasting six hours each. These sessions were conducted between February 19 and February 21, 1680. She was placed in Spanish boots, a popular torture method where the victim's feet were placed in metal boots that were then systematically and gradually tightened. And throughout the interrogation, she was kept quite intoxicated.[58]

TRIAL

Little is known about Monvoison's trial. We do know that the legal proceedings were held within the jurisdiction of the Chambre Ardente. And it has been recorded that the trial took place in 1680.[59]

Monvoison bragged at her trial that she had willfully murdered more than 2,500 infants during her Satanic rituals. She was charged with being both a sorcerer and a poisoner. She was convicted and sentenced to death for witchcraft and poisoning.[60]

This trial was unusual in several respects. For instance, innocent people were imprisoned for life because of their knowledge of incriminating facts. And the degree of censorship was noteworthy: the censorship of trial items insisted on by King Louis was apparent during the trial. The tribunal proceedings and transcripts were incomplete, with substantial amounts of information stricken from the official records.[61]

Monvoison was executed after being tortured. She died on February 22, 1680. According to another account, the date was actually February 23. A February 20, 1680, death date was suggested in an alternate version of the case.[62]

She was executed in Paris at the Place de Greve. The public execution reportedly drew a decent crowd of onlookers.[63] Monvoison was burned at the stake, but she did not exit gracefully and with equanimity. She went to her death singing lewd and bawdy songs and cursing the priests who sought her death.[64]

CONCLUSION

The Monvoison multiple murders were part of a much larger tapestry of poisoning at the very heart of the French aristocracy. The Affaire des Poisons was a major criminal and sociological phenomenon in France, and the killings must be understood as part of the greater set of crimes. In this respect, these were atypical serial murders.

It was believed that Monvoison was a witch and that she praised Satan and prayed to him. The slaughter of babies so that their blood could be used in the celebration of black masses characterized these crimes as especially heinous and horrible. She also was responsible for countless other murders as a professional purveyor of poisons.

GILLES DE RAIS

One of the most enigmatic men in European history is the subject of this chapter. He was also described as "one of the most bizarre figures in European history." Gilles de Rais is thought to have been the model for the fictional character Bluebeard.[1]

A few accounts of his crimes recognized both the positive and the negative aspects of this killer. His distinguished military career was recalled by one authority who also discussed the Frenchman's trial for Satanism, child abduction, and murder. De Rais was both a national hero and an infamous criminal.[2]

De Rais has been remembered in a variety of positive ways. A contemporary account described "a man of rare elegance and almost angelic beauty." He was a national hero who played a major role in the French victory against the British at Orleans. He was called one of the greatest French heroes.[3]

He was one of Europe's most enthusiastic supporters of the arts, sponsoring music, literature, plays, and other art forms. De Rais organized and financed a 25-person youth choir. He created and paid for a music school. And his personal religious entourage included a principal chaplain, a dean, a chanter, two archdeacons, four vicars, 12 assistant chaplains, and an eight-voice choir.[4]

However, numerous negative notions concerning de Rais have also been recorded. He was called a precursor of the contemporary serial killer. His choice of victims made the crimes even worse: he was one of the most sadistic and brutal serial killers of children in history. He was undoubtedly one of Europe's worst child rapists and murderers.[5] One account of his crimes referred to him as a multiple murderer. And it was said that he did not merely murder his victims: he "luxuriated in hideous cruelty."[6]

THE SERIAL MURDERER

Many accounts of the case place de Rais's birth in September or October 1404. In fact, the precise date was September 10, 1404. His birthplace is often reported as being Champtoce, France. A slightly different version reported the location as Champtoce-sur-Loire. Machecoul, France, and Machecoul, Brittany, are sometimes suggested as the place of birth.[7]

His parents were French nobles: Marie de Craon and Guy de Montmorency-Laval. His mother Marie died in 1415, according to one account of the case. Their marriage was purely political and profit motivated in nature. One fact about his parents: they were cousins.[8]

His childhood was much like his life in general. He was raised in luxury, surrounded by every possible privilege. What accounted for this good fortune? De Rais was a son in the ruling house of Brittany.[9]

He had a brother Rene who was a year younger. Rene outlived his older brother, dying in 1474. He and Gilles had a strained but friendly relationship.[10]

Their childhood was privileged yet passionless. The boys were raised in a formal and loveless way because the aristocratic French child-rearing system of the day posited that children should be treated like young adults until the age of seven, the legal age of reason. Gilles and Rene rarely saw their parents and were raised by a nurse.[11]

But then things changed for the worst. Their parents died. Gilles was anywhere from nine to 20 years of age when his father died. One version of the case suggested that their mother survived her husband by two years but that she quickly remarried and abandoned Gilles and Rene.[12] She most likely died before her husband. Both parents died about the same time, according to another version of this case. It was reported that when Gilles was a 10-year-old, both parents died. The year was 1415. Their father wanted his children raised by his cousin Jean Tournemine de la Junaudaye. His will specified that intention. Nevertheless, they were sent to live with their maternal grandfather, Jean de Craon, in the middle of 1416.[13]

De Craon was a suboptimal caregiver. He was described as violent and dissolute. He was definitely a poor influence on the impressionable boys. They received no affection and minimal schooling and were seldom supervised.[14]

De Rais was a French nobleman in an ancient and respected family. He was also known as a Breton baron. "Aristocrat" was another term frequently used to describe him. A similar term might be considered "deranged French aristocrat." One study perfectly described the significance of his social status, referring to de Rais and similar aristocrats whose position placed them beyond the law. It should be noted that wealth was the foundation of that social status and that the de Rais fortune resulted from his father's combining the estate of Jeanne de Rais with that of Marie de Craon.[15]

Gilles was educated in the classics, arts, humanities, and ethics at an early age. He also was taught Latin and Greek by his parents' paid tutors. He read and spoke Latin fluently. He was described as an adequate student. He was considered to be a relatively bright or intelligent child.[16]

Much of his education was pragmatic training in martial arts and military skills. He was trained in combat, war, and chivalry. His two primary instructors in warfare were Guilliaume de la Jumelliere, the lord of Avegnon, and Georges de la Tremoille, a man who was close to King Charles VII.[17]

There is a somewhat balanced depiction of his personality, unlike the unidimensional and negative portrayal of many serial killers. For instance, we know about his "mystical turn of mind." And de Rais loved music as a young boy.[18]

The rest of his personality left something to be desired. He was accused of displaying egomania, being an arrogant bully, and behaving immaturely. On a slightly more serious note, he was also a sadist. "Monstrously depraved" was another term used to explain him. His wife claimed that his bizarre and somber character frightened her.[19]

Other unfortunate personality traits were not lethal but merely objectionable. He was overly ambitious. De Rais was also impetuous and craved excitement and bloodshed. According to a contemporary account, he did not have the moral strength to restrain his impulsive behavior. And he was an alcoholic.[20]

De Rais was a good-looking man, according to legend. "His appearance was fascinating," one account claimed. He was an attractive man who was distinguished by a bluish-black beard.[21]

First and foremost, De Rais was a soldier until his career took a decidedly dark detour into depravity. He came from a long line of knights.[22] He was also a fearless and crafty warrior. And he was considered to be a distinguished soldier.[23]

He was an officer. Early in his military career, he commanded a force of 25 men-at-arms and 11 archers. He served in the French army from 1427 until 1435, it was suggested in one report. He fought in battles between 1426 and 1433 in another version of this case. He reportedly was a hero in the Hundred Years' War, and he rose to the rank of royal commander in the French army.[24]

He fought alongside Joan of Arc. He was standing next to her when she was wounded. Her death reportedly sent him into a deep depression from which some say he never recovered. He left the military after her death, returned to one of his castles, and immediately began his criminal career.[25]

Their relationship went beyond cursory comradeship. De Rais was called a confidante of Joan's. He was a friend of hers in another version. Some claimed that he was assigned to Joan's personal bodyguard detail. One report claimed that he was her primary adviser and most trusted general, while another referred to him as her chief lieutenant.[26]

But their bond may have been even deeper. He was a platonic lover of Joan of Arc, it was contended. De Rais was romantically attracted to and in love with Joan, another version of the case claimed.[27]

De Rais lived in a time of politically arranged marriages. His grandfather tried unsuccessfully to create two advantageous marital unions, one with Jeanne de Paynol and another with the niece of the duke of Brittany, Beatrice Rohan. The third attempt succeeded, but de Rais had to kidnap his bride, Catherine de Thonars, heiress to the La Vendee and Poitou fortunes. They were wed on November 30, 1420.[28]

His daughter Marie was born in 1429. She later married an admiral in the French navy. Little else has been recorded about her.[29]

Two last things about his family life. It was suggested that Catherine and her sister Anne were instrumental in the unraveling of these crimes. And de Rais reportedly left his wife in anger, denouncing her and forsaking sexual intercourse with women.[30]

His extensive ecumenical entourage has already been documented. His generous financial support of the Roman Catholic Church has been commonly described. "A devout Christian," he built a cathedral and several chapels at his own expense.[31]

De Rais earned a number of significant honors. He received the prestigious designation of marechal, one of four soldiers so honored. But perhaps his most impressive military honor was being named a marshal of France at the age of 25, the award signifying his status as France's most distinguished soldier. He was also introduced at the court of Charles VII in 1425.[32]

He received another noteworthy honor in 1429, but the exact nature of this event is obscured by the volume of varying versions. He carried the holy chrism (anointing oil) from Paris to Reims for the coronation of King Charles, it was reported. Or he carried the oriflamme, the ancient French flag, at the coronation ceremony. He was reportedly one of four lords who brought the holy ampula from the Abbey of St. Remy for the king's installation. A final version suggested that he crowned Charles at the coronation.[33]

He was insane since his childhood, according to one authority on the case. "Deranged" was an adjective commonly used to describe him. The betrayal and execution of his comrade-in-arms and friend Joan of Arc badly upset and unsettled him and resulted in what one source called his "descent into madness."[34]

De Rais admitted his homosexual orientation in court. The remainder of his romantic repertoire revealed an aberrant and decidedly abnormal sexuality. This sadistic lust murderer was considered a truly terrible sexual predator. He masturbated on the entrails of his victims as he killed them and in the immediate aftermath. And he confessed that the torture and mutilation gave him an unparalleled sexual thrill.[35]

He was referred to as one of the wealthiest European nobles. He inherited "fifteen princely domains" and huge estates throughout the Loire Valley. De Rais was heir to the largest French fortune of the time. He was frequently called the richest man in France.[36] But his overhead and cost of living were outrageous. He had three very expensive castles to finance and a private army of 200 soldiers. The castles housed and fed approximately 500 people daily. A retinue of workers, soldiers, jugglers, dancers, comics, mimes, and others was expensive. De Rais and his entourage enjoyed more lavish living conditions than the king. His hunting party was said to be more luxurious than that of the pope. He funded extravagant theatrical productions, such as "The Siege of Orleans," and maintained a substantial library of rare manuscripts, including *The City of God* by St. Augustine.[37]

The result of expenses exceeding revenue was a deficit in his budget. He had exhausted all his resources on returning to his castle. By 1432, de Rais was compelled to sell several estates and other property.[38]

De Rais was the target of many fraudulent schemes designed to obtain part of his wealth. His greed made de Rais easy prey for fraudulent alchemists, and he never learned that he was being cheated. Purported spirit conjurer Jean de la Riviere led an expensive but phony black mass in the woods one evening. And de Rais's main priest, Blanchett, offered to locate and obtain herbs that could coerce the Devil into obeying a human master. These herbs grew only in Spain and Africa, and Blanchett volunteered to search for them if de Rais funded the expedition.[39] De Rais never saw Blanchett again.

De Rais resorted to alchemy after depleting his wealth. One authority on Satanism in the Middle Ages suggested that after his vast fortune was squandered, he decided to try alchemy as a way of restoring his estate. He searched throughout Italy, Spain, and Germany for alchemical experts to participate in his research and development efforts. He constructed a state-of-the-art laboratory, but a full year of costly experiments produced nothing.[40]

An event took place in 1440 that catapulted de Rais toward an unkind fate. He decided to renege on the sale of a castle and attempted to repossess it by force. It had been purchased by Geoffrey de Ferron, the royal treasurer to Jean V, duke of Brittany. Even worse, the new owner of the castle, Geoffrey's brother Jean (a priest), was viciously assaulted, and the castle was ransacked. An alternate version of this story situated the fracas in the St. Etienne de Mermote Roman Catholic Church during the celebration of High Mass. De Rais and a gang of brigands broke into the church brandishing a double-edged axe, attacked the priest, and dragged him away.[41]

OTHER CRIMES

Robbery was probably de Rais's first serious crime. After he left the army, he began to engage in illegal conduct. De Rais started to rob travelers for excitement and profit.[42]

There was another de Rais crime prior to the serial murders, a decidedly grave one. It is believed that he sanctioned or even ordered the execution of captured British soldiers. These murders were war crimes. De Rais approved the mass murder of prisoners of war.[43]

De Rais sodomized his victims, frequently violating them before calming them down and apologizing before attacking a second time. He was charged with 140 counts of child molestation. And he was most certainly a pedophile.[44]

De Rais sodomized his victims "before, during and after their death." During evening sex sessions, children would be hung on hooks and tortured until near death, at which point de Rais reportedly sodomized them until after their demise. Eyewitnesses accused him of engaging in frequent acts of necrophilia.[45]

After death, the bodies of the victims were violently abused. The sexual mutilation of the children was an important aspect of the motivation behind these crimes. He enjoyed torturing and mutilating children. Disembowelment was one specific type of mutilation manifested in these murders.[46]

We already know that he viciously and brutally sexually violated his victims. He would hang the children on hooks and rape them as they flailed suspended in midair. He then masturbated on and into holes cut and ripped in their bodies.[47]

He kidnapped his wife and her uncle and a couple of others. Several of their party died in the de Rais dungeon. He reportedly kidnapped Jean le Farron. And in a very bizarre allegation, he was accused of abducting a pregnant woman, killing her, and then tearing the fetus from the womb and raping it.[48]

The severed heads of children were prepared for pageants. He often employed a woman to curl the children's hair and apply makeup to their faces. The heads were then affixed to poles or rods and appreciated. De Rais and his entourage displayed the severed heads of these children in order for them to decide which was "the fairest." The winning head was subsequently used for that evening's sexual gratification.[49]

The final crime was the probable real reason behind the prosecution. De Rais was disposing of family property and selling off his heirs' legacy. His brother Rene requested that King Charles prevent any further property sales and then secured the Champtoce Castle before occupying the Machecoul estate with his cousin Andre de Laval-Loheac to keep it in safe hands. So the king dutifully issued an edict in July 1435 preventing the sale or mortgaging of the remainder of his property. Despite these efforts, de Rais sold the Mal-emont estate and a number of baronies.[50]

THE SERIAL MURDERS

Modus Operandi

The victims were raped and killed. De Rais slit their throats, sodomized them, decapitated and dismembered the bodies, and then masturbated on them. They were reportedly decapitated and dismembered and had their necks broken. A final account suggested that the victims' throats were slit, a brasquemard (a short broadsword) was used to decapitate them, and they were dismembered.[51]

A young man named Poitou was a former de Rais victim-turned-assistant. He testified that the murder methods varied: "sometimes beheading or decapitating them, sometimes cutting their throats, sometimes dismembering them, and sometimes breaking their neck with a cudgel." Always the young victims were sexually abused.[52]

The majority of the bodies were burned or buried. The corpses were set on fire and the ashes buried, thrown in the moat, or scattered on the castle grounds. The bodies were burned slowly in an attempt to reduce the terrible smell of burning flesh. Approximately 50 bodies were discovered in a tower of the Machecoul castle.[53]

An unknown number of accomplices assisted de Rais in these crimes. There were two assistants according to one account. One was Poitou, and another was a servant named Henriet. Two of his cousins, Gilles de Silles and Roger de Briqueville, also served as accomplices. His main helper was Francisco Prelati, a defrocked priest and alchemist from Padua. Prelati was a 22-year-old "conjurer and charlatan," who was intelligent and charming and spoke French, Italian, Latin, and Greek fluently.[54]

Some of the crimes took place in the family chateau at Machecoul. The crime scenes were his castles. The murders occurred around his domain, at Champtoce, the Suze family house, or the castles at Nantes, Tiffauges, and Machecoul.[55]

Number of Victims

De Rais's victimage is uncertain, but it is believed to have been consider-able. At least 50 children was one estimate, similar to the more than 50 vic-tims suggested in another account. Eighty victims were identified in another version of the case.[56]

Several hundred murders was a relatively vague estimate. The most common quantification of the victimage is 140 deaths. He confessed to 140 murders and was indicted for the same number.[57]

Other victimage estimates were higher. The murder of 400 peasant children was reported. There were in excess of 600 victims, it was said. There were as many as 800 victims, one source estimated, while another concluded that there were in excess of 800 deaths.[58]

Some victimage estimates were expressed as ranges. There were between 80 and 200 deaths, it was contended by one study. Another authority estimated that there were at least 200 murders and possibly as many as 300.[59]

There is some doubt about the true death toll accumulated by de Rais. "It is unlikely that Gilles killed [the] hundreds of children he was blamed for," it was concluded. It is doubtful that claims of 500 to 800 victims were accurate, several sources suggested.[60]

Victimology

De Rais's victims were selected with care. He preferred young boys; the victims were mostly boys, and his favorites had blond hair and blue eyes. Peasant children made up by far the largest possible victimology cohort, and they were typically between the ages of eight and 15.[61]

"The prettiest children" were prized as victims. A large number of them were starving children. Many of the victims were referred to as throwaway children.[62]

Time Frame

These atrocious crimes took place in the fifteenth century. They occurred in 1430, according to one authority.[63] Other potential time frames in this case can be considered.

A time frame from 1432 to 1440 was offered by one authority. From 1432 to 1442 was an alternate estimate. A time frame from 1426 to 1442 was also suggested, as was a similar version, from 1426 to 1440.[64]

The duration of the serial slayings is similarly uncertain. They occurred over an eight-year period, according to a pair of respected serial murder authorities. Fourteen years is how long they lasted, in the opinion of another source.[65]

Victims

The names of de Rais's victims (except for one) are lost to time. However, we do know a little about a few of the unlucky children victimized by de Rais.

In 1442, nine-year-old Jeannot Roussin disappeared while looking for animals near her home. The eight-year-old son of Jeanne Eolin, widow of Aimery Eolin, was another victim, as was the 10-year-old son of Jean Le Moine. The child of Alexandre Chastelier was murdered, as were the eight-year-old son of Jeanne Bonneau and Jean Merdon's 12-year-old boy.[66]

Motive

The specific motives are unknown. Pleasure appears to have been the primary motive in this case. De Rais later admitted that he did all the damage possible for the sake of his own pleasure. He seems to have enjoyed killing.[67]

We might consider a pair of additional motives. De Rais admired Roman emperors, such as Caligula and Tiberius, and it was claimed that he murdered because he wanted to emulate the ancient Roman Caesars. And it is possible that he became mentally unhinged after the betrayal and execution of Joan of Arc, whose death apparently caused him to withdraw from his military and public activities and rededicate himself to the pursuit of occult and criminal conduct.[68]

WITCHCRAFT

De Rais was called an infamous sorcerer. He was convicted and executed as a witch. He had made a pact with the Devil in return for wealth.[69]

He practiced and was a devotee of Satanism. He had a "side hobby of Satanism." He attempted to invoke demonic supernatural assistance in his efforts at alchemy.[70]

The murder of children characterized these crimes as being particularly egregious offenses. The child sacrifices began in 1439, de Rais confessed. Infants and children were sacrificed, and their blood was collected for ritual use.[71]

Parts of children were used in the black magic ceremonies. The eyes and hands of a child were sacrificed to Satan, it was said, while another version suggested that the eyes, hands, and feet were offered. According to another account, the sacrifice included the eyes, hands, lungs, heart, and blood of a child.[72]

THE INVESTIGATION

An investigation was launched into the serial murders by a clergyman in 1440. The bishop of Nantes is said to have begun a probe after de Rais kidnapped Jean le Farron.[73] This investigation reportedly turned up evidence of the more serious serial slayings. And it has been contended that there was a separate secular investigation that confirmed the results of the Roman Catholic Church's scrutiny. An alternate version of events contended that Catherine de Rais and her sister discovered the loathsome evidence of her husband's occult activity and that Anne signaled to some passersby for assistance from the top of the Machecoul castle tower.[74]

But there had been suspicions and rumors for years. There were public declarations about dark deeds at the Champtoce estate in particular. Yet no one dared come forward and accuse the reigning monarch or demand an investigation.[75]

Interviews were conducted with the parents of missing children. Pierre L'Hopital, the chief judge of Brittany, and his prosecutor friar, Jean de Touscheronde, interviewed members of 10 families between September 18 and October 8, 1440. The vicar of the Inquisition, Jean Blouyn, also observed the proceedings.[76]

Bishop Malestroit issued an arrest warrant for de Rais on September 14, 1440. That same day. he sent a letter to all French Church officials to assist in the location and apprehension of de Rais. The next day, September 15, the constable of France and the duke of Brittany's men arrested de Rais and his accomplices at the Machecoul castle.[77]

THE TRIAL

De Rais was summoned to trial with a 47-paragraph indictment. He was indicted on October 13, 1440, on 34 charges of murder, sodomy, heresy, and violating the immunity of the Church. He was also indicted by the French Catholic Church on October 11, 1440, for murdering 140 children over 14 years.[78]

He was accused of "sorcery, sodomy, and murder" or murder, sodomy, and heresy. A more extensive list of charges included killing, strangling, massacring children, evoking demons, making pacts with the Devil, and child sacrifice. He was charged with three specific types of heresy: abuse of clerical privilege, conjuration of demons, and sexual perversion against children. A final set of charges included sorcery, violating the immunity of the Church, and sexual perversion against children.[79]

De Rais was tried twice in secular and ecclesiastical courtrooms. One trial concerned the serial murders, and the other involved the black magic activity. The ecclesiastical trial was focused on the heresy charge, while the civil court heard the murder case. An alternate version of the case noted one trial, a combined affair with a commission including the bishop of Nantes, the chancellor of Brittany, the vicar of the Inquisition, and the president of the Provincial Parliament.[80]

The initial trial concerned the attack on the St. Etienne Church. This civil trial was held in the ducal court. On October 23, 1440, de Rais and his accomplices were convicted of murder. He was sentenced to death, and the others received prison terms.[81]

Bishop Malestroit of Nantes also brought him to court. De Rais "came under the jurisdiction of the Catholic Church." Another account asserted that he was tried in an Episcopal-inquisitorial court. On September 13, 1440, Jean, the bishop of Nantes, signed the legal writ resulting in a Church trial for de Rais.[82]

Initially, de Rais vigorously resisted the legal proceedings and denied all charges against him. He verbally castigated the commission and refused each of the four times he was asked to respond to the allegations by making a plea in court. But he returned to court two days later after being refused Communion, tearfully apologizing for his offenses. On October 21, dressed entirely in white, he admitted everything. He confessed to the father superior of the Carmelites and later to Bishop Jean Pregent and Pierre L'Hopital.[83]

Overwhelming evidence was produced against him on a daily basis at these trials. There were approximately 110 witnesses against the defendants. The alleged accomplices testified for five days against de Rais. The most persuasive evidence was that given by the parents of the boys who had vanished and were presumed dead. Etienne Corillait also provided incriminating testimony.[84]

The trials have been called a farce. Most of the evidence was obtained through torture. The facts in the case were exaggerated and distorted, according to one version of events. It was claimed that most of the evidence resulted from witnesses who were tortured, spiteful, or stood to benefit from the trials. Some say that de Rais was framed.[85]

The motive behind the trials was possibly to confiscate his wealth. The bishop, inquisitor, and duke of Brittany gained enormous wealth by prosecuting de Rais and confiscating his property.[86] One result of the trials was the redistribution of the de Rais fortune. Lawsuits and family feuds reallocated the de Rais estate. The titles to his property were promptly transferred to the duke of Brittany, who actually confiscated many de Rais assets before the trials had even concluded.[87]

The convictions were announced on October 23, 1440: guilty on all charges. De Rais was convicted of 140 counts of child molestation, rape, and murder. He was found guilty of torture, rape, and murder, according to another account. De Rais was executed at Nantes, France, on October 26, 1440.[88]

CONCLUSION

Was de Rais one of the worst serial killers ever or an innocent victim of greedy and scheming Church and secular leaders? This colleague of Joan the Arc was once one of the wealthiest men in France until these accusations arose. What actually transpired is unfortunately not clear to us at the present time.

If the allegations against him are true, de Rais was a truly terrible type of monstrous multiple murderer. Sodomy, torture, black magic, witchcraft, and sexual abuse characterized these crimes as especially egregious, even as the victimage of young children did. This mighty marshal of France might have murdered nearly 1,000 children.

PART IV

ARISTOCRATIC SERIAL KILLERS

VLAD THE IMPALER

Vlad the Impaler was the ruler of Wallachia, which, along with Moldavia and Transylvania, became modern-day Romania.[1] He "was a complex and fascinating figure of history."[2] He remains a national hero in Romania, according to a 2010 report.[3]

Vlad was concerned about the peasant class and opposed the boyars, the wealthy Wallachian aristocracy. He championed the cause of the common man against the oppressive boyars. And at a time of military threats from the Ottoman Empire and economic domination by German commercial interests, Vlad protected his people from foreigners: the Turkish invaders as well as German merchants.[4]

Vlad was denounced by some of his contemporaries. He reportedly ruled with an iron hand and had a reputation as an evil leader. One respected serial murder authority recalled that Vlad's atrocious and unspeakable crimes stood out for their brutality.[5]

There is disagreement within the literature on whether Vlad was a serial killer. He was "not a true serial killer," it was claimed in one account. Serial murder authorities disagree on whether tyrants like Vlad should be included as serial slayers.[6] Instead, Vlad was a "mass murderer," according to one report. *The Crime Library* concurred, noting that by modern standards he would be characterized as a mass murderer.[7]

Did Vlad inspire Bram Stoker and facilitate creation of the literary character Dracula? The consensus of opinion has suggested that Stoker's *Dracula* was modeled on Vlad. Yet some accounts have dismissed any similarity between Vlad and Stoker's character as mere coincidence.[8]

THE SERIAL MURDERER

Vlad's name has been variously reported and deserves some clarification. He was named Vlad or Vladislav Basarab at birth. His father was called

Prince Dracul (or dragon), so Vlad was referred to as Dracula, or son of Dracul. He therefore inherited the title or name Dracula.[9]

Other names were used to designate this individual. Vlad Dracolya was one such term, and another was Vlad III. The name Vlad Die Tepes appeared in the literature, as does the more commonly used Vlad Tepes. "Tepes" means "spike" in Romanian, according to one source, while another authority translated the name as "impaler."[10]

His exact date of birth is unknown. It was about 1430. The winter of 1431 was another estimate, as was late 1430. December of 1431 was also suggested as the time of Vlad's birth along with November or December 1431.[11]

His birthplace is also a bit uncertain. Sighisoara, Transylvania, is often said to be the place of birth, but so is Schassburg or Schaasburg. He was probably born in a village named Sighisoara, which was also called Schassburg. This town was located in the Tirvana Mare Valley.[12]

We know something about his parents because they too were nobles. His paternal grandfather was King Mircea the Old. And a great deal is known about Vlad's father and namesake, Vlad Dracul, also known as Vlad II Dracul. He was a very brave soldier and the commander of the Dragon Unit, or heavy cavalry. He was also famous for his cruelty. He was installed in the Order of the Dragon in February 1431 in Nuremburg, Germany, pledging to defend Christianity from the Muslim threat posed by the Ottoman Empire.[13]

His mother was Princess Cneajna of Moldavia. She was the daughter of the Moldavian Prince Alexander cel Bun. She has also been described as a Transylvanian noblewoman. She was considered a deeply devout woman.[14]

Not much is known about his early years. He had three brothers: the older brothers were named Vlad IV the Monk and Mircea, and the younger was named Radu. He also had a sister named Alexandria.[15]

His relations with his siblings varied. He and Mircea frequently engaged in mischief. Radu had been intimate with the Turkish sultan and would eventually die from syphilis. Radu was his political rival, allying with the Turks against his homeland. His half brother Vlad the Monk similarly competed with Vlad for the Wallachian throne.[16]

A significant event happened in 1443 in Vlad's life. He and Radu were left as hostages at the Ottoman court because of Turkish distrust of their father, Vlad II. The boys were kept at Adrianople for seven years as virtual prisoners.[17]

Vlad and his siblings received a much more extensive education than was typical for fifteenth-century children. Most of the instruction was provided by their mother. An elderly Christian knight was also hired to assist in the education. Vlad was recalled as a good pupil.[18]

Instruction included geography, mathematics, science, languages, philosophy, and the classical arts. Etiquette was also taught. Vlad spoke Romanian, Turkish, Greek, and German.[19]

Vlad was much like his famous father. He inherited some of the good qualities of his father, according to one authority. He was famous for his bravery in battles against the Turks.[20]

Other reports of his personality were not as positive. Again, genetics is believed to have been a factor, as Vlad inherited his father's excessive temper and fiery nature. When he and Radu were hostages in Turkey, he was described as having "a belligerent and smothering attitude." And, worst of all, he was a sadist.[21]

He was married more than once. He married the daughter of a Romanian noble who committed suicide rather than risk being taken captive by the Turks. An alternate version of this case declared that his third wife killed herself. This initial marriage produced a son named Mihnea cel Rau. The boy was later known as Mihnea the Bad.[22]

His second marriage was to Ilona Szilagyi, who was related to the Hungarian king Matthias Corvinus. They met while he was incarcerated in a Hungarian prison after fleeing Wallachia. He encountered the lovely and statuesque Countess Szilagy, who was a cousin of the king. According to another version, Vlad "caught the eye" of Ilona, the king's sister.[23]

They quickly became engaged, wed, settled in Badu, and had two boys. One son was named Vlad, and the other boy's name is unknown. Their large home was a lavish palace.[24]

Was Vlad a sincerely religious person? Many at the time and since have doubted the reality of his religious appearance. He was surrounded by bishops, abbots, and priests of both the Greek Orthodox and the Roman Catholic churches. He converted to Catholicism in 1475. He was brought up as a Roman Catholic for political reasons, but he said that he preferred the Romanian Orthodox Church and its monasteries in Tisnava and Snajov.[25]

It does not appear from the available information that Vlad was mentally ill. He was not insane, one authority contended. However, his period of time as a hostage may have injured his psyche, and it could be concluded that his imprisonment traumatized Vlad. The death of his father and brother also definitely affected him; the news about the massacre of his family made him go "berserk."[26]

One particular aspect of his mental health might be examined: his impalement of small animals and insects. While imprisoned, he would capture bugs and mice, kill them, and impale them on slivers of wood that he would proudly display to his captors. He was seen impaling spiders, cockroaches, squirrels, and mice. He also impaled birds.[27]

"Voevod" means "warlord-prince" in the Wallachian language. His father served in this capacity before being assassinated, and Vlad reigned on three different occasions. His initial term in office was for two months in the fall of 1448, and it ended with his exile to Moldavia. Next, he reigned from August 20, 1456, until 1462, the so-called reign of terror. After more than a decade under house arrest in Hungary, he returned to the Wallachian throne in 1476 for a few weeks until his death.[28]

The geographic placement of this kingdom imperiled it, as the Ottoman Empire was on one side and the largely Roman Catholic European continent on the other. Vlad II was required to pay 10,000 ducats a year in tribute to the sultan and send him 500 boys to serve in the Janissary, a corps of foreign-born young male bodyguards. Vlad II was assassinated by Hungarian King Ladislas Poshumous because he thought that he was politically too close to the Turks.[29]

In addition to threats from outside the country, there were definite domestic dangers. Vlad's older brother Mihnea was buried alive by the boyars and merchants of Tirgoviste. The boyars' eternal feuding and power squabbles frustrated attempts at building a unified nation.[30]

Vlad was disliked by many but also had his supporters. He was considered a hero by the Wallachian public because he protected them from the predations of roving bands of Turks and marauding Hungarian Magyars. Tirgoviste, the Wallachian capital, was the safest city on the European continent. And he prevented unfair economic competition from foreign merchants by enacting supportive and protective trade policies.[31]

If anyone ran afoul of the law or Vlad's sensibility, they were cruelly punished. Vlad once saw a planter wearing a caftan that was too short. The planter told him that his wife was too ill to properly care for his clothes and her other duties, so the Voevod promptly dragged her from their hut, killed her by impalement, and selected an unwed neighbor girl as the planter's new spouse.[32]

He did not live most of his life in freedom. He was incarcerated for years in various prisons, totaling 26 of the 46 years of his life.[33] Vlad was imprisoned for four years, according to one estimate. He was reportedly imprisoned by the king of Wallachia for 12 years. When imprisoned in Hungary, he was incarcerated in Solomon's Tower in the Visegrad Palace.[34]

He was exiled to Moldavia and Transylvania from 1448 until 1456. He was reportedly in exile for a total of 14 years. A three-year period of exile in Moldavia was identified in another account of the case.[35]

Vlad was referred to by a nickname that is relatively well known throughout the world even today. That nickname is Vlad the Impaler. He earned that nickname not as a warrior in battle but as a depraved and sadistic killer.[36]

OTHER CRIMES

It is said that Vlad had a secret torture chamber in the dungeon of one of his castles.[37] A variety of torture tactics was tried on his victims. They were skinned, boiled alive, and then impaled. Another account specified the severance of limbs, strangulation, blinding, boiling, and burning. Torture methods included "cutting off the limbs, blinding, strangulation, burning, skinning, boiling alive and the mutilation of sex organs."[38]

There were dark, unsubstantiated rumors of occult practices in this case. No public allegations were ever made, but witchcraft may have been a factor in these crimes. He was considered by some to be the Devil or at least a demon.[39]

Vlad has been accused of terrorism tactics. The extensive public impalement was an obvious attempt to terrorize his subjects into compliance and foreigners into leaving Wallachia alone. He terrorized the churches, and he also frequently used terrorist tactics against his Turkish and Hungarian enemies.[40]

Vlad was a serial killer, but he was also a mass murderer. While most serial killers kill a person (or a few) at a time repeatedly over time, Vlad repeatedly murdered hundreds and sometimes thousands of victims. Vlad destroyed the entire population of a number of villages and towns.[41]

He killed 50 people at a time, it was contended by contemporary reports. On one occasion, he murdered 200 boyars. Five hundred Wallachian nobles were thought to have been slain in another incident. In an event that was extreme even by his standards, 30,000 people were killed at one time.[42]

The Brasov massacre exemplified the scope of his cruelty. On April 2, 1459, thousands of Saxons were impaled in this Carpathian Mountain town. Those who were not impaled were chopped up like cuts of beef for him. In the midst of this murderous mayhem and while the city burned, Vlad requested, was served, and ate an extravagant dinner.[43]

A noteworthy atrocity occurred in Sibu, another Transylvanian town. Vlad was angry with residents of this place because they supported his half brother Vlad the Monk. On one St. Bartholomew's Day, 20,000 citizens were arrested and spiked in one bloody afternoon. On Easter Sunday in 1459, approximately 300 boyars and their families were taken from church and marched to Vlad's personal castle on the Arges River. This was called Vlad's first major act of revenge, and the victims included the individuals responsible for the murder of his father and older brother. No one survived.[44]

The Wallachian poor were the victims in another infamous incident involving Vlad's cruelty. He invited hundreds of the poor to a dinner, and during desert Vlad and his staff unobtrusively filtered out. Archers then fired burning arrows into the dining hall, which quickly was engulfed in a fiery conflagration. Vlad remarked, "The poor unloved creatures, it is best that they leave the world now, on a full stomach."[45]

Vlad was concerned about the rapidly advancing army of Mehmed the Conqueror in May 1462. The invading forces dwarfed Vlad's forces. So he decided to deter the invasion in another way. He poisoned the Wallachian wells, burned the fields and homes and other buildings, and added a final touch.

He gathered all the Turkish prisoners in the area, approximately 20,000, and killed and impaled them on the outskirts of Tirgoviste. Mehmed and his men encountered "a forest of rotting men." The impaled Turkish soldiers covered an area the size of one by three kilometers, or approximately two square miles. Mehmed reportedly became ill and immediately returned home.[46]

There is reason to believe that Vlad was a cannibal. He allegedly roasted and ate babies. Vlad is thought to have eaten a meal from the flesh collected from the bodies of impaled victims. It was reported that "he occasionally had a servant dip his bread in the blood of dying souls so that he could savor the taste of life."[47]

An additional aspect of Vlad's cannibalism warrants mention. Not only did he consume human flesh, but he also coerced a truly terrible act. He compelled mothers to consume their children, frequently forcing mothers to eat their own babies.[48]

THE SERIAL MURDERS

Modus Operandi

Wallachia under Vlad was a society where capital punishment was considered a universal panacea. Virtually every crime was punishable by death from impalement, including idleness. The usual routine in these murders was to sever the hands and feet and then impale the victims on sharpened wooden stakes.[49]

Murder methods might have varied a bit in this case. Boiling, quartering, and decapitation were mentioned as killing techniques. An alternate version suggested being hanged, burned at the stake, boiled alive, and then impaled. Yet another account reported decapitation, blinding, strangling, burning, boiling, skinning alive, and impaling as ways that victims were killed.[50]

A couple of additional murder methods may merit mention. Vlad hated German merchants, and they were "hacked to pieces like cabbage." And some victims were reportedly driven off of a cliff, a relatively unique serial slaying system.[51] But this discussion of his murder methods must focus on impalement.

Vlad learned about impalement from the Turks. He first witnessed this extreme form of execution in a Turkish prison. It was his personal favorite form of torture, and it was so common that there were corpses impaled at every Wallachian crossroads. Most of Vlad's impalements took place in the three years between 1459 and 1461.[52]

Victims were impaled on sharp wooden stakes. The stakes were oiled. There were three types of impalement, corresponding to the three points of entry into the body: oral, anal, and navel. One of his preferred methods involved a horse that was attached to the victim's legs so that a sharpened stake was slowly introduced into his body. The result was an excruciatingly slow and painful death after a few hours to a couple of days of agony. Vlad sometimes adjusted the height of the pole to the victim's rank: the higher the rank or status of the victim, the higher the pole.[53]

Number of Victims

There was a relatively high death toll in this case. Vlad was responsible for what is considered the greatest victimage count by a single ruler until the modern era. Tens of thousands of people were slain.[54]

One hundred thousand victims were attributed to this serial slayer. The total of 100,000 may well be the most accurate. But there were other estimates as well. A total of 40,000 to 100,000 victims was suggested, and another account reported a range of between 20,000 and 300,000 deaths.[55]

Time Frame

Vlad committed these serial murders in the mid-fifteenth century. A more precise time frame has been indicated: 1456 to 1462. The duration of the serial slayings was approximately six years.[56]

Victimology

Is it possible that these were totally random and irrational murders? One version of this case contended that Vlad randomly selected human playthings. A second source suggested that virtually no one was safe from his atrocities.[57] Despite these opinions, it is possible to identify a variety of Vlad's victimology variables.

Specific individuals disliked by Vlad were a primary target. As difficult as it may be to believe, the wives of badly dressed men were regularly killed because Vlad held them responsible for the defects in their husband's attire. The boyars were another favorite victim group for personal and political purposes.[58]

Churches were victimized despite his nice gestures toward those institutions. And Vlad had an unmistakable prejudice against Saxons, Ottomans, and boyars. Germans in particular incurred his wrath. And women were always at risk around him.[59]

Motive

The revenge motive has already been introduced. Revenge became Vlad's inspiration, it was claimed. His childhood experiences motivated the desire to seek revenge from everyone who he felt had done him wrong.[60]

Pleasure was another hypothesized motive. Vlad enjoyed impalement. It was said that he murdered for the sheer pleasure of observing the suffering endured by his victims. He confessed that impalement provided "a pleasure far more exquisite than the thrill of battle."[61]

A pair of alternate motives can be considered. Politics has been suggested as a factor because many of the murders involved political targets. And, believe it or not, boredom may have motivated some of the murders.[62]

ARISTOCRATIC SERIAL MURDER

Vlad was a member of an aristocratic family. His father was Vlad Dracul II, king of Wallachia. His mother was a Transylvanian noblewoman. Vlad was decidedly a member of the aristocracy, a fifteenth-century nobleman.[63]

He was referred to as a Wallachian aristocrat. He was also called Prince Vlad Tepes of Wallachia. He served his native land as Voevod on three different occasions, the longest from 1456 to 1462. He lived in ornate castles at Poenari and Arefu.[64]

Aristocrats at this time in history were virtually unchallenged rulers. They could murder with impunity, and several did just that. According to Kathleen Ramsland, "The homicidal monsters whose names have come down to us from the distant past tend to be aristocrats themselves; Gilles de Rais, for example, or Vlad the Impaler."[65]

MASS COMMUNICATION

The initial stories about Vlad Dracula were the extensively circulated pamphlets produced by German monks. In fact, most of the extant written documents about Vlad are pamphlets printed by German monks. The best-known picture of Vlad is a woodblock print from a pamphlet depicting Vlad eating dinner on a hilltop in the midst of a veritable forest of impaled bodies.[66]

A poem was based on these pamphlets and an interview. Michael Beheim was a German poet who wrote a 1,070-line poem, "Story of a Bloodthirsty

Madman called Dracula of Wallachia." In the preparation of his poem, Beheim interviewed Brother Jacob, who had survived an encounter with Vlad. The verse was set to music and performed several times for the Roman emperor Frederick III.[67]

These propaganda pamphlets were disseminated to rationalize Vlad's arrest by Hungary's King Matthias Corvinus in 1462. Another famous pamphlet, published in Nuremburg in 1476 after his death, tried to convince readers of the evil nature of the Wallachian ruler. It explained Vlad's motive in the incident where he invited the poor to dinner and then killed them: "He felt they were eating the people's food for nothing, and could not repay it." Another pamphlet, this one written in 1462, claimed that he "roasted children of mothers and they had to eat their children themselves."[68]

HIS DEATH

Vlad died the way he lived: as a warrior. He died around Christmas, it is believed. It was the end of December 1476 or early January 1477. One authority specified December 1476, and another identified a January 1477 death.[69]

The Vlasia Forest is where he died. Vlad and his soldiers were reconnoitering enemy positions and serving as a decoy when they encountered a superior force of Turkish soldiers in the Vlasia Forest. This Turkish army was led by Laiota Basarab.[70]

There is controversy over the specific circumstances of his death. He may have been killed in battle by the Turks. An assassin killed him, according to another version of the case. His death reportedly was an accident, a result of friendly fire.[71]

Some say that Vlad was assassinated by disloyal Wallachians, while others say that he was killed in battle. A third theory suggested that he was accidentally killed by one of his own men celebrating their victory. According to another account, "The nobles betrayed him because they were afraid of him. . . . Others say his close followers who confused him for an Ottoman killed Vlad. Because Dracula was wearing Turkish clothes the killer could have been one of his own people." He may have died in battle or been betrayed by one of his own: nothing is known with certainty.[72] They cut Vlad's body into several pieces. An alternate version claimed that the mutilated body was found in a bog. Vlad was decapitated, and his head was missing.[73]

Vlad's head was placed above the gate to the city of Constantinople, it was said. Or it was presented to the Ottoman sultan as a present. The head was publicly displayed to convince Ottomans that Vlad was really dead. His body was placed in a crypt at the Snagov Monastery.[74]

CONCLUSION

Was Vlad a patriotic aristocrat who loved his homeland and sought to protect Wallachia from its enemies foreign and domestic? It cannot be denied that his country was endangered by foreign foes and internal opponents. The neighboring Hungarians had assassinated his father, and his own countrymen had murdered his brother, so the dangers were decidedly real.

He spent most of his life in exile or imprisoned. His father was assassinated and his older brother buried alive. Vlad's violent vendetta against his enemies resulted in perhaps the largest number of serial murders in history.

QUEEN NZINGA

She was referred to as "the Angolan heroine during the period of Portuguese conquest" and the renowned seventeenth-century Queen Nzinga.[1] She was the exception to the rule at a time when royal rulers were typically male. Africa's greatest daughter was one of the most fascinating African women in history. Queen Nzinga was considered a strong ruler and queen to the African people.[2]

Not only was Queen Nzinga a national leader, but she was also an expert in military matters. She was a savvy stateswoman and strategist. One account of her life described her brilliant military tactics.[3] She personally led her troops into battle in her sixties.

Queen Nzinga earned the respect of her subjects and even her enemies. Perhaps this is because of her remarkable character. The leaders and people of Portugal learned to admire her, as did most of the European population. She became a public sensation in Europe after the publication of Jean-Louise Castilhan's *Zingua: Reine d' Angola*.[4]

However, there are alternate perspectives on the subject of Queen Nzinga. "Her rule was a series of repeated mistakes," it was claimed. She upset many of her people by inviting Christian missionaries into Ndongo (Angola). And, perhaps most seriously of all, she opened the door for the Portuguese-African slave trade.[5]

There is disagreement concerning contemporary public opinion among her subjects toward their queen. It is commonly asserted that she was very popular and even loved in Angola. Nzinga was called the "beloved Black Mother." However, it was also claimed that she "ruled as a bloodthirsty tyrant."[6]

And she was a serial killer. She murdered her brother to ascend to the throne, and she murdered her nephew to eliminate him as a potential rival. It is also believed that she killed an unknown but large number of men after a solitary night of intimacy.

THE SERIAL MURDERESS

There is considerable controversy over Nzinga's name. That is not unusual in cases of historic serial murder. But Queen Nzinga's variety of names exceeds the norm in this respect.

Queen Nzinga is the term I have chosen to designate this powerful woman ruler, and it is the most frequently used name in the literature.[7] She was called Queen Zingua by one authority on serial murder.[8] Another name was used: Ana Nzinga. The Portuguese called her Jinga.[9]

Some authorities hedged their bets by using multiple names to refer to Queen Nzinga. Her name was "Anna Nzinga, aka Queen Nzinga and Dona Ana de Souza," one account of the case reported.[10]

She was born in 1581 in Kidonga, the capital of Ndongo.[11] Her life duration was said to have been from 1581 to 1663, although another authority preferred 1583 to 1663.[12]

She was born into the royal family of her country. Her parents were Ndambi Kiluanji and his second wife, Kangela.[13] Nzinga a Mbande Ngola Kiluaje was her father's name, according to one version. His name was Ngola Kiluanji Kia Samba, another authority suggested.[14] He was king of Ndongo.

Her brother's name was Mbande. Ngola Mbande was also used to refer to him. Ngola Ngoli Bbondi was his name, one source suggested. In 1618, he assassinated their father and assumed the throne of Ndongo. He also murdered Queen Nzinga's son and tried to kill her and her husband, who promptly fled for their lives.[15]

Queen Nzinga was highly intelligent, calculating, and cunning. She was characterized as being "an intelligent and visionary political leader." She was known for her political and diplomatic skills, considerable wit and intelligence, and effective mastery of military tactics and strategy. It is said that she successfully manipulated the Portuguese, the Imbangala, and the Dutch.[16]

Her intellect was the foundation for her cognitive abilities. Her uncanny skill at internal Mbundu politics was noteworthy, as was her status as an insightful diplomat. One last thing: "Her wits and audacity" were remarkable.[17]

She was married twice. First was a Mbundu prince named Azeze, who was killed in battle. Later, she married a chieftain to solidify an alliance between her people and another tribe. This was a symbolic ceremonial marriage to Kaza, an Imbangala chief.[18]

In her soul, she was "a warrior queen." Her Dutch allies were surprised to discover that she actually seemed to enjoy fighting. She dressed like a man, it was said. She corrected those who addressed her as "queen," expressing the desire to be called "king."[19]

Was she a deeply religious person or a very pragmatic one? It has been widely suggested that she used religion as a political tactic. For instance, she converted to Christianity to enhance her relationship with the governor of Luanda (a Portuguese colony in Ndongo). She selected either the governor or his wife as godparent and chose as her Christian name Dona Ana de Souza after the governor's wife.[20] But she soon renounced Christianity as a racist social construct intent on subjugating African people.

Then Queen Nzinga confounded everyone toward the end of her life by reconverting to Christianity. It was said that she had an ulterior motive: distancing herself as far as possible from association with the Imbangala tribe. She took a Kongo Catholic priest as her confessor, Calisto Zelotes des Reis Magros.[21]

And she facilitated the influx of Christian missionaries into Africa. Initially, she allowed two Capuchin missionaries, Antonio de Gaetes and Giovanni Antonio Cavazzi De Montecuccolo, to spread their faith. Queen Nzinga made her country accessible to European missionaries.[22]

She was a skillful negotiator.[23] And it was in the realm of negotiation that she initially earned public political prominence. A milestone event occurred in her life in 1622 when her brother asked her to represent their country in negotiations with Correa (or Correia) de Souza, the Portuguese governor of Luanda.

Queen Nzinga arrived for the meeting resplendent in her royal clothes. But de Souza had planned a psychological gambit to place her at a disadvantage in the negotiations. There was only one chair in the room (for him), and he had put a floor mat out for her to sit on, which in Mbundu culture signaled her subordinate status. So she motioned for a servant to kneel on the ground, and she sat on his back; "facing the governor on his level, Nzinga was able to talk as equals."[24]

Queen Nzinga was an abolitionist. She manifested her antislavery inclinations through a number of specific actions. In 1624, she declared Ndongo a free country, meaning that slaves who reached there could not be extradited to the custody of their former owners. Sanctuary was offered to all runaway slaves; she welcomed them, and they were an important segment of her constituency. She vigorously resisted the relentless incursions by Portuguese slave traders and tried her best to prevent the taking of slaves in Ndongo.[25]

Portugal played a significant role in events in Ndongo during the reign of Queen Nzinga. This seafaring power first established a colony in Africa at Ambaca in 1616 under the direction of Governor Luis Mendes de Vasconcelos. It was used as a slave collection center and directly threatened Ndongo. A second base was built at Luanda.

Initially, she tried to ally Ndongo with the Portuguese. But they chose war instead. She fought and beat the Portuguese in several battles. However, they prevailed in important military actions in 1645 and 1646, and they drove her from Ndongo in 1646. The Portuguese leadership decided that Nzinga had to be killed or exiled.[26]

There were six years of negotiations between Nzinga and her European counterparts. In 1656, a peace treaty was concluded and signed. But it was never seriously honored by the Portuguese. Nevertheless, she was officially named the governor of Luanda by the Portuguese from 1643 to 1646.[27]

Queen Nzinga fought for nearly 40 years against Portuguese forces and their indigenous allies. She was called "the greatest military strategist ever to confront the armed forces of Portugal."[28] Her use of guerilla tactics against the Portuguese led to her military successes in the face of her opponent's technological superiority.

She fomented rebellion in the Portuguese army against Philip I (also known as Ari Kiluanji), the puppet ruler placed by Portugal on the Ndongo throne.[29] Queen Nzinga personally selected several of her soldiers to infiltrate the Portuguese forces by inserting agents among the black soldiers under Portuguese control. As a result of her efforts, entire companies rebelled against their Portuguese masters and deserted.[30]

One additional aspect of her military leadership might be mentioned. She invented a new concept in military/social organization known in Ndongo as *kilombo*. In this system, substantial numbers of young boys essentially were turned over to the state for military purposes. Under the *kilombo* system, youth essentially renounced their family and were brought up in communal militia-like collectives.[31]

The Portuguese forced her out of Ndongo, so she "consolidated" a powerful and entirely new political state in the nearby kingdom of Matamba.[32] The *Black History Page* contended that "she fled north, conquered Matamba, and continued the war from there." According to another version, after Portugal betrayed her and broke the treaty in 1626, she and her forces moved west and "founded Matamba." Queen Nzinga and her army fled from the Portuguese to the east, it was also reported.[33]

Queen Nzinga returned to Matamba after the Dutch were defeated by the Portuguese and driven from Africa. She concentrated on the economic development of that nation. As a result of her efforts after her death, Matamba was still a formidable commercial state capable of dealing with the Portuguese on equal terms.[34]

She understood the importance of alliances and coalitions and was skilled in their creation. Queen Nzinga attempted cooperation with the Portuguese, the Dutch, the Jaga, and the Imbangala. Her most loyal constituency was a coalition of ex-slaves, Europeans, and other non-Mbundu people, including the Kongo, Kassanje, Dembos, and Kissama tribes. She created the anti-Portuguese coalition that kept the Europeans out of Ndongo for 30 years.[35]

She died in Matamba on December 17, 1663.[36] In fact, she passed away peacefully at home.[37] Queen Nzinga was reportedly 82 years of age at her death.[38] According to an alternate version, she died of old age at 80.[39]

OTHER CRIMES

It has been suggested that Queen Nzinga was a cannibal. Cannibalism was a part of the lifestyle and dietary practices of the Imbangala tribe of Africa. Stories about Imbangala cannibalism were reported by African witnesses like the kings of Kongo who complained about it.[40]

She declared herself an Imbangala immediately after she fled from her homeland at the suggestion of the Portuguese. Nzinga introduced her people to a ritualistic type of cannibalism.[41] There seems little doubt that Queen Nzinga was a cannibal and encouraged the practice among her people.

THE SERIAL MURDERS

Modus Operandi

Very little is known about the serial murders themselves. It is known that Queen Nzinga's brother Mbande died from poisoning, and rumors abounded that Nzinga had poisoned him.[42] Her lovers were reportedly executed, but the manner of execution remains unknown.[43]

Number of Victims

Queen Nzinga "engaged in indiscriminate killing of her subjects," it was contended. There were two definite murders, and after that little is reliably known. The number of her one-night-stand lovers who were murdered is unknown, and there is no information about the number of women who were killed because they violated the "vulgi-vaguability" statute.[44]

Time Frame

The time frame of these crimes is uncertain, but we can narrow it down to a relatively manageable estimate. An early seventeenth-century time frame was suggested.[45] Queen Nzinga killed between 1623 and 1663, it was also estimated. A 30-year duration of the serial crimes was reported.[46]

Victimology

Queen Nzinga confined herself to a relatively limited type of victim. There were actually three very specific categories of targets in this case. They included relatives, her lovers, and women who did not make themselves sexually available to their husbands. It was dangerous to be a member of her family. Her brother assassinated her father to take control of their country. He also murdered her son and tried to kill her and her husband. Then

Queen Nzinga killed her brother, and for good measure she murdered her nephew so that he could not compete with her for the throne of Ndongo.

Men with whom she spent the night were the second type of victim in this case. It was reported that Queen Nzinga had an unusual sexual habit: after a night of lovemaking, her lover was executed the next morning. The infamous Marquise de Sade mentioned this tendency in *Philosophy in the Bedroom*: "Zingua, Africa's queen, also immolated her lovers."[47]

There was a second, gladiatorial element in this sexual system. Men were allowed to enter a competition with the winner awarded Queen Nzinga for the evening. After she became queen, she created a large harem to sate her sexual needs. These men fought to the death in a contest to spend the night with her. Her lovers were murdered after a single night of lovemaking.[48]

A third type of victim included women who were sexually stingy with their spouse. Queen Nzinga established a policy known as "vulgi- vaguability." She believed that women were obligated to sexually satisfy their husbands whenever the men desired and that wives who were not accommodating in this manner should be put to death. This law mandated that "on pain of death women were to make themselves available at all times for sex."[49]

Victims

Two of Queen Nzinga's victims are known to us. One was her brother Mbande. It was in 1623 that she had him assassinated so that she could succeed him.[50]

Her nephew Kaza (her brother's son) stood to succeed his father as king of Ndongo. Like most of the world's countries, Ndongo was usually governed by males, and despite his young age, he would have ascended to the throne instead of Queen Nzinga. So she assumed control as regent of Kaza, who was residing with the Imbangala. Nzinga sent to have the boy in her charge, and when he returned, he was killed.[51]

Motive

Queen Nzinga's motives remain entirely her own. She never discussed the murders or the reasons behind them. Since there were three types of victims, perhaps there were different motives. It is unknown why she wanted to execute women who did not sexually satisfy their mate, and it is similarly unclear why she would kill her lovers after a solitary night of sexual intimacy. But the murders of her brother and his son were clearly political in nature, intended as they were to eliminate the obstacles to her becoming the queen of Ndongo.

ARISTOCRATIC SERIAL MURDER

There is a genre of serial murderer characterized by the social role of leadership. Aristocratic serial murderers of the past, like their contemporary brothers and sisters, took advantage of their privileged social status to easily procure victims and do what they wish with them.[52] Queen Nzinga typified nicely the genre of aristocratic serial killer.

She was born to the royal family and became the queen in 1623.[53] In her native Kimbundu language, her royal title was Ngola; the Portuguese misunderstood this to be the name of the country, which they thereafter called Angola.[54] Queen Nzinga ascended to the Ndongo throne in 1624. Another account suggested that "she seized the throne during a succession dispute."[55]

In any case, Queen Nzinga succeeded her brother as leader of Ndongo.[56] She was the "most powerful ruler in the interior during the 1640s."[57] She was queen of Ngola and later Matamba, and she dominated Kimbundu politics for 40 years.[58]

CONCLUSION

Queen Nzinga is worthy of close scrutiny not only because of her individual intrinsic importance but also because "she represents remorseless killers who held positions at times and in places that allowed them to exercise their blood lust as an extension of royal privilege."[59] She was a serial killer, but her greater importance had to have been her leadership against Ndongo's enemies. Her political and military skills have been thoroughly documented.

DOWAGER EMPRESS CIXI

Dowager Empress Cixi was one of the most powerful women in the world at the end of the nineteenth century, if not the most powerful. "One of China's most controversial figures," she rose from complete obscurity to the Chinese throne. There is widespread agreement among analysts about her central role in the history of China. On a more personal level, it was said that she was either a loyal and great friend or a treacherous enemy.[1]

Cixi was reputed to be one of the most formidable women in modern history. Particularly impressive was her political acumen. During her political life, she was always clever and mastered most situations.[2]

But this powerful female leader had her share of detractors as well. Cixi usually placed her personal interest ahead of that of her nation, it was asserted. She squandered vast sums of money on lavish banquets, jewels, and other luxuries at a time when most Chinese were impoverished. Twenty million Chinese civilians died during a civil war and series of subsequent starvations, but Cixi was preoccupied with her tomb, which she had demolished and rebuilt in 1895, an ostentatious and grandiose series of temples, gardens, and gazebos covered in gold leaf.[3]

Her conceit, her conservatism, her ignorant and xenophobic antiforeign policies, and her incompetent public administration were recalled by one biographer. Her leadership efforts were considered counterproductive when it came to fending off foreign influence because during her reign, Western nations attained considerable power in China. Corruption is a final failure of her rule: China became increasingly scandalous under Cixi.[4]

The story of her rise to power is compelling. She began her sojourn through life as a concubine to the Chinese emperor and wound up at the pinnacle of political power. She said of herself, "I must say I was a clever woman, for I fought my own battles and I won them, too. When I arrived at court, the late Emperor became very much attached to me. . . . I was lucky in giving birth to a son, as it made me the Emperor's undisputed favorite."[5]

THE SERIAL MURDERESS

Multiple names have been used to describe this important woman in history. Tz'u H'si was one commonly used name. It was the name given to her when she entered the imperial court, and it means virtuous and kind.[6]

Her birth name is disputed. Some maintain that her birth name is unknown. Her given name was her Manchu name, Yehonala, which combined the names of her parents' tribes: the Yeho and the Nala.[7]

Cixi is another term used to designate her. This is the name which is most frequently used in modern reports, but it is neither her birth name nor her family name. It is an honorific name that was bestowed on her in 1861 after her son became emperor.[8]

Most authorities provided multiple names for her. She was Tzu Hsi or Cixi, we are told. The initial name was Tz'u, Tzu, or Tse, according to one account.[9] She was called Yehonala, the Empress Hsaio-ch'in and Old Buddha. Cixi was known by several names, one authority declared, pointing out use of Tzu Hsi, Cixi and Cixi Dowager Empress. Her full ceremonial name after her death was Empress Xiao-Qin Ci-Xi Duan-Yu Kang-Yi Zhao-Yu Zhuang-Cheng Shou-Gong Qin-Xian Chong-Xi Pei- Tian Xing-Sheng Xian.[10]

Her birthday was November 29, 1835. Her life span was reportedly from 1834 until 1908, according to an alternate version. There are several popular tales about her origins; she is believed to have come from one of four places: the Yangtze River region; Changzhi, Shanxi (where she reportedly was a Han Chinese adopted by a Manchu family); Suiyuan, Inner Mongolia; and Bejing.[11]

Wherever her birth occurred, it was a humble affair. Her parents were from the middle class of Manchu society. Cixi was born into the Mauchu Yehe Nara clan on her father's side of the family.[12]

Her father was named Yehenara Huizheng, or Hui-cheng. He was a member of the Bordered Blue Banner of the Eight Banners in Shanxi province. He served as the commissioner of Anhui Province but was dismissed in 1853 (and possibly beheaded) for not resisting an insurrection with sufficient resolve during the Taipei Uprising. He has been called a minor Manchu mandarin and an ordinary public official.[13]

She had two brothers (one named Guixiang, it was believed), and she had sisters as well.[14] Their lives changed abruptly when their father died. Cixi was still quite young but was the eldest child, and she expressed feeling mistreated, neglected, and unappreciated. She claimed, "Ever since I was a young girl, I had a very hard life. I was not happy with my parents, as I was not a favorite. My sisters had everything they wanted, while I was, to a great extent, ignored altogether."[15]

She was literate unlike most Chinese women of her era. She taught herself to read and write. And during her time at the court, she fully utilized the Imperial Palace's library. Cixi was shrewd according to reliable reports. And she exhibited impressive political understanding and skill.[16]

She was said to be beautiful and charming. She was in good shape, being blessed with tremendous physical vitality and strength. Cixi was described as a very pleasant, unusually pretty, and quite bright ex-concubine.[17]

Her personality has been portrayed in positive and negative ways. An exceptionally attractive personality was recalled by one account. Cixi was also strong willed, capable, and ambitious. To some, she was kind and considerate with considerable composure, charm, and grace. It is said that she loved dogs, boating, flowers, Chinese water pipes, and European cigarettes.[18]

Negative personality depictions have also been asserted. For instance, she believed that the Boxers had magic powers, such as being impervious to bullets. And she was described as a power-hungry and ruthless individual. Finally, Cixi was noted for her foul temper, which was ferociously displayed regularly. A witness to these outbursts testified that her eyes "poured out straight rays, her cheekbones were sharp and the veins on her forehead projected; she showed her teeth as if she was suffering from lockjaw."[19]

She loved wealth, it was recognized by one authority, and she enjoyed a wild and lavish lifestyle. After her death, it was discovered that she had stolen approximately eight and a half million English pounds sterling and deposited it in London banks. Her sixtieth birthday fete exemplified her largesse. All imperial employees donated one-quarter of their annual salary to finance the festivities. Cixi received a gift of 10 million taels of silver.[20]

She was served 150 dishes at frequent banquets, drank from a jade cup, and ate with solid gold chopsticks. She accumulated 3,000 ebony boxes full of jewelry. Cixi built her summer palace with funds diverted from the Imperial Navy.[21]

Even her death was decadent and extravagant. She was laid to rest in luxury, covered with gems and diamonds. Cixi's funeral is believed to have cost one and a half million taels.[22]

Cixi enabled the technological and tactical modernization of the Chinese military. She supported the work of three prominent Han Chinese industrial reformers—Zeng Koufang, Li Hongzhang, and Zuo Zongtang—in southern China. She opened Tongwen Guan, an early university, in 1862.[23]

But there has been considerable criticism of Cixi. She allowed financial corruption to get out of control in the Forbidden City. She opposed the construction of railroads and was strongly anti-Western and conservative. She opposed liberal thinking and even prohibited Chinese from studying abroad.[24]

She was a royal consort of the emperor Hsien Feng and produced his only male child and heir, T'ung Chih. She was nominated as a candidate-concubine at 14 years of age. In September 1851, she was one of 60 young girls involved in an audition conducted by Kang Ci, the imperial dowager consort. Cixi was one of 28 girls who were initially selected to serve as a "preparative concubine."[25]

She completed her preparation when she was 18 years old. On June 14, 1852, she earned the title Kuei Sen (honorable person), the lowest level of the concubine hierarchy. She earned this honor when she was 16, according to one account.[26]

Cixi ascended to fifth level, or "Noble Person," status after being selected for the emperor's bed. Then, in December 1854 or January 1855, she was promoted to "imperial concubine" status, the fourth rank. Her pregnancy earned her access to the third level, and after the birth of her son, she was elevated from the third to the second level, with the title Noble Consort Yi.[27]

At that point, she had the virtual status of a wife. When her son turned five, she was given the title Dowager Empress Cixi.[28] Her rise to power was complete.

There are mixed accounts of her relationship with the emperor. He respected her and trusted her advice, consulting her regularly on state affairs, according to one authority. But other reports differed. The relationship between the emperor and Cixi was never a stable one, we are told, and their interactions were always reserved and strained.[29]

Cixi suffered a stroke in 1907 when she was 74. The stroke may have occurred in 1908, an alternate version suggested. She died in the Hall of the Graceful Bird on November 15, 1908.[30]

She had a solitary nickname in addition to all those names and titles. She was called the Dragon Empress. She presided over the Dragon Court.[31]

OTHER CRIMES

Cixi committed a pair of crimes concurrently with her serial murders. In a crime reminiscent of contemporary American politics, she resorted to selling official positions to finance her lavish lifestyle. She began to sell positions of influence in exchange for substantial donations to her private funds.[32]

Torture was her other offense. Palace courtiers claimed that she enjoyed punishing her household servants through physical beatings and other "sundry cruelties." Cixi declared on one occasion, "They have not been punished for several days and they are looking forward to it. I will not disappoint them, but give them all they wish to have."[33]

THE SERIAL MURDERS

Modus Operandi

The modus operandi in these murders varied considerably. But the one unifying theme is that they were mandated by Cixi, who ordered that all foreigners be killed, according to the Smithsonian Institution.[34] Almost a half dozen multiple-murder modi operandi will be considered.

Cixi ordered executions. The decree that all foreign prisoners be decapitated was issued by her. Numerous Chinese and foreigners were killed in this manner.[35]

A torturous method of murder was called "slicing." The victim was slightly cut repeatedly, scores or hundreds of times, until death resulted from shock or loss of blood.[36]

Poisoning was another means of murder used by Cixi's subordinates and associates. It is believed that she poisoned her nephew. Her co-dowager and cousin Ci'an (or Niuhuru) died after an unpleasant encounter with Cixi, with poisoning suspected.[37]

Beatings also resulted in numerous killings during the Boxer Rebellion. The movement's name came from the fact that boxing was a favorite recreational activity of rural youth. Their formal name was Righteous and Harmonious Fists.[38]

A final murder method might be mentioned. When Cixi and her entourage were fleeing the Imperial Palace during the Boxer Rebellion, she was stopped by her son's favorite concubine, known as the Pearl Concubine. The girl begged Cixi to stay and defend Beijing. Cixi ordered that she be tossed into a well in the Forbidden City.[39]

Number of Victims

There were 250 foreigners killed during the Boxer Rebellion, according to one account.[40] The deaths of 16 others have also been documented, so by a conservative estimate, there were 266 victims using these numbers.

Much larger estimates were involved in an alternate version of this case. There were 30,313 deaths during the Boxer Rebellion instead of a mere 250, it was contended.[41] If we add the 16 other deaths to this total, we arrive at a victimage total of 30,329.

Time Frame

When did these serial murders take place? We know that Cixi ruled from 1861 to 1908. The initial murder might have been her son's death at age 25 on January 12, 1875. The last victim may well have been Kuang-hsi, the emperor and her nephew, on November 14, 1908, the day before her own death.[42]

Victims

Several of Cixi's victims are known either by name or through their position and the circumstances of their death. For instance, two corrupt local officials were executed. Quinying tried to avoid a demotion through bribery, and He Guiqing, the viceroy of Lianjiang, deserted his post.[43]

Two aristocrats were allowed to kill themselves. They reportedly were Prince I and Prince Cheng. These two were given ceremonial white silk suicide suits to wear.[44]

Su-Shun was an elderly Chinese gentleman. He was one of the eight regents appointed to help Cixi's five-year-old son govern China. She executed him.[45]

Kuang-hsi was her nephew who she put on the throne, but Cixi later had him poisoned. In 2008, forensic examination disclosed that he died of acute arsenic poisoning. CNN reported that arsenic levels in his body were 2,000 times greater than normal.[46]

Her son was thought to have died from smallpox, although some suspected that syphilis was the man's medical malady. Rumors circulated that Cixi had caused her son's early death. And his wife Alute was another victim; her death was officially called a suicide, but Cixi told someone to murder her and make it appear to be a suicide.[47]

A concubine whose name is unknown to us was another victim. She was pregnant, and if her baby was a boy, he would have been the rightful heir to the Chinese throne. Mysteriously, this concubine died during the unsuccessful delivery. But it is suspected that she was killed under Cixi's orders.[48]

Victimology

Cixi did not kill at random. Several primary victimology variables can be identified. For instance, foreigners were frequently victimized.[49] Missionaries, their Chinese converts, and all nonnative merchants were a favorite target.[50]

Her enemies were another main target. So were prominent public officials who opposed her or were considered potential rivals. Three of the eight regents were murdered or forced to commit suicide.[51]

Her family was the final main victimology cohort. She is suspected in the death of her nephew Kuang-hsi, her son Tun'g Chih, and his wife Alute. And there was also the death of Ci'an.[52]

Motive

A trio of possible motives might be considered in this case. The official rationale behind the public executions was the need to deter official white-collar corruption and crime. Cixi is thought to have executed two prominent officials to serve as examples.[53]

Commercial motives might have been at play in this case. Regent Su-Shun's death liberated his property. His estates and considerable personal property were transferred to Cixi and Ci'an.[54]

The third motive was power. Cixi killed and connived to attain and maintain power. Power was the root of her crimes; "her greed for power became insatiable."[55] She was considered to be the most powerful person in China.

ARISTOCRATIC SERIAL MURDER

This was most decidedly a case of aristocratic serial murder. Although Cixi came from humble beginnings, she ascended into the Manchu Chinese aristocracy by virtue of her ability to bear children. But let there be no doubt: she was a national leader. Cixi effectively governed China for nearly half a century. In fact, she was the de facto leader of the Chinese Manchu Qing dynasty for 47 years.[56]

She sought and attained power through political intrigue, as when her son died and she advocated her nephew's candidacy for emperor. Cixi defied ancient laws and threw Chinese imperial tradition out the window, but she got her way when 15 of the 25 councilors endorsed Kuang-hsi as emperor.[57] When Ci'an died, Cixi became the solitary regent and leader. She ousted the eight regents on a series of pretexts. The rationale behind her assumption of power was contained in the document "The Eight Guilts of Regent Ministers." Historians refer to this incident as the Xinyou Palace Coup.[58]

Her response to the Hundred Days of Reform was predictable and bloody. Supported by Jung Lu and his soldiers, the empress seized control of the Chinese government. At her death, she unsuccessfully tried to crown Punji, a 14-year-old nephew, as crown prince.[59]

CONCLUSION

Dowager Empress Cixi remains an enigma to us today. Was she a sincere, good-intentioned ruler trying her best to govern a complex and gigantic nation? It has been suggested that much of the criticism of Cixi was unfair, inaccurate, and politically motivated by Kuomintang and communist Chinese historians.

By many accounts, though, she was involved in a substantial number of serial slayings. Even discounting the Boxer Rebellion deaths, the victimage of her family members marked her as a deadly foe. She was a murderous monarch whose multiple murders manifested her general criminal ruthlessness.

PART V

COMMERCIAL SERIAL KILLERS

LOCUSTA THE POISONER

"The first documented serial killer" is the subject of this chapter. Locusta is widely believed to be the first known serial killer. She was certainly one of the earliest if not the first publicly identified serial killer. The famed Roman poet and historian Horace included Locusta along with Canidia and Martina as notorious poisoners in his *Satires*. She was referred to as an infamous professional poisoner.[1] A survey of ancient Roman criminals concluded that Locusta was probably the most feared of the female serial poisoners.[2] No prior serial killer has been discovered and generally accepted.[3]

Her lethal skills were legendary. Nero hired her to serve as his personal expert on poison. Locusta was the official poisoner of the Roman imperial court.[4]

Locusta is remembered for her skill at serial slaying. She was quite likely one of the first professional assassins in Western society. Locusta became the Roman professional assassin of choice, concluded a specialized study of famous women of antiquity.[5]

THE SERIAL MURDERESS

"Locusta the Poisoner" is what several sources called her.[6] She was commonly named Locusta.[7] One variant on her name was Lucusta. She has also been referred to as Locusta of Gaul.[8]

During the ancient Roman Empire, modern-day France was known as Gaul.[9] Locusta was born in the first century BCE in this outer province of the Roman Empire.[10] No other information about her birth has been recorded.

Locusta developed an interest in herbal lore that she turned into a profitable career. As a young girl enjoying her days in the country, Locusta evidently learned about the medicinal and lethal properties of the plants she encountered. She was highly educated and skilled in the use of herbs.[11]

Not much is known today about her personality. Her "titanic cruelty" was noteworthy. She has also been credited with infinite inventiveness.[12]

Her botanical studies and herbal instruction have already been alluded to in this section. Not content with her knowledge, Locusta traveled to Messalina to study poisons under Appollodorus of Pergamon.[13] After Locusta established her school of poisoning, she conducted a wide variety of experiments on different types of subjects.

Locusta made more than mere money from murder. She was able to become upwardly mobile in a very class-based culture. Nero rewarded her by granting her enhanced social status.[14]

Locusta discovered that when she poisoned victims, her clients remained grateful. Later, when Locusta needed them after she was arrested, her former patrons found ways to assist her. Her clientele included individuals who were able to extricate her from jail rather quickly.[15]

She sat in jail waiting to be executed for the assassination of Emperor Claudius. But he snuck her out of her cell, and then Nero overturned Locusta's death sentence and named her his adviser on poisons. After Brittanicus died, Nero canceled her death sentence and appointed Locusta his official counselor on poisons.[16]

Locusta was legally forgiven for all the poisonings she had been charged with in the past. A complete and retroactive pardon for all her murders was part of her deal with Nero. She was legally exonerated of culpability for all past and possible future poisonings.[17]

She also received immunity from execution during Nero's lifetime. One thing is certain: she was supremely confident with Nero as emperor and did not fear arrest in the slightest. But Nero lived only another dozen years or so. She would fare quite differently with Nero's replacement emperor, Galba.[18]

OTHER CRIMES

Locusta had a relatively lengthy arrest record, an occupational hazard confronting professional killers. She was frequently arrested for her criminal activities.[19] They weren't just arrests on her record—she was convicted. She was found guilty of several criminal offenses when Claudius was emperor. Locusta was reportedly convicted of numerous poisoning-related offenses.[20]

Locusta believed in alchemy, a popular science of the times, the proponents of which believed that it was possible to turn base metals into valuable substances like gold. This transformation required potent chemical assistance. Many alchemists used blood from children as a sort of enzyme or facilitating resource. In this case, she murdered and molested small children for the sake of pleasure and also used their blood in her alchemy activity.[21]

Locusta and Agrippina conspired to kill Claudius, according to one account. Locusta and Agrippina planned to murder Claudius together.[22] The murder of Brittanicus most assuredly involved a conspiracy as well.

Locusta opened her school to teach others her extensive knowledge about poisonous herbs.[23] But others believed that the school was begun by Nero. He created and organized an institute of poisoning where Locusta trained others in poisoning technology and techniques. No matter who initiated the school, it is known that Nero supported Locusta in this endeavor. Nero referred a number of potential poisoners to Locusta to enable them to pass her lethal knowledge to future generations.[24]

Her research and service overlapped when she was called on to document the effectiveness of a poison for a potential customer by using it on one of the slaves kept for that specific purpose.[25] Nero allowed her to conduct experiments on animals, slaves, and condemned criminals. Studies planned to determine the qualities of various poisons and methods of defending the emperor against poison were conducted by Locusta.[26]

One more point is in order regarding her school. As an individual poisoner, she was limited in the number of victims she could attain. But by virtue of her role as a teacher of poisoning techniques, she could facilitate many more poisoning deaths. It is no exaggeration to suggest that through her students, she was responsible for as many as 10,000 deaths.[27]

THE SERIAL MURDERS

Modus Operandi

Locusta was a poisoner, so the general modus operandi involved the administration of poison into the bloodstream of a victim. It is said that Claudius ingested belladonna alkaloid made from hemlock, yew, or aconite. He was killed by *Amanita phalloides*, the so-called death cap mushroom, according to others. Brittanicus was reportedly killed by cyanide.[28]

A tasty, tantalizing tempting dish of toxic mushrooms was used to poison Claudius. The mushrooms were concealed within the ingredients of a stew. Agrippina knew that Claudius greatly enjoyed mushrooms. The unsuspecting emperor Claudius hungrily gobbled the poisoned delicacy down.[29]

Both Agrippina and Locusta had noted an oddity of Claudius's dining behavior. He liked to "eat and purge." He carried with him a feather used to induce vomiting, after which he would resume eating.[30]

Agrippina and Locusta struck at Claudius at an opportune time. One night, Claudius's most protective right-hand man called in sick. The evening that the emperor's most trusted aide was ill, Agrippina persuaded the food taster to ignore his responsibility (and thereby save his life).[31]

Claudius was rendered mute by the initial dose of poison. But he was clearly in distress. His wife Agrippina hovered over him with the feather, a fatal feather containing another massive dose of poison.[32] When it appeared that Claudius was troubled or merely wanted to purge, Agrippina administered the fatal feather.[33]

There are alternate versions of the binge-and-purge story. Xenophon was the emperor's personal physician, and he gave Claudius a purgative enema into which he injected a very toxic colocynth. Another version of this story suggested that Agrippina gave him a poison-laden enema.[34]

Brittanicus was also murdered while dining with family. The Romans had a habit of drinking wine diluted with hot water, which sometimes had to be chilled a bit to suit the imperial palate. When Brittanicus requested that his wine be cooled, his taster chose not to taste the clear water that had been added to Brittanicus's goblet, which was precisely where Locusta had added the deadly poison. The Roman historian Tacitus wrote that the poisoned cold water "circulated so rapidly in his veins that it deprived him of speech and life."[35]

Nero took advantage of the fact that Brittanicus had epilepsy, a relatively open secret and well-known fact within the royal family. When Brittanicus ingested the poisoned wine, he became incapacitated and lost the ability to speak, much like a grand mal seizure. As Brittanicus convulsed, Nero merely reminded his dinner guests that Brittanicus suffered from severe epilepsy and that there was no need to summon assistance for him.[36]

"Don't worry. Brittanicus has the sacred disease—epilepsy. He'll soon come out of his fit and regain his sight and voice. Let's just enjoy the dinner—he'll be fine," Nero told the dinner party. When Brittanicus began to experience convulsions, Nero seemed unconcerned about the event. He declared that Brittanicus was only having an epileptic seizure and would soon be back to normal. So the meal resumed.[37]

But Brittanicus did not recover. So Nero instructed the servants to assist the boy in leaving the room. Little if anything was done to revive Brittanicus.[38]

It was commonly believed that poisoning deaths resulted in the victim's skin either turning blue or acquiring a reddish tinge.[39] Brittanicus was buried the same night he died, with his face covered with chalk to conceal the blue or red evidence of murder.[40] Fate foiled the effectiveness of the chalking because it rained that evening. Cassius wrote, "A shower of rain washed the chalk away and revealed to the people the evidence of the crime."[41]

The successful assassination of Brittanicus was not accomplished on the initial attempt. Locusta successfully killed her young victim on the second try. Her first poisoning attempt (about which little is known) on Brittanicus failed.[42]

Number of Victims

There was a relatively wide range of lethality estimates and body counts in Locusta's case. Some estimates were specific and quantitative, and others were verbal and vague. She had five definite victims, it was suggested. There were five or six victims, according to another report.[43] Locusta may have killed Claudius, Brittanicus, and up to five others.[44]

It is quite probable that Locusta had other unknown victims. Besides the seven certain victims, there is a possibility that more victims are attributable to this poisoner, so the exact death toll is a bit uncertain.[45]

Victims

Claudius was one victim. He was murdered before he could turn over his empire to Brittanicus. He died on October 13, 54 BCE.[46]

The other known victim was Brittanicus. Locusta was called on to eliminate Nero's rival to the throne. Brittanicus was 14 years old at the time of his death. He was Nero's half brother.[47]

Time Frame

The era of Locusta's crimes is long gone, consigned to the distant past. She was a female serial killer in Rome during the first century BCE. Historians have placed her crimes between 68 and 54 BCE.[48]

Victimology

Imperial Rome was populated with greedy and ambitious individuals seeking to expedite the demise of wealthy relatives or their personal and professional rivals. The trick was to make the deaths appear to be natural, and that is why poisoning was popular.[49] That was the key to Locusta's appeal.

The other group of likely victims inhabited the world of Roman politics. The deaths of Claudius and Brittanicus documented the dangers facing politicians at that time. But the danger extended to their family as well, as Locusta killed a number of wives.[50]

Motive

We might conclude that Locusta was a commercial serial killer who was motivated by the profit to be realized from the successful completion of the crimes. However, there could be more to these murders than is apparent at first glance. There may have been an emotional aspect to her motive as well.

Some serial slayers seem to savor their crimes, somehow deriving a sense of satisfaction from the suffering and death they inflict on others. Was Locusta one of these affect-driven killers? It was said that Locusta killed for profit but also for personal enjoyment.[51]

A final motive might be considered: alchemy. We have already recognized the prevalent public perception that alchemy could alter materials and turn lead into gold, for instance. After molesting and killing her children victims, Locusta used their blood in her attempts at turning lead to gold.[52]

COMMERCIAL SERIAL MURDER

Locusta was a notorious paid assassin who was quite prominent at the time. She became a professional poisoner after she realized the tremendous need for her services in Rome.[53] Some have called her the preferred Roman hit woman of choice.[54]

She was a premodern paid killer, a hired gun.[55] She poisoned victims on behalf of private, cash-paying citizens.[56] Agrippina solicited Locusta's assistance, and she reportedly ordered Locusta to prepare a large batch of poisoned mushrooms. Locusta received "a secret summons" from Agrippina seeking her assistance with the death of Claudius.[57]

The same thing was true regarding the assassination of Brittanicus. Nero took the initiative by calling Locusta and asking her to prepare an effective and instant-acting poison. He engaged the services of Locusta. There is no doubt about her involvement in the murder of Brittanicus.[58]

She was kept occupied with her contract murder work as a poisoner-for-hire. It was said that Locusta was employed by political opponents of Emperor Claudius. An appropriate term was coined to describe this type of a killer: "necro-entrepreneur."[59]

Locusta received a considerable amount of compensation for her services in both the public and the private sector. Locusta was put on Nero's pension list, and he made her a wealthy woman. In return for her services, she received money and referrals for additional business opportunities. Because Nero was so pleased with her labor, Locusta also received a valuable parcel of property, gifts, and other valuables.[60]

THE INVESTIGATION

After his death, Nero's opponents went after the contract killer. Locusta tried to protect herself as best she could by keeping a relatively low profile. But her widespread public reputation as a poisoner betrayed her. As a result, when the new Roman emperor took the throne, the stage was set for her downfall.[61]

So how did Locusta come to the attention of Emperor Galba? Details are unfortunately unavailable. Most likely, when Emperor Galba implemented a law-and-order initiative throughout the Roman Empire resulting in the public execution of a considerable number of criminals, Locusta was one of them.[62]

THE TRIAL

The facts of Locusta's trial are lost to history. Few official records of any type from that era have survived. She was condemned to die by Emperor Galba in 69 BCE.[63]

"Justice" is a relative term, and there is a cultural element in what is perceived to be just. Locusta's punishment manifested this notion of indigenous justice. For one thing, the timing of her execution was attuned to the ancient Roman reality of providing public spectacles on major Roman holidays. The Agonalia festival celebrated the Roman god Janus on January 8, and Locusta was publicly executed on that day.[64]

But it was the means of execution that characterized this judicial exercise as rather unusual. Legend has it that she was raped by a specially trained giraffe in a public ceremony, then she was torn limb from limb by several wild animals. Her body had been smeared with vaginal juices of the female animal to provoke the male to bestiality.

That is a good story, but is it true? At least one study claims to have debunked this tale.[65]

There is an alternate version of the end of Locusta's life. The facts are very different in this story and not nearly as dramatic or salacious. She reportedly was strangled to death and then burned after a church-instigated trial in January 69 BCE.[66]

CONCLUSION

Very little is known about Locusta the person. Was she friendly and playful as a child? Her family life is unknown to us, and we are similarly unaware of any marriages or significant others in her life. What we do know about are her crimes.

She was at the very summit of her profession. She was a professional killer and professor of poison. She killed an emperor of Rome and the heir to his throne among her victims. Her reputation as a mistress of death marked her as a person to be taken seriously.

LA TOFANIA

La Tofania was a controversial figure in Naples, Italy, in the early seventeenth century. She was a commercial serial killer, although she was also motivated by her hatred of men. La Tofania was referred to as a notable woman poisoner and one of the most notorious poisoners. Along with La Voison and another Italian poisoner named Spara, she was considered one of the three most lethal poisoners of her era.[1]

One of the most prolific murderers in history is how one serial murder authority described her.[2] Was she also a mass murderer? That was the conclusion of one study that decided that she was "one of history's biggest mass murderers."[3]

Her poisonous career caused a sensation, and her arrest and trial induced pandemonium throughout Italy but particularly in Naples and Rome. During her serial murders, her poison produced dread in every royal family in Italy. Making matters even worse, she implicated numerous members of Italian royalty and society, and the result was chaotic. All of Italy was thrown into a frenzy, and many of her former clients fled, while others were quietly killed in prison and many publicly executed.[4]

This chapter differs slightly from the others in this book in one respect. We don't know much at all about the killer, but considerable information is available about her specific poison. So our focus will similarly be on her elixir, which was labeled as "Manna of St. Nicholas of Bari" but better known popularly as "Acqa Tofania."

THE SERIAL MURDERESS

La Tofania's birth name and life history are unfortunately lost to us today. A study of women mass murderers and serial slayers concurred, noting that she is known to us only as La Tofania (or Toffania) because her name was forgotten years ago.[5] But numerous other names have been applied to this infamous poisoner. For instance, La Tofannia has been identified as her name.[6] Some authorities shortened the name to Tofania.[7] Toffana was another version of her name.[8] Toffania was used by one authority on this case. An alternate name was given in another account: Tophania. We might consider a final suggested name: Tofana.[9]

She was born in 1653. The place of her birth, her parents' names, and related details are unavailable. It has been suggested that she was from Palermo.[10]

There was another prominent female poisoner, Heironyma La Spara, plying her trade in Italy in the same general era as La Tofania. Sometimes the two are confused and mistaken for each other. La Tofania was a mentor and teacher to La Spara, according to one account: Spara was said to be Tofania's student and also a reputed witch.[11] However, the *Chamber's Edinburgh Journal* reported an opposite set of facts: "Spara was supposedly taught by Tofania, but it was more likely that Spara taught Tofania."[12] Spara reportedly lived 50 years before La Tofania. Spara was actually the teacher and La Tofania the student.[13]

One more factor about the relationship between La Tofania and Spara might be considered. Spara might have been the original inventor of the poison usually attributed to La Tofania. *The Medical Record* reported in 1903 that she made a poison that was very similar to Spara's.[14]

Where did La Tofania concoct and dispense her deadly poison products? Italy was identified as the location of the crimes. In 1889, *The Calcutta Review* contended, "It remained for the ever-to-be-abhorred Heironyma Spara, and the equally detestable Tofania to obtain for Italy the unenviable reputation of the cradle of modern poisoners."[15]

Naples, Italy, was where she made murderous materials and administered them herself or dispensed them to others.[16] La Tofania's homicidal activity also occurred in southern Italy and Sicily. Her poisons were extensively used throughout Naples and Rome.[17]

Did her victimage occur beyond the borders of Italy? That was the opinion of one history of these crimes. Murders caused by La Tofania took place in France, Spain, and England.[18]

Little is reliably known about her personal life. She lived to old age, it was noted. She was in her late sixties or as old as seventy when arrested and executed.[19]

"A psychopath" is how her mental health status was characterized.[20] It is believed that she was originally from the countryside around Palermo, Italy.[21] She was very popular, particularly among Italian women.[22] One last personal topic warrants mention: she hated men. La Tofania was an early and ardent feminist, but her focus seemed to have been not on the advancement of women but rather on the destruction of men.[23]

AQUA TOFANIA

The lethal liquid she prepared was referred to by a variety of names, just as was La Tofania herself. Aqua Tofania, Acqua Tofana, and Acqua Toffana were suggested as the name of her poison. A relatively similar version of the name was Aqua Tofana.[24] Another authority offered three names, including Aqua Toffania, Aqua Della Toffania, and Acquitta di Napoli.[25] Similarly, Aquetta di Napoli, was suggested by one version of the case. Another name used was Acquetti di Napoli.[26]

Those were the popular names for the poisonous product. The inscription on the label read "Manna of St. Nicholas of Bari," and there was a drawing of the saint on the product label. The name on the label was "Manna de San Nicola," according to an alternate perspective.[27]

It might be interesting to consider how the product was marketed to seventeenth-century Neapolitan customers. There were a couple of ostensible product uses besides the deadly ulterior purpose. The vials were positioned in the consumer marketplace as a cosmetic, according to some accounts. But women were quietly instructed to ask La Tofania in person about administering the poison, information not provided on the label. It was also sold as a medicine to improve facial health.[28]

This dangerous substance was created sometime around 1650. There are a couple of similar slightly supernatural stories concerning the invention. This allegedly miraculous substance was discovered "oozing" on St. Nicholas of Bari's tomb, it was contended.[29] A slightly different version of events observed that it was named after a curative oil taken from St. Nicholas's tomb.[30]

What was in this widely heralded and publicly popular poison? Arsenic was the main ingredient, it was believed. To be a bit more specific, it was crystallized arsenic mixed with the herb cymbalaria. An alternate version suggested instead that the poison was mostly arsenic, with some lead and possibly belladonna.[31]

Just a few drops administered over time could slowly and imperceptibly kill someone.[32] And this poison was so deadly that a very small dose was all that was required to kill someone. A doctor estimated that four to six drops could kill a man.[33]

Aqua Tofania was said to be an evil and especially effective elixir for another main reason: it was almost impossible to detect because it was a clear and insipid liquid. One report from 1833 declared that the poison was as tasteless as pure water and that it was impossible to guard against its use.[34] According to another account, the poison was without color, odor, and taste.[35]

A contemporary description of the effects of this poison can be considered:

A certain indescribable change is felt in the whole body, which leads the person to complain to a physician. The physician examines and reflects, but finds no symptoms internal or external, no vomiting, no inflammation, no fever. In short, he can only advise patience, strict regimen and laxatives. . . . Meanwhile, the poison takes firmer hold of the system; languor, wearisomeness, and loathing of food continue; the nobler organs gradually become torpid, and the lungs in particular at length begin to suffer. In a word, the malady from the first is incurable.[36]

OTHER CRIMES

Some people La Tofania murdered herself, but more often she was merely the supplier. Most of the murders resulted from poison sales. The poison was sold to women clients who were also given instructions for its use.[37]

A second criminal conduct concerned conspiracy. La Tofania organized a group of poisoners. The membership of this secret society of slayers was restricted to women.[38]

Her third crime was related to the organization of poisoners. And maybe this other group is actually the same as the poisoners. A militant feminist organization was created to plot against males.[39]

Torture was the final additional crime committed by La Tofania. If her poison was administered in microdoses over a lengthy period of time, the killer could enjoy their victim's agony as long as possible. She encouraged her clients to prolong their victim's suffering.[40]

THE SERIAL MURDERS

Modus Operandi

The modus operandi was poisoning. Victims ingested the poison in water and wine. The colorless and tasteless potion was easily mixed in a variety of beverages.[41]

Number of Victims

There is almost consensus on the number of victims in this case. That seldom happens because, as the reader knows by now, there is usually controversy over the number of victims attributed to serial killers. But in this case there was near unanimity among the estimates of her death toll.

La Tofania confessed to a total of 600 victims, and it was estimated that by 1723, she had killed or assisted in the murder of approximately 600 people.[42] One alternative estimate prevented unanimity in this case. This outlier quantified the serial murders at a much higher level. According to Neapolitan gossip, La Tofania had killed 1,000 people.[43]

Time Frame

We might locate these serial slayings in time through exploration of their time frame and duration. The initial murder was thought to have occurred in Palermo in 1650, but a time frame of 1670 to 1719 was suggested.[44]

The murders lasted from La Tofania's adolescence until she was executed at the age of 70. They took place over nearly 50 years.[45] This is among the longest serial murder durations in history.

Victims

None of the names of La Tofania's victims is available to us today. But we can nevertheless identify a few of her victims in some manner. She gave the police a list of her victims, but unfortunately that list has not been preserved.[46] Her initial victim may have been her husband. In any case, he was a very close male relative.[47] Additionally, she reportedly poisoned two Roman Catholic popes.[48]

Victimology

More is known about La Tofania's victimology choices than about the specific individuals murdered. Husbands, obviously, were her primary target group. There was an important subset of males when it came to victimology variables: men with money were definitely more endangered than their less affluent brethren. Virtually all her victims were men.[49]

But not all. La Tofania was directly or indirectly responsible for the murder of some women but not nearly as many as men. Tiresome and unpopular relatives were another specific (and nongendered) victimology cohort.[50]

What about her clients, the women who sought to expedite the passing of a loved one or associate? They were unhappy adulterous and jealous wives who came to La Tofania for help. They were typically society women seeking to slay a husband or lover.[51]

Motive

La Tofania was a commercial serial killer. But it is not at all uncommon and, in fact, is rather typical for serial killers to have multiple motives. That was the case with La Tofania.

She hated men. La Tofania reportedly offered her assistance for free if a woman lacked the resources to purchase poison. A specialized study of women who commit multicide concluded that she was motivated by her hatred of men.[52]

COMMERCIAL SERIAL MURDER

It appears that La Tofania was motivated primarily by commercial factors. It is true that she hated men, but she did not have to charge for her services. She risked her life to assist in these murders and was richly rewarded for her efforts. The preponderance of evidence in this case casts these as commercial crimes.

Greed was her primary motive, according to one authority on serial murder, along with her disdain for men. La Tofania made poison her profession.[53] And business was very good. La Tofania provided lethal concoctions to a specific clientele: those with the means who could afford it.[54]

According to the *Calcutta Review*, "It was the business of these wretches to assist ladies in ridding themselves of their husbands."[55] La Tofania was a businesswoman whose nefarious trade was death. Her preparation and sale of poisons was the basic element in the commission of a staggering number of murders.[56]

INVESTIGATION

Married men were dying at such an excessive rate that the authorities finally noticed. This perspective does not credit the Naples, Rome, and Vatican police forces with much diligence. It is a critical reality that authorities uncovered La Tofania's crimes only after 600 murders.[57]

In fairness to Italian law enforcement, La Tofania actively worked to make their job difficult. Because she dreaded being found by the police, she continually changed her name and residence. She also adopted a variety of disguises in addition to changing abodes.[58]

She was apprehended in 1719. There are two versions of how she came to the attention of the authorities. The viceroy of Naples personally launched an investigation because of the substantial inexplicable male murder rate.[59]

La Tofania was warned about her impending arrest because her spies warned her about her imminent apprehension. She sought ecclesiastical protection by taking sanctuary in a convent.[60] But she took advantage of the good graces of her protectors by continuing to sell poison from within convent walls.[61]

The viceroy appealed to the convent leadership to turn La Tofania over to his soldiers but was refused. Because of her public popularity, it was difficult for the authorities to evict her by force, so rumors were spread that she had poisoned some wells, reducing her popularity somewhat. Finally, the viceroy felt it was safe to issue an arrest order. Soldiers invaded the convent, and she "was dragged out by force."[62] The archbishop of Naples demanded her release but to no avail.[63]

There is an alternate version of her apprehension. La Tofania came to the attention of the Italian police because they were able to trace the poison back to her. A search of her residence turned up vials of her deadly potion as well as a quantity of arsenic. The day before her arrest, she had dispatched two boxes of her poison to Rome that were intercepted in the Rome Customs House, leading police to her.[64]

After her arrest, she was subjected to torture during her interrogation. She confessed to the serial murders during and after being tortured on the rack. La Tofania was arrested and tortured and confessed within a relatively brief period of time, although it undoubtedly must have seemed like an eternity to her.[65]

TRIAL

La Tofania's trial remains as much of a mystery today as was the defendant. It is believed that she was tried in 1723. She enthusiastically implicated a substantial number of others, the women who had been her clients. She readily named her customers, and because of her candor (perhaps coerced), she identified the women who had patronized her and who were immediately arrested at home, in various churches and monasteries, and elsewhere.[66] She was convicted and sentenced to death.[67]

It must be apparent by now that there are conflicting accounts of several pertinent aspects of these serial murders. The specific facts in the La Tofania crimes vary between renditions. A report from the nineteenth century concluded,

> In the accounts of her fate there is considerable discrepancy. For Labat says that she was arrested in 1709; Keysler, another traveler, affirms, on the contrary, that she was still living in Naples in 1730, and resided in a convent . . . and Gaelli, who was a physician to Charles the Sixth, writes to a friend about 1719 that she was still in prison in Naples.[68]

It has been repeatedly reported that her execution occurred in 1709, but it actually took place in 1723. Strangulation was the mode of execution. Her body was thrown back over the walls into the convent as a final gesture of contempt for those who had tried to use the Roman Catholic Church to protect La Tofania and thwart justice.[69]

CONCLUSION

La Tofania was a prominent professional poisoner if the accounts available to us are accurate. She seems to have been fiercely and criminally unhappy with men. Her organization of a society of female poisoners characterized her as an ardent and fervent male hater.

But she was also a canny criminal capable of profiting from her sexist serial slayings. La Tofania made sure that she profited from these crimes. That qualifies her for inclusion in the category of commercial serial murderer.

ANDREAS BICHEL

Andreas Bichel's blood lust characterized these serial murders as being particularly atrocious events. He was "a creature with a lust for blood and devoid of all sense and pity."[1] Because of Andreas Bichel, Bavaria suffered a series of sex murders.[2]

The violent and cold-blooded nature of the murders outraged Bichel's contemporaries. But was he a serial slayer or a mass murderer? It was suggested that Bichel was one of the worst mass murderers of the nineteenth century.[3]

He was referred to as a prototype of the contemporary serial slayer. Bichel has even been considered a precursor to the infamous Jack the Ripper. It was speculated that these Ripper-like multiple murders may have inspired the Whitechapel murderer.[4]

Bichel elicited strong reactions from those he encountered in the course of his investigation and trial. The judge presiding over his trial remarked that Bichel was "beneath even the dignity of the common criminal."[5] Perhaps that is attributable to his disclosures at trial. He admitted that a strange passion overwhelmed him after which he explored the bodies of his victims in an intimate, firsthand and criminal manner.[6] Richard Krafft-Ebing, in his landmark publication *Psychopathia Sexualis, with Especial Reference to the Antipathic Sexual Instinct: A Medico-Forensic Study*, called him "the most horrible example."[7]

THE SERIAL MURDERER

Bichel had his good points as well as his bad, and his character has not been depicted in a unidimensional and unflattering manner. He was said to be quiet and industrious. Observers noted that Bichel maintained a seemingly respectable front.[8]

Other depictions of his character were not as positive. His cruel and piti-less nature was observed. One report mentioned his somewhat effeminate and anxious character. A quartet of undesirable traits was ascribed to him, including cruelty, harshness, avarice, and timidity. Worst of all, "his stubborn lying" resulted in a bad reputation because his honesty was not entirely above reproach.[9]

We have mixed reviews of his personality just as his character received inconsistent assessments. He was thought by some to be a harmless person. Major Arthur Griffith described Bichel in positive terms: "Not a drunkard, nor gambler, nor quarrelsome."[10] Other personality portrayals were not so kind. Bichel's behavior was said to be beneath desirable levels and revealed the limitations of his character, his lack of education, and the absence of even limited intelligence. Unlike most local men, he did not patronize the alehouse regularly because he had a relatively reserved and unsocial disposi-tion. It was thought that he was afraid of the jeers and jokes and rough man-ner of the village toughs.[11]

He was a day laborer, and he worked at an inn. But he is best known by his main vocation: fortune-teller. Bichel earned a little money by telling fortunes.[12]

It is not unusual for serial murderers to maintain stable marriages and have seemingly normal family existences. That was true in this case as well. Bichel was blessed with a wife, children, and a home.[13]

There was no mention of children in some versions of events. We know a little about his relationship with his wife; Bichel valued his wife, "to whom he appeared to be warmly attached."[14] She had the reputation of being as reserved as him, and as a result they were not highly regarded by their neigh-bors, mostly because they did not socialize and kept to themselves.[15]

Bichel committed his crimes in the early 1800s while Jack the Ripper's murders took place at the other end of the century in the 1880s. Thus, his crimes were in the public record and a publicized reality before the Ripper was born. This suggests that Bichel's crimes were a model for the crimes com-mitted by Jack the Ripper.[16]

He was born a Bavarian citizen, and that is where he killed.[17] Regensdorf was his Bavarian hometown, and he never left.[18] His nickname was the "Bavarian Ripper."[19]

OTHER CRIMES

A petty criminal at heart, Bichel was a known property crime miscreant. He often purloined fresh produce from his neighbor's garden. And he lost a job at the local inn when he was caught stealing hay from his employer's barn.[20]

Bichel engaged in a couple different types of sexual misconduct during the commission of the serial slayings. He raped his victims before killing them, according to numerous accounts.[21] But he wasn't done with the sexual aspect of the crimes. Later, as the victims lay dying, he "masturbated over the writhing bodies."[22]

Various terms have been used to explain what he did to the bodies of his victims after death. A trio will be considered. First, he dissected them, it was observed at the time.[23] Bichel also mutilated his young victims. This body desecration was intentional and deliberate. Bichel himself reportedly admitted the enjoyment he experienced from the mutilations.[24] I suspect that dissection and mutilation referred to the same activity. The same is true of the third term, disembowelment: numerous accounts specifically mentioned that Bichel disemboweled the victims.[25]

Mutilation occurs after death. The very same treatment before death would be called torture. It is fair to say that he tortured his victims to death. He reportedly preferred to begin to dissect his victims while they were still alive.[26]

Bichel may not have been a cannibal. He was not accused of such criminal conduct, nor was there evidence of cannibalism. Nevertheless, he confessed "his desire at the time to eat a piece."[27]

A final concurrent crime might be considered: the removal of body parts. Perhaps he ate them. They were not in the victims' bodies. It is believed that Bichel tore their hearts out and removed them from the scene.[28]

THE SERIAL MURDERS

Modus Operandi

Victims were "ravished, killed and dissected."[29] Bichel raped and then tortured his victims prior to killing them.[30] And there was considerable similarities in his murder modus operandi since he had murdered several girls in an identical manner.[31]

There are competing beliefs about how Bichel accomplished his crimes. Victims arrived at his residence in search of employment as servants, one report claimed. In a very different and generally more accepted version, they were enticed to his home through promises of having their fortunes told.[32] His victims were knocked out and then stripped. They reportedly awoke to find that they had been bound and gagged. Baring-Gould reversed that order of action in her authoritative account: "when he had them in his power he bound their hands behind their backs, and stunned them with a blow."[33] What actually happened is somewhat more improbable, but sometimes reality is stranger than fiction. Bichel explained to the gullible young girls that his magic mirror would show their future husbands to them, but first they had to be bound and blindfolded to enhance the mirror's comfort level.[34]

Some victims were slashed to death. One was stabbed in the neck. Others faced a more terrible fate: they were hacked to pieces while still alive.[35]

Number of Victims

The Bichel victimage is uncertain. Many women were reportedly killed. It was also contended that several girls were victimized.[36] Fifty victims is the most common estimate reported in the literature. Several sources indicated more than 50, while one specified nearly 50 victims. Although 50 victims is the common estimate, the more credible accounts provide lower victimage totals.[37] The victimage could easily have been higher than it was. After a few murders, he attempted the same thing with three other young women. But each time, the potential victims resisted his overtures and rejected his invitation.[38]

Time Frame

These crimes took place in the early years of the nineteenth century. Two time frame estimates were expressed as ranges. The 1790s to 1808 was one version of the time frame, and the alternate notion was 1806 to 1809.[39] Other perspectives on the Bichel serial murder time frame were more specific. The year 1800 was one authority's estimate, while another version was 1807. Most specific of all was this estimate: the early months of 1808.[40]

Victims

Barbara Reisenger was killed in 1807. It is believed that she was offered a position as a domestic servant and arrived at the Bichel residence expecting a job interview. Once there, Bichel convinced her to let the magic mirror reveal her future husband to her.[41] She agreed to be bound and blindfolded. Then Bichel repeatedly stabbed her in the neck. He nearly severed her spinal column, so ferocious were the wounds, and he even stabbed her lungs.[42]

The other known victim was Catherine Seidel, sometimes referred to as Katherina Leidel. She mysteriously vanished after visiting with Bichel. Seidel told her sister Walburga of Bichel's readiness to help her see her future husband at her convenience. Seidel said that Bichel had "a wonderful glass in which those who looked could see their future."[43]

When the police asked Bichel about where Seidel was, he admitted that she had seen him. But he claimed that she left town abruptly with someone he had never seen before and was unable to identify.[44] This was in 1807.[45]

Bichel had made a strange request of Seidel. He asked her to wear her best dress and bring three others. She did so and was rewarded with being slain by a crushing blow to the head. And then came his coup de grâce: "He then cut open the body—as it might seem, out of pure devilishness—and bathed his hands and covered the house floor with her blood."[46]

Victimology

Victimology considerations in this case were relatively simple. Bichel had very exclusive victim requirements—pretty young females.[47] A contemporary newspaper account of the case reported on Bichel's apparent limited victimology: "It is highly significant that it never seems to have occurred to him to inveigh into his house either a man or boy."[48]

Motive

Bichel's main motive was monetary.[49] But most serial murderers have more than one factor impelling their homicidal activity, and Bichel was no exception to this general rule. A trio of additional motives might be considered.

Fetishism was suggested as a Bichel motive. He had a decided fetish for women's clothes. A second motive might have been lust: that was the opinion of Krafft-Ebing. Pleasure was the final possible alternate motive because Bichel allegedly admitted that he murdered because he took pleasure in killing.[50]

COMMERCIAL SERIAL MURDER

These were fundamentally simple crimes in one respect. They were committed so that Bichel could steal clothing and the victims' other belongings. Baring-Gould recorded the fact that he "despoiled them of their clothes, for the sake of which he committed the murders."[51]

He testified that his motive was to steal the girls' clothing, which he admitted he didn't need and could dispense of only after considerable difficulty, the *Pall Mall Gazette* reported in 1888. He further confessed that he killed Reisenger because he was tempted by her expensive garments. Bichel admitted murdering the women to steal their personal belongings.[52]

Bichel is believed to have contacted Reisenger's parents after her murder and told them that she had married and left the area. He claimed that she had asked him to obtain her other garments and possessions and take them to her. Reisenger's gullible parents gave him what he asked for.[53]

The spoils of the serial slayings wound up incriminating him, as is usually the case. Bichel's wife sold items of Reisenger's clothing to Barbara's friends that they knew had belonged to their friend. And when police searched the house, chests full of women's clothes were found. A contemporary media story reported that his greed was aroused by any display of wealth and that greed resulted in his arrest.[54]

INVESTIGATION

Although Bichel's residence was thoroughly searched at the time, no evidence of murder was discovered by the police. He confused investigators, too, making admissions at one point only to later retract them. After Reisenger's death, there was no evidence implicating Bichel in the crime.[55]

Bichel toyed with the investigators. During the investigation, his conduct showed him to be a determined criminal who openly admitted only those things that were previously confirmed by other sources. The *Pall Mall Gazette* characterized him as acting guilty, noting that many of his answers were contradictory and clearly false.[56]

There are two versions of how he came to the attention of the authorities. The initial tale tells that after the Seidel murder, the police used bloodhounds to track the killer. The dog followed the olfactory trail to Bichel's woodshed, where bodies were found buried. Bichel was subsequently apprehended.[57]

Seidel's sister solved the case in the alternate perspective on events. She was looking for her missing sister when she noticed an unusual fabric in a tailor's window: a distinctive corded cloth. It was material from her sister's petticoat.[58] She notified the police, who immediately traced the fabric to Bichel. They went to his residence and interrogated him there. Bichel claimed that Seidel had visited him but had met a wealthy man and run off with him, so she no longer needed her old clothes. The police greeted his explanation with skepticism.[59]

They searched his house and found a large assortment of women's clothing. Some were identified by her sister as belonging to Seidel. A police dog insistently led searchers to the woodshed located behind the house.[60] They dug in the outbuilding and found a layer of straw. Underneath that, a head was found first, followed soon after by the discovery of a bisected headless corpse. Nearby beneath a rubbish pile, a second body cut in two was also unearthed along with the other head.[61]

However all this occurred, Bichel was arrested. Both he and his wife were apprehended, according to one account. It was also claimed that he alone was arrested and subsequently voluntarily confessed.[62]

TRIAL

Not a great deal is known about Bichel's trial. He was reportedly brought to court in late 1808 or 1809.[63] He was initially uncooperative and admitted nothing.[64] Stymied, Bavarian authorities were limited because their nation had recently outlawed torture and they needed a confession. So they used an idiosyncratic provision of Bavarian law to induce Bichel's cooperation.

Bichel was forced to examine the clothing of his victims in the courtroom, causing him to collapse in his chair. He was shown the mutilated bodies of his victims in the courtroom, according to another version, and he was taken to his home and shown the bodies, according to an alternate perspective. Three days later, he broke down in his cell and confessed to everything.[65]

His trial testimony tended to incriminate him. Here is the account of Baring-Gould: " 'I must say,' he remarked at his trial, 'that during the operation I was so eager, that I trembled all over, and I longed to rive off a piece and eat it.' " Additional testimony by Bichel was reported by Krafft-Ebing: "I opened her breast and with a knife cut through the fleshy parts of the body. Then I arranged the body as a butcher does beef, and hacked it with an axe into pieces of a size to fit the hole which I had dug up in the mountains for burying it. I may say that while opening the body I was so greedy that I trembled, and could have cut out a piece and eaten it."[66]

His conviction was a forgone conclusion. In light of the kind of testimony against him, his guilt was not in doubt, and he was easily convicted. The judge castigated him for lacking "the energy or courage to rob on the highway or break into a house." Instead, Bichel chose to "cunningly induce young girls to go to him, and then murder them in cold blood for the sake of their clothes or a few pence."[67]

The judge sentenced Bichel to be "broken" on the wheel. This ancient Germanic method of execution involved the breaking of a man's bones, which are systematically smashed to bits.[68] Instead, as an act of mercy, he was decapitated. The execution occurred in 1809.[69]

CONCLUSION

Bichel was a complicated man. He is considered a serial slayer who was motivated by money. Yet his victims were young girls who were sexually abused. And he mutilated the corpses of the girls he tortured to death. That does not sound like the typical commercial serial murderer.

Yet he admitted in court that he acted out of greed. He was not tortured, unlike many of the confessed serial killers covered in this book. Bichel remains a bit of an enigma, but he most likely got what he deserved.

16

CONCLUSION

This final chapter assesses what has been introduced in the 15 previous chapters and attempts to synthesize that information into a set of specific and salient conclusions. A considerable quantity of concepts, facts, and details have been discussed in this book, and it might be useful to offer the reader some perspective by focusing this conclusion on a few subjects. Therefore, this summary will be limited to three main subjects: main findings, implications, and reservations.

MAIN FINDINGS

The case study method has been used along with integrative research techniques to analyze the information gathered in this study. Fourteen specific serial murder cases were selected because they illustrated one of the types or categories of historic serial murder. As a result of this analysis, some conclusions can be confidently presented. Four main sets of conclusions will be discussed: the historic serial murder thesis confirmed, aggregate analysis of the serial murderers, aggregate analysis of the serial murders, and unusual findings.

The Historic Serial Murder Thesis Confirmed

This book asserts a solitary but significant position: serial murder is not a relatively recent crime but is a time-honored and ancient human activity. The only reason we do not know more about these crimes from the past is the fact that time has limited our ability to discover and research them. And, of course, ancient people did not understand serial murder and instead attributed the atrocities to supernatural entities. But make no mistake about it: serial murder took place in prehistoric times, the Middle Ages, and the entire premodern world.

Aggregate Analysis of the Serial Murderers

Fourteen killers have been analyzed in this book. I have reviewed as much information about these killers as is available. More information exists about some of these historic figures than others, but we can nevertheless consider some aggregate facts about our sample of serial slayers. These basic facts are presented in Table 16.1.

Table 16.1
Basic Serial Killer Facts

Killer	Multiple Names	Maximum Number of Murders	Minimum Number of Murders	Family	Intellect
Bathory	Yes	650	30	Yes	Highly
Verzini	Yes	12	2	No	Average
Vacher	No	23	10	No	Not very
Garnier	No	5	3	Yes	?
Stubbe	Yes	17	15	Yes	?
Chalons	Yes	23	12	Yes	?
Monovoison	Yes	3,000	100	Yes	?
De Rais	No	800	50	Yes	Very
Vlad	Yes	300,000	20,000	Yes	Highly
Nzinga	Yes	?	2	Yes	Very
Cixi	Yes	30,313	266	Yes	Very
Locusta	Yes	6	5	?	Very
Tofania	Yes	1,000	600	Yes	?
Bichel	No	50	2	Yes	Not very

Killer	Sadism	Mental Health	Animal Mutilation	Tortured?	Death
Bathory	Yes	Psychotic	No	No	Old age
Verzini	No	Partly insane	Yes	No	Suicide
Vacher	Yes	Persecution complex	Yes	No	Guillotine
Garnier	No	?	No	No	Burned alive
Stubbe	Yes	?	No	Yes	Decapitated
Chalons	No	?	No	Yes	Burned alive
La Voison	No	Deranged	No	Yes	Burned alive
De Rais	Yes	Healthy	No	Yes	Strangled
Vlad	Yes	Healthy	Yes	No	Died in battle
Nzinga	Yes	Healthy	No	No	Old age
Cixi	Yes	Healthy	No	No	Old age
Locusta	No	Healthy	No	Yes	Torn apart by wild animals
Tofania	No	Psychopath	No	Yes	Strangled
Bichel	Yes	Healthy	No	No	Decapitated

Ten of these 14 murderers have been referred to by more than one name over the years, and in at least one case (Monvoison), the killer is known by two entirely different names in the literature. Analysis of the maximum number of murders per killer reveals two clusters or categories of carnage: the top six killers (Vlad, Cixi, Monvoison, La Tofania, de Rais, and Bathory) accounted for a total of 335,763 deaths, a mean average of 55,960 per killer. The others (Vacher, Verzini, Garnier, the Werewolf of Chalons, Stubbe, Locusta, and Bichel) collectively killed about 136 people, a mean average of 19.42 victims per killer.

The range between the maximum and minimum estimated victimage in these cases revealed three types: narrow, intermediate, and extensive. The Garnier, Stubbe, and Locusta crimes involved ranges of fewer than three murders. In the intermediate-range cases (Bichel, Werewolf of Chalons, Vacher, and Verzini), the ranges varied between 10 and 48 murders. There were also extensive ranges: Vlad, 300,000 to 20,000; Cixi, 30,313 to 266; Monvoison, 3,000 to 100; La Tofania, 1,000 to 600; de Rais, 800 to 50; and Bathory, 650 to 30. The smallest range in the extensive category was 620 murders, and the greatest was 280,000.

Most of these serial slayers had families; only Vacher and Verzini did not. The intellectual level of our sample varied greatly. Two were called highly intelligent (Bathory and Vlad), and four were very smart, including de Rais, Nzinga, Cixi, and Locusta. Eight of these serial murderers were sadists: Bathory, Vacher, Stubbe, de Rais, Vlad, Nzinga, Cixi, and Bichel.

Mental health issues were not as prevalent or frequently documented as you might think. Six of these individuals (de Rais, Vlad, Cixi, Nzinga, Locusta, and Bichel) were considered mentally healthy, or at least there were no reported issues. Bathory was called psychotic and La Tofania psychopathic. Monvoison was said to be deranged, Verzini was partly insane, and Vacher was treated repeatedly for a persecution complex.

We might consider a final dimension of these killers: their denouement. Bathory, Cixi, and Nzinga died of old age, although Bathory was confined to a very small space. Verzini killed himself, and nine of the remaining 10 were executed. Three were decapitated, three others were burned alive, two were strangled, one was ripped apart by wild animals, and Vlad died in battle.

Aggregate Analysis of the Serial Murders

The diversity of these serial murders frustrates easy summarization. The modi operandi, time frames, and victimology were quite different from case to case. Nevertheless, it is possible to discuss three aspects of these cases in a systematic and comparative manner. We will consider motive, other and concurrent crimes, and sexually oriented crimes.

Our initial issue involves the causes of these crimes. The motivation of these serial killers is of salience to this study of the crimes. Table 16.2 summarizes these findings.

It is not uncommon for multiple motives to be manifested in multicide cases. Indeed, in the 14 cases examined, only two (Garnier and Monvoison) were considered to involve a solitary motive. Aristocratic motives were evident in five cases, and there were a half dozen instances of commercial serial murder. Seven of these killers expressed pleasure from the act, while there were three cases of revenge and the same number of instances of religious motivation.

Table 16.2
Serial Murder Motivation

Killer	Aristocrat	Profit	Pleasure	Revenge	Religion
Bathory	Yes	No	Yes	No	Yes
Verzini	No	No	Yes	No	No
Vacher	No	No	No	Yes	Yes
Garnier	No	No	No	No	No
Stubbe	No	No	Yes	Yes	Yes
Chalons	No	No	No	No	No
Monovoison	No	Yes	No	No	No
De Rais	Yes	No	Yes	Yes	No
Vlad	Yes	Yes	Yes	No	No
Nzinga	Yes	No	No	No	No
Cixi	Yes	Yes	No	No	No
Locusta	No	Yes	Yes	No	No
Tofania	No	Yes	No	No	No
Bichel	No	Yes	Yes	No	No
Total	5	6	7	3	3

Killer	Politics	Sex	Multiple Motives
Bathory	Yes	No	Yes
Verzini	No	Yes	Yes
Vacher	Yes	No	Yes
Garnier	No	No	No
Stubbe	No	No	Yes
Chalons	No	Yes	Yes
Monovoison	No	No	No
De Rais	Yes	Yes	Yes
Vlad	Yes	No	Yes
Nzinga	Yes	No	Yes
Cixi	Yes	No	Yes
Locusta	No	No	Yes
Tofania	No	No	Yes
Bichel	No	No	Yes
Total	6	3	12

Serial killers typically have committed other crimes prior to the initiation of the serial slayings, and also common is the commission of concurrent crimes. Every killer included in this book either committed a crime before the serial murders and/or engaged in other offenses at the same time. These offenses are shown in Table 16.3.

Table 16.3
Other Crimes

Killer	Devil Worship	Witchcraft	Cannibalism	Torture	Mutilation
Bathory	Yes	Yes	Yes	Yes	No
Verzini	No	No	Yes	No	Yes
Vacher	No	No	Yes	No	Yes
Garnier	Yes	Yes	Yes	No	Yes
Stubbe	Yes	Yes	Yes	No	Yes
Chalons	No	No	Yes	Yes	Yes
Monovoison	Yes	Yes	No	No	No
De Rais	Yes	Yes	Yes	Yes	Yes
Vlad	No	Yes	Yes	Yes	Yes
Nzinga	No	No	Yes	No	No
Cixi	No	No	No	Yes	No
Locusta	No	No	No	Yes	No
Tofania	No	No	No	Yes	No
Bichel	No	No	No	Yes	Yes
Total	5	6	9	8	8

Killer	Vampire	Werewolf	Kidnapping	Body Part Theft	Infanticide
Bathory	Yes	Yes	Yes	No	No
Verzini	Yes	No	No	Yes	No
Vacher	Yes	No	No	Yes	No
Garnier	No	Yes	No	No	No
Stubbe	Yes	Yes	No	No	No
Chalons	No	Yes	No	No	No
Monovoison	No	No	No	No	Yes
De Rais	Yes	Yes	Yes	No	Yes
Vlad	No	No	Yes	Yes	No
Nzinga	No	No	No	No	Yes
Cixi	No	No	No	No	No
Locusta	No	No	No	No	No
Tofania	No	No	No	No	No

(Continued)

Table 16.3 (Continued)

Killer	Vampire	Werewolf	Kidnapping	Body Part Theft	Infanticide
Bichel	No	No	No	Yes	No
Total	5	5	3	4	3

Killer	Dismember- ment	Decapitation	Disembow- elment	Theft	Other Crimes
Bathory	No	No	No	No	Yes
Verzini	No	No	Yes	No	Yes
Vacher	No	No	Yes	No	Yes
Garnier	No	No	No	No	Yes
Stubbe	No	No	No	No	Yes
Chalons	Yes	Yes	No	No	Yes
Monovoison	No	No	No	No	Yes
De Rais	Yes	Yes	Yes	Yes	Yes
Vlad	Yes	Yes	Yes	No	Yes
Nzinga	No	No	No	No	Yes
Cixi	No	No	No	No	Yes
Locusta	No	No	No	No	Yes
Tofania	No	No	No	No	Yes
Bichel	Yes	No	Yes	Yes	Yes
Total	4	3	5	2	14

Five of these serial murderers were alleged to have consorted with or prayed to the Devil, and six were suspected of witchcraft. Nine of the 14 cases involved suspected cannibalism, and in eight of these instances, the victims were tortured and mutilated. Vampirism was alleged in five cases, the same number of werewolf assertions. Three of these serial killers were kidnappers, the same number that was accused of infanticide.

Two of the cases involved common theft. There were five cases involving disemboweling, four sets of dismemberments, and three series of decapitations. Parts of bodies were taken away by the killer in four instances.

A significant amount of the concurrent criminal conduct by these serial killers involved sex. There were several specific types of sexual misconduct. They are quantified in Table 16.4.

Two of these serial killers were incestuous: Bathory and Stubbe. A quartet of serial murdering rapists included Vacher, Stubbe, de Rais, and Bichel. Vacher, the Werewolf of Chalons, de Rais, Locusta, and Bichel were sexual predators and child molesters. Necrophilia was committed by Verzini, Vacher, the Werewolf of Chalons, and Bichel. And four of these serial murderers masturbated during the killings: Verzini, Vacher, de Rais, and Bichel.

Table 16.4
Serial Murderer Sex Offenses

Killer	Incest	Rape	Child Molestation	Necrophilia	Masturbation during Crimes
Bathory	Yes	No	No	No	No
Verzini	No	No	No	Yes	Yes
Vacher	No	Yes	Yes	Yes	Yes
Garnier	No	No	No	No	No
Stubbe	Yes	Yes	No	?	No
Chalons	No	No	Yes	Yes	No
Monovoison	No	No	No	No	No
De Rais	No	Yes	Yes	Yes	Yes
Vlad	No	No	No	No	No
Nzinga	No	No	No	No	No
Cixi	No	No	No	No	No
Locusta	No	No	Yes	No	No
Tofania	No	No	No	No	No
Bichel	No	Yes	Yes	No	Yes
Total	2	4	5	4	4

Unusual Findings

There were a few surprises in my findings. These unanticipated factors warrant recognition and discussion. Basic quantification of the occurrence of these unexpected findings is offered in Table 16.5.

The ancient justice systems dealing with these serial murderers were not very concerned with defendants' rights or due process. Six of these murderers were tortured, including Garnier, the Werewolf of Chalons, Monvoison, de Rais, Locusta, and La Tofania, and at least four of these trials were censored (Bathory, the Werewolf of Chalons, Monvoison, and de Rais).

Serial murder and mass murder were combined in an astonishing six cases, nearly half the sample. De Rais, Vlad, Nzinga, Cixi, La Tofania, and Bichel were alleged to be mass murderers. These killers merged the two crimes: while typical serial killers slay one person at a time on several occasions, these killers committed mass murder repeatedly, although most also killed a person or two at a time on occasion.

The role of the embryonic mass media was manifested in several cases. Much of the information available to us about five killers (Vacher, Garnier, Stubbe, Vlad, and Nzinga) was included in broadsheets, posters, pamphlets, and other print mass communication media. It is an accepted fact that there is a significant interrelationship between contemporary serial slayers and the modern media, but it appears that this relationship extends back considerably farther than was previously realized.

Table 16.5
Unusual Aspects of Serial Murder Cases

Killer	Tortured?	Mass Murderer	Mass Media	Trial Censored	Framed?
Bathory	No	No	No	Yes	Yes
Verzini	No	No	No	No	No
Vacher	No	No	Yes	No	No
Garnier	Yes	No	Yes	No	Yes
Stubbe	No	No	Yes	No	Yes
Chalons	Yes	No	No	Yes	No
Monovoison	Yes	No	No	Yes	No
De Rais	Yes	Yes	No	Yes	Yes
Vlad	No	Yes	Yes	No	Yes
Nzinga	No	Yes	Yes	No	No
Cixi	No	Yes	No	No	Yes
Locusta	Yes	No	No	No	No
Tofania	Yes	Yes	No	No	No
Bichel	No	Yes	No	No	No
Total	6	6	5	4	6

Were these individuals really guilty, or is it possible that they were framed or set up in some way? That was alleged in a half dozen cases, involving Bathory, Garnier, Stubbe, de Rais, Vlad, and Cixi. Bathory, de Rais, and Vlad were said to be the victim of profit-motivated autocrats who coveted their possessions, while Garnier and Stubbe were said to be scapegoats for unsolved killings. Cixi was castigated by Chinese Kuomintang and communist historians seeking to create the revisionist rewriting of history through criticism aided by communist Chinese leaders.

IMPLICATIONS

There are two sets of salient implications to be examined: the serial murder and the supernatural science dimensions of this work. If it is correct that serial murder is an ancient reality and not the contemporary concern that it is often considered to be, then some revision of common knowledge will be appropriate. Two specific types of implications might be considered: serial murder and supernatural subjects.

Serial Murder Implications

It has been commonly accepted in the serial murder literature that this is a relatively recent type of crime. Little is known about premodern instances of this offense, so it has been assumed that there were not any. But that is an invalid conclusion, reflecting the difficulty inherent in historic research more than the truth of the situation.

Serial murder did not begin suddenly in the 1970s or the 1950s. Nor was it a product of the age of industrialization. Jack the Ripper did not initiate the crime. Chances are good that it began early in the history of man. The recency of serial murder is another myth deserving of relegation to the circular file of mistaken concepts.

Supernatural Science Implications

But this work has meaning far beyond the domain of serial slaying studies. The disciplines involved with myth, folklore, and the emerging field of supernatural sciences might be interested in this research. This book offers a very different and empirically grounded explanation for the phenomenon previously rationalized through belief in the existence of supernatural entities.

Such creatures most likely never existed. If they did, they certainly were not responsible for the human carnage actually generated by premodern serial killers. So one of two things is true: either vampires and their supernatural kin were and are actual living creatures with the ability to kill people and a historic record of accomplishing just that, or someone or something else was the culprit. The most reasonable and efficient answer to these questions is the historic reality of serial murderers.

RESERVATIONS

My conclusions are the result of a scholarly study of serial slayers, but some reservations or caveats should nevertheless be recognized. For one, I used a purposive or convenience sample, meaning that the cases were selected to illustrate the salient types of serial killers. Therefore, there are no claims to representativeness in statistical terms, although such claims are irrelevant to case studies anyway.

A second caveat involves research. My use of secondary sources along with available primary sources makes me reliant on those earlier informational inputs. But this is not usually an issue because I have used every source available, and, taken collectively, this literature basis allows me to overcome the deficiencies or problems with any individual source.

The third caveat is a recognition of another liability of integrative research: inconsistent facts. In every case in this book, there were disputed facts and varying versions of virtually everything. That makes effective integration difficult, and my solution is to share all the data with the reader and allow you to arrive at your own interpretation.

CONCLUSION

Serial killers have been around since mankind became civilized. Recognition of this fact should be an accepted aspect of common knowledge. America does not have a monopoly on this crime and never has, nor was it an American invention.

Every part of the ancient world, from Africa to Asia and including Europe and the Americas, has accepted the reality of a variety of supernatural dangers, such as vampires and werewolves. This book has documented how premodern serial killers were thought to be vampires, werewolves, and witches instead of other human beings. It is time to discredit mythic monsters as historic threats to humans and replace them with the serial murderers who were the real villains all along. Anything less is a disservice to the market-place of ideas.

NOTES

INTRODUCTION

1. Colin Wilson and Donald Seaman, *The Serial Killers: A Study in the Psychology of Violence* (New York: Carol Publishing Group, 1992), 7.

2. David Lester, *Serial Killers: The Insatiable Passion* (Philadelphia: The Charles Press, 1995), 31.

3. Gini G. Scott, *Homicide: 100 Years of Murder in America* (New York: Lowell House, 1998), 13.

4. Mark Fuhrman, *Murder in Spokane* (New York: Cliff Street Books, 2001), 226.

5. Katherine Ramsland, *The Human Predator* (New York: Berkley Books, 2005), viii.

6. Ronald M. Holmes and James De Burger, *Serial Murder* (Newbury Park, CA: Sage, 1998), 21.

7. Steven A. Eggar, *The Need to Kill: Inside the World of the Serial Killer* (Upper Saddle River, NJ: Prentice Hall, 2003), 28.

CHAPTER ONE: INVISIBLE SERIAL MURDER

1. Ernest Drake, *The Dragonology Handbook* (Cambridge, MA: Candlewick Press, 2005), 10.

2. Joseph Gambit, "A Philosophical Exploration: Are Dragons Real?," *Ezine Articles*, January 15, 2009, retrieved December 1, 2009, from http://ezinearticles.com/?A-Philosophical-Exploration—Are, 1.

3. Kevin Owens, "Dragons across Cultures," *Dragonika*, 2000–2009, retrieved December 1, 2009, from http://www.dragonika.com/culture.php, 1; Robert Bast, "Real Dragons?" 2000–2009, retrieved December 1, 2009, from http://survive2012.com/index/php/dragons-were-they-once-real.html, 1–2.

4. Kevin Owens, "The History of Dragons," *Dragonika*, 2000–2009, retrieved December 1, 2009, from http://www.dragonika.com/history.php, 1; Kevin Owens,

"Chinese Dragons," *Dragonika*, 2000–2009, retrieved December 1, 2009, from http://www.dragonika.com/chinese.php, 2.

5. Kevin Owens, "Western Dragons," *Dragonika*, 2000–2009, retrieved December 1, 2009, from http://www.dragonika.com/cultures/western.php, 1.

6. Owens, "Dragons across Cultures," 4.

7. James John Frazier, *The Golden Bough* (New York: Macmillan, 1922), 215–16.

8. Rossell Hope Robbins, *The Encyclopedia of Witchcraft and Demonology* (New York: Crown, 1959), 127–29.

9. James N. Watkins, "Are Demons, Exorcism Real?," Christian Broadcasting Network, 2009, retrieved December 1, 2009, from http://www.cbn.com/spirituallife/BibleStudyAndTheology/Perspective, 2.

10. Merrill F. Unger, *Demons in the World Today* (Wheaton, IL: Coverdale House, 1971), 21, 26–27.

11. Colin Wilson, *Beyond the Occult: Twenty Years' Research into the Paranormal* (London: Watkins, 2008), 373.

12. Colin Wilson, *The Occult* (New York: Doubleday, 1971), 433.

13. Milton Meltzer, *Witches and Witch-Hunts: A History of Persecution* (New York: Blue Sky Press, 1997), 9–11, 60.

14. John Demos, *The Enemy Within: 200 Years of Witch Hunting* (New York: Viking Press, 2008), 2.

15. Robbins, *The Encyclopedia of Witchcraft and Demonology*, 4, 17; Demos, *The Enemy Within*, 38–39.

16. Meltzer, *Witches and Witch-Hunts*, 16, 20, 22–23, 62.

17. Robbins, *The Encyclopedia of Witchcraft and Demonology*, 5, 160.

18. Janis Masyk-Jackson, "Are Werewolves Real? History of the Werewolf and Its Legends and Myths," November 21, 2009, retrieved December 1, 2009, from http://paranormal.suite101.com/article.cfm/are_werewolves_real, 1.

19. Daniel Cohen, *Werewolves* (New York: Dutton, 1996), 51.

20. John Quinones, Laura Viddy, and Cecile Bouchardeau, "Real-Life Werewolves: Five Generations of a Family Suffer from Excessive Hair, Like the Mythical Werewolf," ABC News, September 12, 2007, retrieved December 1, 2009, from http://abcnews.go.com/print?id=2259069, 1–3; Cohen, *Werewolves*, 2.

21. Cohen, *Werewolves*, 9–10; Wilson, *The Occult*, 443.

22. Cohen, *Werewolves*, 19; Will Bradbury, *Into the Unknown* (Pleasantville, NY: Readers' Digest Association, 1981), 95.

23. Tom Sleman, "Werewolves," BBC, December 2, 2009, retrieved December 17, 2010, from http://www.bbc.co.uk/wales/northeast/guides/weird/myths andlegends, 1.

24. Cohen, *Werewolves*, 22–23.

25. Cohen, *Werewolves*, 38–39.

26. Bradbury, *Into the Unknown*, 100.

27. Tom Harris, "How Vampires Work," 1998–2009, retrieved on December 1, 2009, from http://science.howstuffworks.com/vampire1.htm, 1; Robbins, *The Encyclopedia of Witchcraft and Demonology*, 522.

28. Robbins, *The Encyclopedia of Witchcraft and Demonology*, 524.

29. Wilson, *The Occult*, 449.

30. Ray T. McNally, *A Clutch of Vampires* (New York: Bell, 1974), 12–13, 33.

31. Benjamin Radford, "The Real Science and History of Vampires," November 30, 2009, retrieved December 1, 2009, from http://www.livescience.com/ strangenews/091130-vampire-science-h, 1.

32. Robbins, *The Encyclopedia of Witchcraft and Demonology*, 524.

33. John Heinrich Zopft, *Dissertatio de Vampiris Serviensibus* (Leipzig, 1795), 75.

34. Harris, "How Vampires Work," 1–2; Robbins, *The Encyclopedia of Witchcraft and Demonology*, 524; Jeremy A. Kaplan, "Are Vampires Real? The Science Behind the Myth," November 25, 2009, retrieved December 1, 2009, from http://www.fox news.com/printer_friendly_story/0.3566.577037.00.html, 1–2.

35. Don Nardo, *Monsters: Discovering Mythology* (San Diego: Lucent Books, 2002), 7, 31, 37.

36. Nardo, *Monsters*, 89.

37. Bradbury, *Into the Unknown*, 93.

38. Nardo, *Monsters*, 4, 8, 17, 74, 88.

39. Nardo, *Monsters*, 88.

40. Bradbury, *Into the Unknown*, 93, 95, 100.

41. Nardo, *Monsters*, 44, 51, 61.

42. Leanne Perry, "A Summarized History of Forensic Science," *Casebook: Jack the Ripper*, n.d., retrieved February 11, 2009, from http://www.casebook.org/ dissertations/ripperoo-forensic.html, 1.

43. Harold Schechter, *The Serial Killer Files* (New York: Ballantine Books, 2003), 130.

CHAPTER TWO: COUNTESS ERZSEBET BATHORY

1. Denise Noe, "Elizabeth Bathory, 'The Blood Countess,'" n.d., retrieved November 28, 2009, from http://www.francesfarmersrevenge.com/stuff/serialkillers/ bathory.htm, 1; Katherine Ramsland, "For the Record," in "Lady of Blood: Countess Bathory," *Crime Library*, 2009, retrieved November 28, 2009, from http://www .trutv.com/library/crime/serial_killers/predators/bathory/countess 1 html, 1; David Rodriguez, "Erzebet Bathory," April 5, 2009, retrieved November 28, 2009, from http://departments.kings.edu/womens_history/erzebet.html, 1.

2. Helen Morrison and Harold Goldberg, *My Life among the Serial Killers* (New York: William Morrow, 2004), 59; *Elizabethan Era*, "Elizabeth Bathory," 2009, retrieved November 28, 2009, from http://www.elizabethan-era.org.uk/elizabethan -bathory.html, 2.

3. Jerome C. Krause, "Erzsebet (Elizabeth) Bathory," n.d., retrieved November 28, 2009, from http://www.abacom.com/~jkrause/bathory.htm, 3; Todd Frye, "Countess Elizabeth Bathory," *Weird Encyclopedia*, 2009, retrieved November 28, 2009, from http://www.weird-encyclopedia.com/Bathory-Elizabeth.php, 2.

4. Peter Vronsky, *Serial Killers: The Method and Madness of Monsters* (New York: Berkley Books, 2004), 50; Kerry Seagrave, *Women Serial and Mass Murderers: A Worldwide Reference, 1580 through 1990* (Jefferson, NC: McFarland, 1992), 20.

5. Colin Wilson and Donald Seaman, *Serial Killers: A Study in the Psychology of Violence* (New York: Carol Publishing Group, 1992), 260; Eric Hickey, *Serial Murderers and Their Victims* (Belmont, CA: Wadsworth, 1997), 33; Donald J. Skaal,

V Is for Vampire (New York: Penguin Books, 1996), 23; *Elizabethan Era*, "Elizabeth Bathory," 1; BBC, "Elizabeth Bathory—The Blood Countess," August 2, 2001, retrieved November 28, 2009, from http://www.bbc.co.uk/dna/h2g2/A593084, 2

6. Katherine Ramsland, "The Lady," in "Lady of Blood: Countess Bathory," *Crime Library*, 2009, retrieved on December 1, 2009, from http://www.trutv.com/library/crime/serial_killers/predators/bathory, 1; Frye, "Countess Elizabeth Bathory," 1.

7. Vronsky, *Serial Killers*, 50; Seagrave, *Women Serial and Mass Murderers*, 20; and BBC, "Elizabeth Bathory," 1.

8. Noe, "Elizabeth Bathory," 2; Seagrave, *Women Serial and Mass Murderers*, 20.

9. Will Bradbury, *Into the Unknown* (Pleasantville, NY: Reader's Digest Association, 1981), 101.

10. Ramsland, "The Lady," 1.

11. Krause, "Erzsebet (Elizabeth) Bathory," 2; Vronsky, *Serial Killers*, 50; Bradbury, *Into the Unknown*, 102; Frye, "Countess Elizabeth Bathory," 1.

12. *Elizabethan Era*, "Elizabeth Bathory," 1; Seagrave, *Women Serial and Mass Murderers*, 20.

13. Frye, "Countess Elizabeth Bathory," 1.

14. Bradbury, *Into the Unknown*, 102; Vronsky, *Serial Killers*, 50; David Everitt, *Human Monsters: An Illustrated Encyclopedia of the World's Most Vicious Murderers* (Chicago: Contemporary Books, 1993), 11.

15. BBC, "Elizabeth Bathory," 1.

16. Bradbury, *Into the Unknown*, 102.

17. Krause, "Erzsebet (Elizabeth) Bathory," 2; BBC, "Elizabeth Bathory," 2.

18. BBC, "Elizabeth Bathory," 3.

19. Bradbury, *Into the Unknown*, 102.

20. BBC, "Elizabeth Bathory," 3.

21. *Elizabethan Era*, "Elizabeth Bathory," 2.

22. Skaal, *V Is for Vampire*, 23; Frye, "Countess Elizabeth Bathory," 2; Rodriguez, "Erzebet Bathory," 1.

23. BBC, "Elizabeth Bathory," 1; *Elizabethan Era*, "Elizabeth Bathory," 2; Frye, "Countess Elizabeth Bathory," 2; Krause, "Erzsebet (Elizabeth) Bathory," 3.

24. Frye, "Countess Elizabeth Bathory," 2; Noe, "Elizabeth Bathory," 1; Rodriguez, "Erzebet Bathory," 1–2; Krause, "Erzsebet (Elizabeth) Bathory," 1.

25. BBC, "Elizabeth Bathory," 2.

26. BBC, "Elizabeth Bathory," 1, 7; Ramsland, "The Lady," 1; Seagrave, *Women Serial and Mass Murderers*, 20–21; Katherine Ramsland, *The Human Predator: A Historical Chronicle of Serial Murder and Forensic Investigation* (New York: Berkley Books, 2005), 26.

27. BBC, "Elizabeth Bathory," 1; Katherine Ramsland, "Training," in "Lady of Blood: Countess Bathory," *Crime Library*, 2009, retrieved November 28, 2009, from http://www.trutv.com/library/crime/serial_killers/predators/bathory, 1; Frye, "Countess Elizabeth Bathory," 2; *Elizabethan Era*, "Elizabeth Bathory," 2.

28. Ramsland, "The Lady," 1; Noe, "Elizabeth Bathory," 2.

29. Ramsland, "Training," 1.

30. BBC, "Elizabeth Bathory," 3.

31. Hickey, *Serial Murderers and Their Victims*, 33.

32. BBC, "Elizabeth Bathory," 3.

33. Everitt, *Human Monsters*, 12; Hickey, *Serial Murderers and Their Victims*, 33.

34. Katherine Ramsland, "Testimony of the Torturers," in "Lady of Blood: Countess Bathory," *Crime Library*, 2009, retrieved November 28, 2009, from http://www.trutv.com/library/crime/serial_killers/predators/bathory, 1; BBC, "Elizabeth Bathory," 3.

35. Krause, "Erzsebet (Elizabeth) Bathory," 1–2.

36. Ramsland, "The Lady," 2; Morrison and Goldberg, *My Life among the Serial Killers*, 59.

37. Ronald M. Holmes and Stephen Holmes, *Contemporary Perspectives on Serial Murder* (Thousand Oaks, CA: Sage, 1998), 33; *Elizabethan Era*, "Elizabeth Bathory," 1; Frye, "Countess Elizabeth Bathory," 2.

38. Bradbury, *Into the Unknown*, 102.

39. BBC, "Elizabeth Bathory," 1; Frye, "Countess Elizabeth Bathory," 2; Ramsland, "For the Record," 1.

40. Ramsland, "Training," 2; Noe, "Elizabeth Bathory," 3.

41. Frye, "Countess Elizabeth Bathory," 2; Seagrave, *Women Serial and Mass Murderers*, 21; Richard Glyn Jones, *The Mammoth Book of Women Who Kill* (New York: Carroll & Graf, 2004), 61.

42. Noe, "Elizabeth Bathory," 4.

43. Hickey, *Serial Murderers and Their Victims*, 33; Everitt, *Human Monsters*, 12.

44. Ramsland, "Training," 1.

45. Rodriguez, "Erzebet Bathory," 1–3; Noe, "Elizabeth Bathory," 2; Krause, "Erzsebet (Elizabeth) Bathory," 3; Katherine Ramsland, "Current Notions," in "Lady of Blood: Countess Bathory," *Crime Library*, 2009, retrieved November 28, 2009, from http://www.trutv.com/library/crime/serial_killers/predators/bathory, 2; BBC, "Elizabeth Bathory," 7.

46. Noe, "Elizabeth Bathory," 2.

47. BBC, "Elizabeth Bathory," 2.

48. Seagrave, *Women Serial and Mass Murderers*, 21; Vronsky, *Serial Killers*, 50.

49. Krause, "Erzsebet (Elizabeth) Bathory," 4; Katherine Ramsland, "Addiction," in "Lady of Blood: Countess Bathory," *Crime Library*, 2009, retrieved November 28, 2009, from http://www.trutv.com/library/crime/serial_killers/predators/bathory, 1.

50. Bradbury, *Into the Unknown*, 102; Ramsland, "Training," 2.

51. Ramsland, "Testimony of the Torturers," 1.

52. Morrison and Goldberg, *My Life among the Serial Killers*, 59; Bradbury, *Into the Unknown*, 102; Krause, "Erzsebet (Elizabeth) Bathory," 4; Ramsland, "Addiction," 1.

53. Krause, "Erzsebet (Elizabeth) Bathory," 4; Ramsland, "Training," 2; Ramsland, "Testimony of the Torturers," 1–2; Katherine Ramsland, "Beyond Belief," in "Lady of Blood: Countess Bathory," *Crime Library*, 2009, retrieved November 28, 2009, from http://www.trutv.com/library/crime/serial_killers/predators/bathory, 1–2; Bradbury, *Into the Unknown*, 102.

54. Frye, "Countess Elizabeth Bathory," 2; Skaal, *V Is for Vampire*, 23.

55. Everitt, *Human Monsters*, 13; Ramsland, "Testimony of the Torturers," 2.

56. Hickey, *Serial Murderers and Their Victims*, 33; Morrison and Goldberg, *My Life among the Serial Killers*, 59; Seagrave, *Women Serial and Mass Murderers*, 20; Jones, *The Mammoth Book of Women Who Kill*, 70.

57. Rodriguez, "Erzebet Bathory," 1–4; Peter Vronsky, *Female Serial Killers: How and Why Women Become Monsters* (New York: Berkley Books, 2007), 79.

58. Krause, "Erzsebet (Elizabeth) Bathory," 5; Bradbury, *Into the Unknown*, 102; Vronsky, *Serial Killers*, 52, 79; Jones, *The Mammoth Book of Women Who Kill*, 64; Noe, "Elizabeth Bathory," 3; Morrison and Goldberg, *My Life among the Serial Killers*, 59.

59. Holmes and Holmes, *Contemporary Perspectives on Serial Murder*, 33; Seagrave, *Women Serial and Mass Murderers*, 20; Hickey, *Serial Murderers and Their Victims*, 3.

60. Frye, "Countess Elizabeth Bathory," 2.

61. Vronsky, *Serial Killers*, 50; Noe, "Elizabeth Bathory," 2.

62. Ramsland, "Testimony of the Torturers," 1.

63. BBC, "Elizabeth Bathory," 7; Ramsland, "Training," 2.

64. Krause, "Erzsebet (Elizabeth) Bathory," 4.

65. Ramsland, "The Lady," 1.

66. Ramsland, "Training," 1.

67. BBC, "Elizabeth Bathory," 2–3; *Elizabethan Era*, "Elizabeth Bathory," 2.

68. BBC, "Elizabeth Bathory," 1.

69. Ramsland, "Training," 1.

70. Katherine Ramsland, "The Disposition," in "Lady of Blood: Countess Bathory," *Crime Library*, 2009, retrieved November 28, 2009, from http://www .trutv.com/library/crime/serial_killers/predators/bathory, 1; Ramsland, "The Lady," 1.

71. Everitt, *Human Monsters*, 13; Ramsland, "For the Record," 1.

72. Frye, "Countess Elizabeth Bathory," 1; BBC, "Elizabeth Bathory," 4.

73. Ramsland, "Testimony of the Torturers," 2.

74. BBC, "Elizabeth Bathory," 4.

75. Frye, "Countess Elizabeth Bathory," 1; Rodriguez, "Erzebet Bathory," 3; Seagrave, *Women Serial and Mass Murderers*, 22; Vronsky, *Serial Killers*, 53.

76. Frye, "Countess Elizabeth Bathory," 1; Ramsland, "Beyond Belief," 1; Bradbury, *Into the Unknown*, 102.

77. Bradbury, *Into the Unknown*, 102; Katherine Ramsland, "Judgment Day," In "Lady of Blood: Countess Bathory," 1; BBC, "Elizabeth Bathory," 3.

78. BBC, "Elizabeth Bathory," 3; Krause, "Erzsebet (Elizabeth) Bathory," 4.

79. Everitt, *Human Monsters*, 13; Ramsland, "Clandestine," 1–2.

80. *Elizabethan Era*, "Elizabeth Bathory," 2; Morrison and Goldberg, *My Life among the Serial Killers*, 59; Vronsky, *Serial Killers*, 52.

81. Ramsland, "Addiction," 1.

82. Noe, "Elizabeth Bathory," 3.

83. Ramsland, "The Disposition," 1; *Elizabethan Era*, "Elizabeth Bathory," 2.

84. Ramsland, "Clandestine," 1; Bradbury, *Into the Unknown*, 102; Jones, *The Mammoth Book of Women Who Kill*, 68.

85. Katherine Ramsland, "Judgment Day," In "Lady of Blood: Countess Bathory," Crime Library. 2009, retrieved November 28, 2009 from http://www .trytv.com/library/crime/serial_killers/predators/bathory, 1–2; Katherine Ramsland, "Clandestine Entry," In "Lady of Blood: Countess Bathory," Crime Library, 2009, retrieved November 28, 2009 from http://www.trutv.com/library/crime/serial_killers/ predators/bathory, 1–2.

86. Frye, "Countess Elizabeth Bathory," 1.

87. Seagrave, *Women Serial and Mass Murderers*, 22; BBC, "Elizabeth Bathory," 4; Noe, "Elizabeth Bathory," 3; Bradbury, *Into the Unknown*, 102; Ramsland, "The Disposition," 1; Vronsky, *Female Serial Killers*, 8.

88. Ramsland, "Current Notions," 2; Ramsland, "Judgment," 1; Ramsland, "Testimony of the Torturers," 2.

89. Ramsland, "The Disposition," 1; Vronsky, *Serial Killers*, 53; BBC, "Elizabeth Bathory," 3.

90. Krause, "Erzsebet (Elizabeth) Bathory," 4; Noe, "Elizabeth Bathory," 3.

91. Everitt, *Human Monsters*, 13; Bradbury, *Into the Unknown*, 102.

92. Vronsky, *Serial Killers*, 53; BBC, "Elizabeth Bathory," 5; Bradbury, *Into the Unknown*, 102.

CHAPTER THREE: VINCENZO VERZINI

1. Peter Vronsky, *Serial Killers: The Method and Madness of Monsters* (New York: Berkley Books, 2004), 60.

2. Vronsky, *Serial Killers*, 60.

3. "The Mystery of Whitechapel, Him or Her? Dark Conjectures," *El Universal*, November 5, 1889, retrieved May 22, 2010, from http://www.casebook.org/forum/messages/4927/7365.html, 2.

4. Leon Henri Thoinot and Arthur W. Weysse, *Medicolegal Aspects of Moral Offenses* (Philadelphia: F. A. Davis, 1920), 422.

5. Vronsky, *Serial Killers*, 60.

6. Vronsky, *Serial Killers*, 60; David Everitt, *Human Monsters: An Illustrated Encyclopedia of the World's Most Vicious Murderers* (Chicago: Contemporary Books, 1993), 43; Harold Schechter, *The Serial Killer Files* (New York: Ballantine Books, 2003), 209; Katherine Ramsland, *The Human Predator: A Historical Chronicle of Serial Murder and Forensic Investigation* (New York: Berkley Books, 2005), 74.

7. Michael H. Stone, "Serial Sexual Homicide: Biological, Psychological, and Sociological Aspects," *Journal of Personality Disorders* 15, no. 1 (February 2001): 1–18; Colin Wilson and Donald Seaman, *The Serial Killers: A Study in the Psychology of Violence* (New York: Carol Publishing Group, 1992); 7; Eric W. Hickey, *Serial Murderers and Their Victims* (Belmont, CA: Wadsworth, 1997), 248.

8. Schechter, *The Serial Killer Files*, 209; Everitt, *Human Monsters*, 43; Vronsky, *Serial Killers*, 60.

9. *El Universal*, "The Mystery of Whitechapel, Him or Her?," 2.

10. Ramsland, *The Human Predator*, 74.

11. Vronsky, *Serial Killers*, 60; *El Universal*, "The Mystery of Whitechapel, Him or Her?," 2.

12. Ramsland, *The Human Predator*, 74.

13. Vronsky, *Serial Killers*, 60.

14. Ramsland, *The Human Predator*, 74.

15. Vronsky, *Serial Killers*, 60.

16. *El Universal*, "The Mystery of Whitechapel, Him or Her?," 2; Vronsky, *Serial Killers*, 59–60.

17. Everitt, *Human Monsters*, 44.

18. Schechter, *The Serial Killer Files*, 210.

19. Schechter, *The Serial Killer Files*, 209; Everitt, *Human Monsters*, 43; Vronsky, *Serial Killers*, 59.

20. Stone, "Serial Sexual Homicide," 1–18.

21. Thoinot and Weysse, *Medicolegal Aspects of Moral Offenses*, 422.

22. Schechter, *The Serial Killer Files*, 210; Everitt, *Human Monsters*, 43; Ramsland, *The Human Predator*, 74; Vronsky, *Serial Killers*, 60.

23. Everitt, *Human Monsters*, 43.

24. *El Universal*, "The Mystery of Whitechapel, Him or Her?," 2.

25. Everitt, *Human Monsters*, 43; Vronsky, *Serial Killers*, 58.

26. Schechter, *The Serial Killer Files*, 223.

27. Schechter, *The Serial Killer Files*, 210; Everitt, *Human Monsters*, 43.

28. Ramsland, *The Human Predator*, 74; Schechter, *The Serial Killer Files*, 210.

29. *El Universal*, "The Mystery of Whitechapel, Him or Her?," 2; Everitt, *Human Monsters*, 43–44; Ramsland, *The Human Predator*, 74.

30. Vronsky, *Serial Killers*, 59; Everitt, *Human Monsters*, 43.

31. Everitt, *Human Monsters*, 43; Vronsky, *Serial Killers*, 58–59.

32. Everitt, *Human Monsters*, 44; *El Universal*, "The Mystery of Whitechapel, Him or Her?," 2.

33. Hickey, *Serial Murderers and Their Victims*, 248; Ramsland, *The Human Predator*, 74.

34. *El Universal*, "The Mystery of Whitechapel, Him or Her?," 2.

35. *El Universal*, "The Mystery of Whitechapel, Him or Her?," 2.

36. *El Universal*, "The Mystery of Whitechapel, Him or Her?," 2.

37. Everitt, *Human Monsters*, 43.

38. Everitt, *Human Monsters*, 43.

39. Hickey, *Serial Murderers and Their Victims*, 248; Vronsky, *Serial Killers*, 58; *El Universal*, "The Mystery of Whitechapel, Him or Her?," 2.

40. Schechter, *The Serial Killer Files*, 210.

41. *El Universal*, "The Mystery of Whitechapel, Him or Her?," 2.

42. Everitt, *Human Monsters*, 43.

43. Ramsland, *The Human Predator*, 74.

44. Vronsky, *Serial Killers*, 58; Everitt, *Human Monsters*, 43; Schechter, *The Serial Killer Files*, 210.

45. Schechter, *The Serial Killer Files*, 210.

46. Everitt, *Human Monsters*, 43; Schechter, *The Serial Killer Files*, 210; Vronsky, *Serial Killers*, 58.

47. Everitt, *Human Monsters*, 44; Vronsky, *Serial Killers*, 58.

48. Schechter, *The Serial Killer Files*, 210; Vronsky, *Serial Killers*, 59; Ramsland, *The Human Predator*, 74.

49. Schechter, *The Serial Killer Files*, 210; Thoinot and Weysse, *Medicolegal Aspects of Moral Offenses*, 422.

50. Everitt, *Human Monsters*, 43.

51. Vronsky, *Serial Killers*, 60.

52. *El Universal*, "The Mystery of Whitechapel, Him or Her?," 2.

53. Everitt, *Human Monsters*, 44.

54. Schechter, *The Serial Killer Files*, 210.

55. *El Universal*, "The Mystery of Whitechapel, Him or Her?," 2.

56. Everitt, *Human Monsters*, 44.

57. Ramsland, *The Human Predator*, 74; Schechter, *The Serial Killer Files*, 210.

58. Vronsky, *Serial Killers*, 58–59.

59. Schechter, *The Serial Killer Files*, 210.

60. Ramsland, *The Human Predator*, 74.

CHAPTER FOUR: JOSEPH VACHER

1. Harold Schechter, *The Serial Killer Files* (New York: Ballantine Books, 2003), 58.

2. Schechter, The *Serial Killer Files*, 57.

3. "French 'Ripper' Guillotined. Joseph Vacher, Who Murdered More Than a Score of Persons, Executed at Bourg-en-Bresse," *New York Times*, January 1, 1899, 7.

4. *New York Times*, "French 'Ripper' Guillotined," 7.

5. Michael Newton, *The Encyclopedia of Serial Killers* (New York: Checkmark Books, 2000), 227.

6. *ExecutedToday.com*, "1898: Joseph Vacher," 2010, retrieved May 21, 2010, from http://www.executedtoday.com/2007/12/31/1898-joseph-vacher, 1.

7. Timothy B. Smith, "Assistance and Repression: Rural Exodus, Vagabondage and Social Crisis in France, 1880–1914," *Journal of Social History* (Summer 1999), retrieved May 21, 2010, from http://findarticles.com/p/articles/mi_m2005/is_4_32/ai_55084001, 1–2.

8. *ExecutedToday.com*, "1898," 1.

9. Smith, "Assistance and Repression," 1.

10. Schechter, *The Serial Killer Files*, 57.

11. Smith, "Assistance and Repression," 1.

12. Newton, *The Encyclopedia of Serial Killers*, 227; Smith, "Assistance and Repression," 1.

13. Brian Lane and Wilfred Gregg, *The Encyclopedia of Serial Killers* (New York: Berkley Books, 1995), 343; *Execution of the Day*, "31 December 1898—Joseph Vacher," 2010, retrieved May 21, 2010, from http://eotd.wordpress.com/2008/12/31/31-december-1898-josephvacher, 1.

14. Schechter, *The Serial Killer Files*, 57.

15. Lane and Gregg, The *Encyclopedia of Serial Killers*, 343; Newton, *The Encyclopedia of Serial Killers*, 227; and Colin Wilson and Donald Seaman, *The Serial Killers: A Study in the Psychology of Violence* (New York: Carol Publishing Group, 1992), 9.

16. Newton, *The Encyclopedia of Serial Killers*, 227.

17. Newton, *The Encyclopedia of Serial Killers*, 227; Smith, "Assistance and Repression," 2; Everitt, *Human Monsters*, 62; Peter Vronsky, *Serial Killers: The Method and Madness of Monsters* (New York: Berkley Books, 2004), 63.

18. Everitt, *Human Monsters*, 61.

19. Lane and Gregg, *The Encyclopedia of Serial Killers*, 343; Newton, *The Encyclopedia of Serial Killers*, 227.

20. Katherine Ramsland, "Vacher the Ripper," in "The Werewolf Syndrome: Compulsive Bestial Slaughterers," *Crime Library*, 2010, retrieved May 21, 2010, from http://www.trutv.com/library/crime/criminal_mind/psychology/werewolves, 1; Smith, "Repression and Assistance," 2; Schechter, *The Serial Killer Files*, 57.

21. Newton, *The Encyclopedia of Serial Killers*, 227.

22. Lane and Gregg, *The Encyclopedia of Serial Killers*, 343.

23. Smith, "Repression and Assistance," 2; Everitt, *Human Monsters*, 62.

24. Ramsland, "Vacher the Ripper," 1.

25. Smith, "Repression and Assistance," 2; Schechter, *The Serial Killer Files*, 57.

26. Robin Odell and Wilfred Gregg, *Murderers' Row* (Phoenix Mill: Sutton, 2006), 343; Smith, "Assistance and Repression," 1–2.

27. Odell and Gregg, *Murderers' Row*, 435.

28. Schechter, *The Serial Killer Files*, 57; Everitt, *Human Monsters*, 61; Odell and Gregg, *Murderers' Row*, 435; Lane and Gregg, *The Encyclopedia of Serial Killers*, 343.

29. *Execution of the Day*, "31 December 1898," 1; Wilson and Seaman, *The Serial Killers*, 48, 64; Schechter, *The Serial Killer Files*, 57.

30. *New York Times*, "French 'Ripper' Guillotined," 7; Katherine Ramsland, The *Human Predator: A Historical Chronicle of Serial Murder and Forensic Investigation* (New York: Berkley Books, 2005), 92.

31. Ramsland, *The Human Predator*, 92; Lane and Gregg, *The Encyclopedia of Serial Killers*, 343; Newton, *The Encyclopedia of Serial Killers*, 227; Vronsky, *Serial Killers*, 63; Smith, "Repression and Assistance," 1.

32. Newton, *The Encyclopedia of Serial Killers*, 227.

33. Newton, *The Encyclopedia of Serial Killers*, 227.

34. Wilson and Seaman, *The Serial Killers*, 3, 8; Lane and Gregg, *The Encyclopedia of Serial Killers*, 343.

35. Everitt, *Human Monsters*, 62; Newton, *The Encyclopedia of Serial Killers*, 227; Schechter, *The Serial Killer Files*, 58–59; Vronsky, *Serial Killers*, 63–64.

36. Wilson and Seaman, *The Serial Killers*, 3.

37. Schechter, *The Serial Killer Files*, 58.

38. Schechter, *The Serial Killer Files*, 300; Ramsland, "Vacher the Ripper," 1.

39. Smith, "Repression and Assistance," 1.

40. Wilson and Seaman, *The Serial Killers*, 8; Newton, *The Encyclopedia of Serial Killers*, 227.

41. Wilson and Seaman, *The Serial Killers*, 49.

42. Ramsland, "Vacher the Ripper," 1; *Execution of the Day*, "31 December 1898," 1; Wilson and Seaman, *The Serial Killers*, 49; Newton, *The Encyclopedia of Serial Killers*, 227.

43. Wilson and Seaman, *The Serial Killers*, 49; Everitt, *Human Monsters*, 62.

44. Odell and Gregg, *Murderers' Row*, 435; Smith, "Repression and Assistance," 1; Lane and Gregg, *The Encyclopedia of Serial Killers*, 343; *Execution of the Day*, "31 December 1898," 1; Wilson and Seaman, *The Serial Killers*, 49; Vronsky, *Serial Killers*, 63.

45. *New York Times*, "French 'Ripper' Guillotined," 7; Schechter, *The Serial Killer Files*, 223.

46. Odell and Gregg, *Murderers' Row*, 435; Smith, "Repression and Assistance," 1; Everitt, *Human Monsters*, 63; Wilson and Seaman, *The Serial Killers*,61; *New York*

Times, "French 'Ripper' Guillotined," 7; Newton, *The Encyclopedia of Serial Killers,* 227.

47. Eric Hickey, *Serial Murderers and Their Victims* (Belmont, CA: Sage, 1997), 248; Everitt, *Human Monsters,* 61; *Execution of the Day,* "31 December 1898," 1; Lane and Gregg, *The Encyclopedia of Serial Killers,* 344.

48. Smith, "Repression and Assistance," 1; Wilson and Seaman, *The Serial Killers,* 48–49.

49. Wilson and Seaman, *The Serial Killers,* 8, 49; Smith, "Repression and Assistance," 1.

50. Smith, "Repression and Assistance," 1; Everitt, *Human Monsters,* 62.

51. Wilson and Seaman, *The Serial Killers,* 3; Smith, "Repression and Assistance," 1; Schechter, *The Serial Killer Files,* 58–59.

52. Everitt, *Human Monsters,* 62; Lane and Gregg, *The Encyclopedia of Serial Killers,* 343.

53. Odell and Gregg, *Murderers' Row,* 435.

54. Schechter, *The Serial Killer Files,* 57.

55. Everitt, *Human Monsters,* 62.

56. Newton, *The Encyclopedia of Serial Killers,* 227.

57. Schechter, *The Serial Killer Files,* 58.

58. Schechter, *The Serial Killer Files,* 58; Vronsky, *Serial Killers,* 64.

59. Schechter, *The Serial Killer Files,* 58–59.

60. Ramsland, *The Human Predator,* 93; Schechter, *The Serial Killer Files,* 223; *New York Times,* "French 'Ripper' Guillotined," 7.

61. Smith, "Repression and Assistance," 1–2.

62. *New York Times,* "French 'Ripper' Guillotined," 7.

63. Wilson and Seaman, *The Serial Killers,* 9; Everitt, *Human Monsters,* 62.

64. Lane and Gregg, *The Encyclopedia of Serial Killers,* 343.

65. Everitt, *Human Monsters,* 63.

66. Everitt, *Human Monsters,* 63; Schechter, *The Serial Killer Files,* 59; Ramsland, "Vacher the Ripper," 1; Newton, *The Encyclopedia of Serial Killers,* 227.

67. Wilson and Seaman, *The Serial Killers,* 9.

68. Everitt, *Human Monsters,* 62–63.

69. Lane and Gregg, *The Encyclopedia of Serial Killers,* 343.

70. Odell and Gregg, *Murderers' Row,* 435; Ramsland, "Vacher the Ripper," 1.

71. Smith, "Repression and Assistance," 1; Lane and Gregg, *The Encyclopedia of Serial Killers,* 344.

72. Ramsland, "Vacher the Ripper," 1.

73. Odell and Gregg, *Murderers' Row,* 435.

74. *New York Times,* "French 'Ripper' Guillotined," 7; Newton, *The Encyclopedia of Serial Killers,* 227.

75. Odell and Gregg, *Murderers' Row,* 435.

76. Ramsland, "Vacher the Ripper," 1; Schechter, *The Serial Killer Files,* 59; Everitt, *Human Monsters,* 63.

77. *New York Times,* "French 'Ripper' Guillotined," 7; Schechter, *The Serial Killer Files,* 59.

78. *Execution of the Day,* "31 December 1898," 1.

79. Odell and Gregg, *Murderers' Row,* 435; Smith, "Repression and Assistance," 2.

80. Odell and Gregg, *Murderers' Row*, 435; Smith, "Repression and Assistance," 1–2.

CHAPTER FIVE: GILLES GARNIER

1. Harold Schechter, *The Serial Killer Files* (New York: Ballantine Books, 2003), 127.

2. David Everitt, *Human Monsters: An Illustrated Encyclopedia of the World's Most Vicious Murderers* (Chicago: Contemporary Books, 1993), 13.

3. Katherine Ramsland, "The Spectral Man," in "The Werewolf Syndrome: Compulsive Bestial Slaughterers," 2010, retrieved May 15, 2010, from http://www.trutv.com/library/crime/criminal_mind/psychology/werewolves, 1.

4. Sabine Baring-Gould, *The Book of Werewolves* (London: Smith, Elder & Co., 1865), 5.

5. *Werewolves.com*, "Gilles Garnier: The Werewolf of Dole," April 10, 2010, retrieved May 15, 2010, from http://www.werewolves.com/gilles-garnier-the-werewolf-of-dole, 1.

6. Ramsland, "The Spectral Man," 1.

7. *Werewolves.com*, "Gilles Garnier," 1.

8. *Werewolves.com*, "Gilles Garnier," 1.

9. Schechter, *The Serial Killer Files*, 127.

10. *Werewolves.com*, "Gilles Garnier," 1.

11. Ramsland, "The Spectral Man," 1.

12. Baring-Gould, *The Book of Werewolves*, 5.

13. Baring-Gould, *The Book of Werewolves*, 5.

14. Ramsland, "The Spectral Man," 1.

15. Everitt, *Human Monsters*, 14.

16. *Werewolves.com*, "Gilles Garnier," 1.

17. *Werewolves.com*, "Gilles Garnier," 1.

18. Ramsland, "The Spectral Man," 1.

19. Baring-Gould, *The Book of Werewolves*, 5; Homayun Sidky, *Witchcraft, Lycanthropy, Drugs and Disease* (Eugene, OR: Wipf & Stock, 1997), 224.

20. Schechter, *The Serial Killer Files*, 127.

21. Everitt, *Human Monsters*, 15.

22. Schechter, *The Serial Killer Files*, 127.

23. *Werewolves.com*, "Gilles Garnier," 1.

24. Ramsland, "The Spectral Man," 1.

25. *Werewolves.com*, "Gilles Garnier," 1.

26. Schechter, *The Serial Killer Files*, 128.

27. *Werewolves.com*, "Gilles Garnier," 1.

28. Sidky, *Witchcraft, Lycanthropy, Drugs and Disease*, 227.

29. Everitt, *Human Monsters*, 15.

30. Schechter, *The Serial Killer Files*, 128.

31. Everitt, *Human Monsters*, 13; Schechter, *The Serial Killer Files*, 126.

32. *Werewolves.com*, "Gilles Garnier," 1.

33. Everitt, *Human Monsters*, 15.

34. Baring-Gould, *The Book of Werewolves*, 5.

35. Schechter, *The Serial Killer Files*, 127.

36. Everitt, *Human Monsters*, 15.

37. Baring-Gould, *The Book of Werewolves*, 5; Ramsland, "The Spectral Man," 1.

38. Ramsland, "The Spectral Man," 1.

39. Ramsland, "The Spectral Man," 1; Baring-Gould, *The Book of Werewolves*, 5.

40. Baring-Gould, *The Book of Werewolves*, 5.

41. Schechter, *The Serial Killer Files*, 127; Everitt, *Human Monsters*, 15.

42. Sidky, *Witchcraft, Lycanthropy, Drugs and Disease*, 227.

43. Schechter, *The Serial Killer Files*, 127; Everitt, *Human Monsters*, 14; Ramsland, "The Spectral Man," 1.

44. *Werewolves.com*, "Gilles Garnier," 1.

45. *Serial Killer Central*, "Gilles Garnier: Werewolf or Just a Murderer?," August 17, 2008, retrieved May 15, 2010, from http://www.skcentral.com/forum/viewthread.php?thread_id=3659, 1.

46. Baring-Gould, *The Book of Werewolves*, 5.

47. Ramsland, "The Spectral Man," 1.

48. Ramsland, "The Spectral Man," 1.

49. Schechter, *The Serial Killer Files*, 128.

50. Ramsland, "The Spectral Man," 1; Everitt, *Human Monsters*, 14; Ramsland, *The Human Predator*, 22; Sidky, *Witchcraft, Lycanthropy, Drugs and Disease*, 224.

51. Baring-Gould, *The Book of Werewolves*, 5.

52. Ramsland, "The Spectral Man," 1.

53. Sidky, *Witchcraft, Lycanthropy, Drugs and Disease*, 225.

54. Everitt, *Human Monsters*, 15.

55. Ramsland, "The Spectral Man," 1.

56. Shantell Powell, "Gilles Garnier, Werewolf of Dole," 1996, retrieved May 15, 2010, from http://www.shanmonster.com/witch/werewolf/garnier.html, 2.

57. Baring-Gould, *The Book of Werewolves*, 5.

58. Ramsland, *Human Predator*, 22.

59. Baring-Gould, *The Book of Werewolves*, 5.

60. Baring-Gould, *The Book of Werewolves*, 5.

61. Ramsland, "The Spectral Man," 1.

62. *Werewolves.com*, "Gilles Garnier," 1.

63. Barry Lopez, *Of Wolves and Men* (New York: Charles Scribner's Sons, 1978), 241; Sidky, *Witchcraft, Lycanthropy, Drugs and Disease*, 225, 227.

64. Ramsland, *Human Predator*, 22; Baring-Gould, *The Book of Werewolves*, 5.

65. Everitt, *Human Monsters*, 15.

66. Schechter, *The Serial Killer Files*, 128–29.

67. Sidky, *Witchcraft, Lycanthropy, Drugs and Disease*, 227.

CHAPTER SIX: PETER STUBBE

1. Katherine Ramsland, "The Wolf Girdle," in "The Werewolf Syndrome: Compulsive Bestial Slaughterers," 2010, retrieved May 20, 2010, from http://www.trutv.com/library/crime/criminal_mind/psychology/werewolves, 1.

2. Ramsland, "The Wolf Girdle," 1.

3. Peter Vronsky, *Serial Killers: The Method and Madness of Monsters* (New York: Berkley Books, 2004), 54; Homayun Sidky, *Witchcraft, Lycanthropy, Drugs and Diseases: An Anthropological Study of the European Witch-Hunt* (Eugene, OR: Wipf & Stock, 1997), 235.

4. David Everitt, *Human Monsters: An Illustrated Encyclopedia of the World's Most Vicious Murderers* (Chicago: Contemporary Books, 1993), 15–16; Harold Schechter, *The Serial Killer Files* (New York: Ballantine Books, 2003), 126; Eric Hickey, *Serial Murderers and Their Victims* (Belmont, CA: Wadsworth, 1997), 30.

5. Everitt, *Human Monsters*, 15; Katherine Ramsland, *The Human Predator: A Historical Chronicle of Serial Murder and Forensic Investigation* (New York: Berkley Books, 2005), 23.

6. Vronsky, *Serial Killers*, 53; Hickey, *Serial Murderers and Their Victims*, 30.

7. Amanda Howard, "Jack the Ripper—Not the First," March 29, 2009, retrieved November 28, 2009, from http://www.amandahoward.com.au/not_the _first.htm, 1; Ramsland, "The Wolf Girdle," 1.

8. Schechter, *The Serial Killer Files*, 126; Everitt, *Human Monsters*, 15; Ramsland, The *Human Predator*, 23.

9. ExecutedToday.com, "1589: Peter Stubbe, Sybil Stubbe and Katharina Trump," October 31, 2007, retrieved May 20, 2010, from http://www.executed today.com/2007/10/31/1589-peter-stubbe-sybil-stubbe-katharina, 1; Everitt, *Human Monsters*, 16.

10. Everitt, *Human Monsters*, 16; ExecutedToday.com, "1589," 1; Howard, "Jack- the-Ripper," 1.

11. Sidky, *Witchcraft, Lycanthropy, Drugs and Diseases*, 235; George Bores, "A True Discourse Declaring the Damnable Life and Death of One Stubbe Peter, 1590," 1996–2010, retrieved May 20, 2010, from http://www.werewolfpage.com/ myths/stubbe.html, 2.

12. ExecutedToday.com, "1589," 1.

13. Everitt, *Human Monsters*, 16.

14. Bores, "A True Discourse Declaring the Damnable Life and Death of One Stubbe Peter, 1590," 1; Schechter, *The Serial Killer Files*, 127.

15. Schechter, *The Serial Killer Files*, 127.

16. ExecutedToday.com, "1589," 1.

17. Sidky, *Witchcraft, Lycanthropy, Drugs and Diseases*, 236; Howard, "Jack-the -Ripper," 1; Ramsland, "The Wolf- Girdle," 1; Schechter, *The Serial Killer Files*, 128.

18. Hickey, *Serial Murderers and Their Victims*, 127; Sabine Baring-Gould, *The Book of Werewolves* (London: Smith, Elder & Co., 1865), 5; Ramsland, "The Wolf Girdle," 1; Schechter, *The Serial Killer Files*, 128.

19. Schechter, *The Serial Killer Files*, 128; Ramsland, "The Wolf Girdle," 1.

20. Baring-Gould, *The Book of Werewolves*, 5.

21. Baring-Gould, *The Book of Werewolves*, 5.

22. Vronsky, *Serial Killers*, 54.

23. Ramsland, "The Wolf Girdle," 1.

24. Hickey, *Serial Murderers and Their Victims*, 31.

25. ExecutedToday.com, "1589," 1.

26. ExecutedToday.com, "1589," 1.

27. Schechter, *The Serial Killer Files*, 128.

28. Howard, "Jack-the-Ripper," 1; ExecutedToday.com, "1589," 1; Schechter, *The Serial Killer Files*, 128.

29. Hickey, *Serial Murderers and Their Victims*, 30–31; Ramsland, "The Wolf Girdle," 1; Baring-Gould, *The Book of Werewolves*, 5.

30. Vronsky, *Serial Killers*, 53; Baring-Gould, *The Book of Werewolves*, 5.

31. Vronsky, *Serial Killers*, 54; Baring-Gould, *The Book of Werewolves*, 5.

32. Baring-Gould, *The Book of Werewolves*, 5.

33. Ramsland, "The Wolf Girdle," 1; Schechter, *The Serial Killer Files*, 128.

34. Baring-Gould, *The Book of Werewolves*, 5; Schechter, *The Serial Killer Files*, 127; Ramsland, "The Wolf Girdle," 1; Hickey, *Serial Murderers and Their Victims*, 31.

35. Baring-Gould, *The Book of Werewolves*, 5; Hickey, *Serial Murderers and Their Victims*, 31.

36. Hickey, *Serial Murderers and Their Victims*, 31.

37. Everitt, *Human Monsters*, 17.

38. Howard, "Jack-the-Ripper," 1.

39. Howard, "Jack-the-Ripper," 1.

40. Schechter, *The Serial Killer Files*, 127.

41. ExecutedToday.com, "1589," 1.

42. Hickey, *Serial Murderers and Their Victims*, 31; Schechter, *The Serial Killer Files*, 128; Baring-Gould, *The Book of Werewolves*, 5; ExecutedToday.com, "1589," 1.

43. Sidky, *Witchcraft, Lycanthropy, Drugs and Diseases*, 236; Hickey, *Serial Murderers and Their Victims*, 31; Everitt, *Human Monsters*, 16.

44. Everitt, *Human Monsters*, 17; Baring-Gould, *The Book of Werewolves*, 5.

45. Bores, "A True Discourse Declaring the Damnable Life and Death of One Stubbe Peter, 1590," 1, 4; Schechter, *The Serial Killer Files*, 127.

46. Ramsland, "The Wolf Girdle," 1; Schechter, *The Serial Killer Files*, 127.

47. ExecutedToday.com, "1589," 1.

48. Bores, "A True Discourse Declaring the Damnable Life and Death of One Stubbe Peter, 1590," 3.

49. Baring-Gould, *The Book of Werewolves*, 5; Everitt, *Human Monsters*, 17; Ramsland, "The Wolf Girdle," 1.

50. Everitt, *Human Monsters*, 17.

51. Everitt, *Human Monsters*, 17.

52. ExecutedToday.com, "1589," 1.

53. Sidky, *Witchcraft, Lycanthropy, Drugs and Diseases*, 236; Baring-Gould, *The Book of Werewolves*, 5; and Ramsland, "The Wolf Girdle," 1.

54. Ramsland, "The Wolf Girdle," 1.

55. Everitt, *Human Monsters*, 18; Ramsland, "The Wolf Girdle," 1.

56. Baring-Gould, *The Book of Werewolves*, 5.

57. Bores, "A True Discourse Declaring the Damnable Life and Death of One Stubbe Peter, 1590," 3; Baring-Gould, *The Book of Werewolves*, 5.

58. Everitt, *Human Monsters*, 18; Baring-Gould, *The Book of Werewolves*, 5.

59. Ramsland, "The Wolf Girdle," 1.

60. Ramsland, "The Wolf Girdle," 1; Everitt, *Human Monsters*, 18; Howard, "Jack-the-Ripper," 1.

61. Vronsky, *Serial Killers*, 54; ExecutedToday.com, "1589," 1.

62. Baring-Gould, *The Book of Werewolves*, 5.

63. Ramsland, "The Wolf Girdle," 1; Schechter, *The Serial Killer Files*, 355.

64. Sidky, *Witchcraft, Lycanthropy, Drugs and Diseases*, 234.

65. Ramsland, "The Wolf Girdle," 1.

66. Sidky, *Witchcraft, Lycanthropy, Drugs and Diseases*, 234.

CHAPTER SEVEN: WEREWOLF OF CHALONS

1. Bob Curran, *Encyclopedia of the Undead: A Field Guide to Those Creatures That Cannot Rest in Peace* (Franklin Lakes, NJ: New Page Books, 2006), 105.

2. Werewolfpage.com, "The Werewolf of Chalons," 1996–2010, retrieved August 3, 2010, from http://www.werewolfpage.com/myths/Chalons.htm, 1.

3. Katherine Ramsland, *The Human Predator: A Historical Chronicle of Serial Murder and Forensic Investigation* (New York: Berkley Books, 2005), 22; Curran, *Encyclopedia of the Undead*, 105.

4. Elisabeth Wetsch, "Shortlist Serial Killers by Name {W}," *Serial Killer True Crime Library*, 1995–2005, retrieved September 1, 2010, from http://www.crimezzz .net/serialkiller_index/xserienkiller_w.php, 1.

5. Katherine Ramsland, "Werewolf of Chalons," in "The Werewolf Syndrome: Compulsive Bestial Slaughterers," *Crime Library*, 2010, retrieved May 3, 2010, from http://www.trutv.com/library/crime/criminal_mind/psychology/werewolfkillers, 1.

6. Sabine Baring-Gould, *The Book of Werewolves* (London: Smith, Elder & Co., 1865), 27.

7. Louis J. Sheehan, "Didn't See It Coming," February 21, 2010, retrieved September 2, 2010, from http://louisljlsheehan.blogspot.com/2010/02/ointment -33oin993-lou, 1–2.

8. Werewolfpage.com, "Werewolf of Chalons," 1; Curran, *Encyclopedia of the Undead*, 105.

9. Baring-Gould, *The Book of Werewolves*, 27.

10. Werewolfpage.com, "Werewolf of Chalons," 1.

11. Ramsland, *The Human Predator*, 22.

12. Ramsland, *The Human Predator*, 22.

13. Ramsland, "Werewolf of Chalons," 1.

14. Ramsland, "Werewolf of Chalons," 1.

15. Baring-Gould, *The Book of Werewolves*, 27.

16. Ramsland, "Werewolf of Chalons,"1.

17. Werewolfpage.com, "Werewolf of Chalons," 1; Deane P. Lewis, "Pieces: A Brief History of Werewolves," 2006, retrieved May 2, 2010, from http://dl.id.au/ ?f=1, 1.

18. Sheehan, "Didn't See It Coming," 1.

19. John Fiske, "Werewolves & Swan-Maidens: The Mediaeval Belief in Werewolves is Especially Adapted to Illustrate the Complicated Manner in which Divers Mythical Conceptions & Misunderstood Natural Occurrences Will Combine to Generate a Long-Enduring Superstition," *Atlantic Monthly* (August, 1871),

retrieved August 31, 2010, from http://www.theatlantic.com/past/docs/issues/1871Aug/fiskej.htm, 1.

20. *Werewolfpage.com*, "Werewolf of Chalons," 1.

21. Sheehan, "Didn't See It Coming," 1.

22. "Werewolf of Chalons," 1.

23. Wetsch, "Shortlist Serial Killers by Name {W}," 1; Ramsland, *The Human Predator*, 22.

24. Baring-Gould, *The Book of Werewolves*, 27.

25. Ramsland, *The Human Predator*, 22.

26. Werewolfpage.com, "Werewolf of Chalons," 1.

27. Curran, *Encyclopedia of the Undead*, 105.

28. Wetsch, "Shortlist Serial Killers by Name {W}," 1; Skeptic World—Cryptozoology, "Werewolves A.K.A. Lycanthrope A.K.A. Wolfman," 2006–2010, retrieved May 21, 2010, from http://www.skepticworld.com/cryptozoology/werewolves.asp, 1.

29. Baring-Gould, *The Book of Werewolves*, 27.

30. Skeptic World, "Werewolves A.K.A. Lycanthrope A.K.A. Wolfman," 2.

31. Fiske, "Werewolves & Swan-Maidens," 1.

32. Baring-Gould, *The Book of Werewolves*, 27.

33. Ramsland, *The Human Predator*, 22.

34. *Werewolfpage.com*, "Werewolf of Chalons," 1.

35. Curran, *Encyclopedia of the Undead*, 105.

36. Sheehan, "Didn't See It Coming," 1.

37. Curran, *Encyclopedia of the Undead*, 105.

38. Curran, *Encyclopedia of the Undead*, 105; Baring-Gould, *The Book of Werewolves*, 27.

39. Ramsland, *The Human Predator*, 22; Sheehan, "Didn't See It Coming," 1.

40. Sheehan, "Didn't See It Coming," 1.

41. Ramsland, "Werewolf of Chalons," 1.

42. *Werewolfpage.com*, "Werewolf of Chalons," 1.

43. Ramsland, "Werewolf of Chalons," 1.

44. Ramsland, "Werewolf of Chalons," 1; Homayun Sidky, *Witchcraft, Lycanthropy, Drugs and Disease: An Anthropological Study of the European Witch-Trials* (Eugene, OR: Wipf & Stock, 1997), 232.

45. Sheehan, "Didn't See It Coming," 1.

46. Baring-Gould, *The Book of Werewolves*, 27.

47. Sheehan, "Didn't See It Coming," 1.

48. Ramsland, "Werewolf of Chalons," 1.

49. *Werewolfpage.com*, "Werewolf of Chalons," 1.

50. Curran, *Encyclopedia of the Undead*, 105; Montague Summers, *The Werewolf* (London: Kegan Paul, Trench and Trubner, 1933), 230.

51. Baring-Gould, *The Book of Werewolves*, 27.

52. Ramsland, "Werewolf of Chalons," 1.

53. Summers, The *Werewolf*, 230.

54. *Werewolfpage.com*, "Werewolf of Chalons," 1; Ramsland, "Werewolf of Chalons," 1.

55. Ramsland, "Werewolf of Chalons," 1.

56. *Werewolfpage.com*, "Werewolf of Chalons," 1; Ramsland, "Werewolf of Chalons," 1.

57. Summers, *The Werewolf*, 230.

CHAPTER EIGHT: CATHERINE DESHAYES MONVOISON

1. BBC, "Infamous Historical Poisoners," July 15, 2005, retrieved May 22, 2010, from http://www.bbc.co.uk/dna/h2g2/A419785, 1.

2. ExecutedToday.com, "1680: La Voison, Poisoner to the Stars," February 22, 2008, retrieved May 22, 2010, from http://www.executedtoday.com/2008/02/22/1680-la-voison, 1.

3. Nigel Cawthorne, *Black Magic Killers: Real-Life Accounts of Satanic Murderers* (London: Magpie Books, 2008), 17; *Columbia Encyclopedia*, "Poison Affair," 2010, retrieved May 22, 2010, from http://www.answers.com/topic/poison-affair 1.

4. Katherine Ramsland, *The Human Predator: A Historical Chronicle of Serial Murder and Forensic Investigation* (New York: Berkley Books, 2005), 32; Executed Today.com, "1680," 1.

5. Richard Glyn Jones, *The Mammoth Book of Women Who Kill* (New York: Carroll & Graf, 2002), 430; Cawthorne, *Black Magic Killers*, 17.

6. Cawthorne, *Black Magic Killers*, 20; Jones, *The Mammoth Book of Women Who Kill*, 434.

7. For example, see Kerry Seagrave, *Women Serial and Mass Murderers: A Worldwide Reference, 1580 through 1990* (Jefferson, NC: McFarland, 1992), 89; *Toxipedia*, "Catherine Deshayes Monvoison," n.d., retrieved May 22, 2010, from http://toxipedia.org/display/toxipedia/Catherine+Deshayes+Monvoison, 1; Jones, *The Mammoth Book of Women Who Kill*, 430; and Eric Hickey, *Serial Murderers and Their Victims* (Belmont, CA: Wadsworth, 1997), 243, 251.

8. Jones, *The Mammoth Book of Women Who Kill*, 435; *Toxipedia*, "Catherine Deshayes Monvoison," 1; Seagrave, *Women Serial and Mass Murderers*, 89.

9. Seagrave, *Women Serial and Mass Murderers*, 89; The Rise of Satanism in the Middle Ages Forum, "Catherine Montvoison," 2008, retrieved May 22, 2010, from http://www.unexplainedstuff.com/Religious-Phenomenon/The-Rise-of-Satanism, 1.

10. Jones, *The Mammoth Book of Women Who Kill*, 435; The Rise of Satanism in the Middle Ages Forum, "Catherine Montvoison," 1; Cawthorne, *Black Magic Killers*, 18.

11. Cawthorne, *Black Magic Killers*, 18; The Rise of Satanism in the Middle Ages Forum, "Catherine Montvoison," 1; Seagrave, *Women Serial and Mass Murderers*, 89.

12. Seagrave, *Women Serial and Mass Murderers*, 89.

13. Seagrave, *Women Serial and Mass Murderers*, 89; Cawthorne, *Black Magic Killers*, 18.

14. The Rise of Satanism in the Middle Ages Forum, "Catherine Montvoison," 1; Cawthorne, *Black Magic Killers*, 18.

15. The Rise of Satanism in the Middle Ages Forum, "Catherine Montvoison," 1; BBC, "Infamous Historical Poisoners," 2; Seagrave, *Women Serial and Mass Murderers*, 89.

16. ExecutedToday.com, "1680," 1.

17. Cawthorne, *Black Magic Killers*, 18.

18. Seagrave, *Women Serial and Mass Murderers*, 89; Jones, *The Mammoth Book of Women Who Kill*, 436.

19. Jones, *The Mammoth Book of Women Who Kill*, 435.

20. The Rise of Satanism in the Middle Ages Forum, "Catherine Montvoison," 1; Seagrave, *Women Serial and Mass Murderers*, 89.

21. Jones, *The Mammoth Book of Women Who Kill*, 436.

22. The Rise of Satanism in the Middle Ages Forum, "Catherine Montvoison," 1.

23. Seagrave, *Women Serial and Mass Murderers*, 89; The Rise of Satanism in the Middle Ages Forum, "Catherine Montvoison," 1; Cawthorne, *Black Magic Killers*, 18.

24. The Rise of Satanism in the Middle Ages Forum, "Catherine Montvoison," 1.

25. For example, see Jones, *The Mammoth Book of Women Who Kill*, 430, 439; Seagrave, *Women Serial and Mass Murderers*, 90; and Cawthorne, *Black Magic Killers*, 19.

26. Seagrave, *Women Serial and Mass Murderers*, 90; The Rise of Satanism in the Middle Ages Forum, "Catherine Montvoison," 1.

27. The Rise of Satanism in the Middle Ages Forum, "Catherine Montvoison," 1; Ramsland, *The Human Predator*, 31–32.

28. Seagrave, *Women Serial and Mass Murderers*, 89.

29. *Toxipedia*, "Catherine Deshayes Monvoison," 1.

30. Ramsland, *The Human Predator*, 31.

31. Seagrave, *Women Serial and Mass Murderers*, 91; Cawthorne, *Black Magic Killers*, 20.

32. Ramsland, *The Human Predator*, 32; Hickey, *Serial Murderers and Their Victims*, 251; Jones, *The Mammoth Book of Women Who Kill*, 430; Peter Vronsky, *Female Serial Killers: Why and How Women Become Monsters* (New York: Berkley Books, 2007), 440.

33. The Rise of Satanism in the Middle Ages Forum, "Catherine Montvoison," 1.

34. BBC, "Infamous Historical Poisoners," 2; Cawthorne, *Black Magic Killers*, 17.

35. Hickey, *Serial Murderers and Their Victims*, 251; Seagrave, *Women Serial and Mass Murderers*, 89; Cawthorne, *Black Magic Killers*, 20.

36. BBC, "Infamous Historical Poisoners," 2.

37. Seagrave, *Women Serial and Mass Murderers*, 89.

38. Cawthorne, *Black Magic Killers*, 19; BBC, "Infamous Historical Poisoners," 2; *Columbia Encyclopedia*, "Poison Affair," 1.

39. BBC, "Infamous Historical Poisoners," 2; Seagrave, *Women Serial and Mass Murderers*, 90.

40. Seagrave, *Women Serial and Mass Murderers*, 89.

41. ExecutedToday.com, "1680," 1.

42. Cawthorne, *Black Magic Killers*, 18; Ramsland, *The Human Predator*, 31.

43. The Rise of Satanism in the Middle Ages Forum, "Catherine Montvoison," 1.

44. *Toxipedia*, "Catherine Deshayes Monvoison," 1; Ramsland, *The Human Predator*, 31; BBC, "Infamous Historical Poisoners," 2.

45. Jones, *The Mammoth Book of Women Who Kill*, 438.

46. Ramsland, *The Human Predator*, 31; The Rise of Satanism in the Middle Ages Forum, "Catherine Montvoison," 1.

47. Cawthorne, *Black Magic Killers*, 16–18.

48. Ramsland, *The Human Predator*, 32; BBC, "Infamous Historical Poisoners," 2.

49. The Rise of Satanism in the Middle Ages Forum, "Catherine Montvoison," 1.

50. The Rise of Satanism in the Middle Ages Forum, "Catherine Montvoison," 1.

51. Ramsland, *The Human Predator*, 31–32; ExecutedToday.com, "1680," 1.

52. ExecutedToday.com, "1680," 1; Cawthorne, *Black Magic Killers*, 17.

53. Cawthorne, *Black Magic Killers*, 20; Seagrave, *Women Serial and Mass Murderers*, 90.

54. The Rise of Satanism in the Middle Ages Forum, "Catherine Montvoison," 1; *Columbia Encyclopedia*, "Poison Affair," 1.

55. *Columbia Encyclopedia*, "Poison Affair," 1; ExecutedToday.com, "1680," 1.

56. *Columbia Encyclopedia*, "Poison Affair," 1.

57. *Columbia Encyclopedia*, "Poison Affair," 1; Seagrave, *Women Serial and Mass Murderers*, 90; The Rise of Satanism in the Middle Ages Forum, "Catherine Montvoison," 1.

58. The Rise of Satanism in the Middle Ages Forum, "Catherine Montvoison," 1.

59. BBC, "Infamous Historical Poisoners," 2; Middle Ages Forum, "Montvoison," 1.

60. The Rise of Satanism in the Middle Ages Forum, "Catherine Montvoison," 1.

61. Cawthorne, *Black Magic Killers*, 20; The Rise of Satanism in the Middle Ages Forum, "Catherine Montvoison," 1.

62. Seagrave, *Women Serial and Mass Murderers*, 91; Jones, *The Mammoth Book of Women Who Kill*, 444; The Rise of Satanism in the Middle Ages Forum, "Catherine Montvoison," 1.

63. ExecutedToday.com, "1680," 1.

64. The Rise of Satanism in the Middle Ages Forum, "Catherine Montvoison," 1.

CHAPTER NINE: GILLES DE RAIS

1. Harold Schechter, *The Serial Killer Files* (New York: Ballantine Books, 2003), 87, 275; Helen Morrison and Harold Goldberg, *My Life among the Serial Killers* (New York: William Morrow, 2004), 53.

2. *Britannica Online Encyclopedia*, "Gilles de Rais," 2010, retrieved October 15, 2010, from http://www.brittanica.com/EBchecked/topic/489979/Gilles-de-Rais, 1; Schechter, The *Serial Killer Files*, 87.

3. The Rise of Satanism in the Middle Ages Forum, "Gilles de Rais (1404–1440)," 2008, retrieved October 15, 2010, from http://www.unexplained-stuff.com/Religious-Phenomenon/The-Rise-of-Satanism-in-the-MiddleAges.com, 1; David Everitt, *Human Monsters: An Illustrated Encyclopedia of the World's Most Vicious Murderers* (Chicago: Contemporary Books, 1993), 6.

4. Everitt, *Human Monsters*, 6; *Occult and Parapsychology Encyclopedia*, "Gilles de Rais," 2010, retrieved October 15, 2010, from http://www.answers.com/topic/retz-gilles-de-laval-seigneur; Morrison and Goldberg, *My Life among the Serial Killers*, 54.

5. Everitt, *Human Monsters*, 6; Katherine Ramsland, *The Human Predator: A Historical Chronicle of Serial Murder and Forensic Investigation* (New York: Berkley Books, 2005), 12.

6. Colin Wilson and Donald Seaman, *The Serial Killers: A Study in the Psychology of Violence* (New York: Carol Publishing Group, 1992), 297; Schechter, *The Serial Killer Files*, 326.

7. *Britannica Online Encyclopedia*, "Gilles de Rais," 1; Sandrine Nouvel, "Gilles De Rais, History's First and Worst Serial Killer?," September 7, 2009, retrieved October 15, 2010, from http://www.associatedcontent.com/article/2149609/gilles _de_rais, 1; Cheri Lasswell, "Gilles de Rais—Piety to Monster or Victim of Greed?," June 7, 2010, retrieved October 15, 2010, from http://www.suite101.com/content/ gilles-de-rais—piety-to-monster-o, 2.

8. Nouvel, "Gilles De Rais, History's First and Worst Serial Killer?," 1; Mark Gribben, "Childhood," in "Gilles De Rais," *Crime Library*, 2010, retrieved October 15, 2010, from http://www.trutv.com/library/crime/serial_killers/predators/ rais/ma, 1; Ramsland, *The Human Predator*, 12.

9. Ramsland, *The Human Predator*, 12.

10. Nouvel, "Gilles De Rais, History's First and Worst Serial Killer?," 1; Mark Gribben, "Epilogue," in "Gilles De Rais," *Crime Library*, 2010, retrieved October 15, 2010, from http://www/trutv.com/library/crime/serial_killers/predators/ rais/ma, 1.

11. Gribben, "Childhood," 1.

12. Lasswell, "Gilles de Rais," 2; *Occult and Parapsychology Encyclopedia*, "Gilles de Rais," 1.

13. Ramsland, *The Human Predator*, 12; Lasswell, "Gilles de Rais," 2; Gribben, "Childhood," 1.

14. Morrison and Goldberg, *My Life among the Serial Killers*, 54–55.

15. Ronald M. Holmes and Stephen T. Holmes, *Contemporary Perspectives on Serial Murder* (Thousand Oaks, CA: Sage, 1998), 8; *Britannica Online Encyclopedia*, "Gilles de Rais," 1; Nouvel, "Gilles De Rais, History's First and Worst Serial Killer?," 1; Ramsland, *The Human Predator*, 17; Schechter, *The Serial Killer Files*, 275; Everitt, *Human Monsters*, 6; Wilson and Seaman, *The Serial Killers*, 260.

16. Lasswell, "Gilles de Rais," 2; Morrison and Goldberg, *My Life among the Serial Killers*, 55; Schechter, *The Serial Killer Files*, 275.

17. Schechter, *The Serial Killer Files*, 275; Lasswell, "Gilles de Rais," 2.

18. Lasswell, "Gilles de Rais," 2; The Rise of Satanism in the Middle Ages Forum, "Gilles de Rais (1404–1440)," 1.

19. Ramsland, *The Human Predator*, 13; Schechter, *The Serial Killer Files*, 275; Holmes and Holmes, *Contemporary Perspectives on Serial Murder*, 8; Wilson and Seaman, *The Serial Killers*, 2; *Occult and Parapsychology Encyclopedia*, "Gilles de Rais," 2.

20. *Occult and Parapsychology Encyclopedia*, "Gilles de Rais," 1; Mark Gribben, "Murders Begin," in "Gilles De Rais," *Crime Library*, 2010, retrieved October 15, 2010, from http://www.trutv.com/library/crime/serial_killers/predators/rais/ma, 1; Mark Gribben, "Monster or Victim?," in "Gilles De Rais," *Crime Library*, 2010, retrieved October 15, 2010, from http://www.trutv/com/library/crime/serial_killers/ predators/rais/ma, 1; Morrison and Goldberg, *My Life among the Serial Killers*, 54–55.

21. *Occult and Parapsychology Encyclopedia*, "Gilles de Rais," 1; Morrison and Goldberg, *My Life among the Serial Killers*, 52.

22. Gribben, "Childhood," 1; Schechter, *The Serial Killer Files*, 87.

23. Gribben, "Monster or Victim?," 1.

24. Schechter, *The Serial Killer Files*, 87.

25. Schechter, *The Serial Killer Files*, 87; Ramsland, *The Human Predator*, 14.

26. Everitt, *Human Monsters*, 6; Mark Gribben, "The Saint and the Sinner," in "Gilles De Rais," *Crime Library*, 2010, retrieved October 15, 2010, from http://www/trutv.com/library/crime/serial_killers/predators/rais/sin, 1; The Rise of Satanism in the Middle Ages Forum, "Gilles de Rais (1404–1440)," 1.

27. The Rise of Satanism in the Middle Ages Forum, "Gilles de Rais (1404–1440)," 1.

28. Mark Gribben, "Unbridled," in "Gilles De Rais," *Crime Library*, 2010, retrieved on October 15, 2010, from http://www.trutv.com/library/crime/serial_killers/predators/rais/unb, 1.

29. Lasswell, "Gilles de Rais," 2; Gribben, "Epilogue," 1.

30. The Rise of Satanism in the Middle Ages Forum, "Gilles de Rais (1404–1440)," 1.

31. Ramsland, *The Human Predator*, 1; Mark Gribben, "Black Magic," in "Gilles De Rais," *Crime Library*, 2010, retrieved October 15, 2010, from http://www.trutv.com/library/crime/serial_killers/predators/rais/ma, 1.

32. Holmes and Holmes, *Contemporary Perspectives on Serial Murder*, 8; Ramsland, *The Human Predator*, 13; Schechter, *The Serial Killer Files*, 88; Everitt, *Human Monsters*, 6.

33. Gribben, "Monster or Victim?," 1.

34. Everitt, *Human Monsters*, 5–6; Schechter, *The Serial Killer Files*, 87–88.

35. Schechter, *The Serial Killer Files*, 275; Ramsland, *The Human Predator*, 14.

36. Brian Lane and Wilfred Gregg, *The Encyclopedia of Serial Killers* (New York: Berkley Books, 1995), 138; Lasswell, "Gilles de Rais," 2; Gribben, "Monster or Victim?," 1; Michael Jones, "Gilles De Rais," *French Literature Companion*, 2010, retrieved October 15, 2010, from http://www.answers.com/topic/retz-gilles-de-laval-seigneur-de, 1; *Occult and Parapsychology Encyclopedia*, "Gilles de Rais," 1; Schechter, *The Serial Killer Files*, 87.

37. Lane and Gregg, *The Encyclopedia of Serial Killers*, 138; Lasswell, "Gilles de Rais," 2; Morrison and Goldberg, *My Life among the Serial Killers*, 53–54; *Occult and Parapsychology Encyclopedia*, "Gilles de Rais," 2.

38. Nouvel, "Gilles De Rais, History's First and Worst Serial Killer?," 1; Lasswell, "Gilles de Rais," 2.

39. Gribben, "Black Magic," 1.

40. Nouvel, "Gilles De Rais, History's First and Worst Serial Killer?," 1; Everitt, *Human Monsters*, 7; *Occult and Parapsychology Encyclopedia*, "Gilles de Rais," 1.

41. Ramsland, *The Human Predator*, 14.

42. Ramsland, *The Human Predator*, 14.

43. Everitt, *Human Monsters*, 6.

44. Schechter, *The Serial Killer Files*, 88; Gribben, "Murders Begin," 1.

45. *Serial Killer Central*, "Gilles de Rais: Ancestor of Gore," October 15, 2010, retrieved October 15, 2010, from http://www.skcentral.com/articles.php?article_id=435, 3.

46. Holmes and Holmes, *Contemporary Perspectives on Serial Murder*, 8.

47. Holmes and Holmes, *Contemporary Perspectives on Serial Murder*, 8.

48. Nouvel, "Gilles De Rais, History's First and Worst Serial Killer?," 1.

49. Schechter, *The Serial Killer Files*, 88.

50. *Occult and Parapsychology Encyclopedia*, "Gilles de Rais," 2.

51. Wilson and Seaman, *The Serial Killers*, 297; Schechter, *The Serial Killer Files*, 88; Everitt, *Human Monsters*, 6–7; Mark Gribben, "Castle of Horrors," in "Gilles De Rais," *Crime Library*, 2010, retrieved October 15, 2010, from http://www.trutv.com/library/crimeserial_killers/predators/rais/cas, 1.

52. Morrison and Goldberg, *My Life among the Serial Killers*, 56; Ramsland, *The Human Predator*, 14.

53. Gribben, "Castle of Horrors," 1; Mark Gribben, "Downfall," in "Gilles De Rais," *Crime Library*, 2010, retrieved October 15, 2010, from http://www.trutv.com/library/crime/serial_killers/predators/rais/do, 1.

54. Everitt, *Human Monsters*, 8; Mark Gribben, "Conspirators," in "Gilles De Rais," *Crime Library*, 2010, retrieved October 15, 2010, from http://www/trutv.com/library/crime/serial_killers/predators/rais/con, 1; *Occult and Parapsychology Encyclopedia*, "Gilles de Rais," 2; Mark Gribben, "Summoning the Devil," in "Gilles De Rais," *Crime Library*, 2010, retrieved October 15, 2010, from http://www.trutv.com/library/crime/serial_killers/predators/rais/dev, 1.

55. Wilson and Seaman, *The Serial Killers*, 297.

56. Wilson and Seaman, *The Serial Killers*, 297; Colin Wilson, *Serial Killer Investigations* (Chichester: Summersdale, 2007), 5.

57. Morrison and Goldberg, *My Life among the Serial Killers*, 56; Everitt, *Human Monsters*, 6, 8; Eric Hickey, *Serial Killers and Their Victims* (Belmont, CA: Wadsworth, 1997), 3; Ramsland, *The Human Predator*, 15.

58. The Rise of Satanism in the Middle Ages Forum, "Gilles de Rais (1404–1440)," 1; Everitt, *Human Monsters*, 6; Hickey, *Serial Killers and Their Victims*, 32; Holmes and Holmes, *Contemporary Perspectives on Serial Murder*, 8.

59. Everitt, *Human Monsters*, 8.

60. Lane and Gregg, *The Encyclopedia of Serial Killers*, 140; Mark Gribben, "An Innocent Man?," in "Gilles De Rais," *Crime Library*, 2010, retrieved October 15, 2010, from http://www.trutv.com/library/crime/serial_killers/predators/rais/an, 1.

61. Ramsland, *The Human Predator*, 14; Everitt, *Human Monsters*, 6; Nouvel, "Gilles De Rais, History's First and Worst Serial Killer?," 1; Morrison and Goldberg, *My Life among the Serial Killers*, 55; Schechter, *The Serial Killer Files*, 88; Gribben, "Monster or Victim?," 1.

62. Morrison and Goldberg, *My Life among the Serial Killers*, 55.

63. Wilson and Seaman, *The Serial Killers*, 297; Hickey, *Serial Killers and Their Victims*, 248.

64. Morrison and Goldberg, *My Life among the Serial Killers*, 55–56.

65. Morrison and Goldberg, *My Life among the Serial Killers*, 56; Schechter, *The Serial Killer Files*, 88; Everitt, *Human Monsters*, 7.

66. Nouvel, "Gilles De Rais, History's First and Worst Serial Killer?," 1.

67. Lane and Gregg, *The Encyclopedia of Serial Killers*, 140; Gribben, "Monster or Victim?," 1; Ramsland, *The Human Predator*, 14.

68. The Rise of Satanism in the Middle Ages Forum, "Gilles de Rais (1404–1440)," 1.

69. Hickey, *Serial Killers and Their Victims*, 32; *Occult and Parapsychology Encyclopedia*, "Gilles de Rais," 1.

70. Schechter, *The Serial Killer Files*, 88; Gribben, "Monster or Victim?," 1.

71. *Occult and Parapsychology Encyclopedia*, "Gilles de Rais," 2; Ramsland, *The Human Predator*, 14; Everitt, *Human Monsters*, 7.

72. Mark Gribben, "Confession," in "Gilles De Rais," *Crime Library*, 2010, Retrieved October 15, 2010, from http://www.trutv.com/library/crime/serial/killers/predators/rais/con, 1; *Occult and Parapsychology Encyclopedia*, "Gilles de Rais," 2.

73. Gribben, "Confession," 1.

74. *Occult and Parapsychology Encyclopedia*, "Gilles de Rais," 3.

75. *Occult and Parapsychology Encyclopedia*, "Gilles de Rais," 4.

76. Gribben, "Inquisition," in "Gilles De Rais," *Crime Library*, 2010, retrieved October 15, 2010, from http//www.trutv.com/library/crime/serialkillers/predators/rais/inq, 1.

77. Gribben, "Downfall," 1.

78. Morrison and Goldberg, My *Life among the Serial Killers*, 56; Gribben, "Inquisition," 1.

79. The Rise of Satanism in the Middle Ages Forum, "Gilles de Rais (1404–1440)," 1; Morrison and Goldberg, My *Life among the Serial Killers*, 56; Lane and Gregg, *The Encyclopedia of Serial Killers*, 139.

80. *Occult and Parapsychology Encyclopedia*, "Gilles de Rais," 4; Schechter, *The Serial Killer Files*, 88; Everitt, *Human Monsters*, 8.

81. Gribben, "Inquisition," 1; Lasswell, "Gilles de Rais," 3.

82. The Rise of Satanism in the Middle Ages Forum, "Gilles de Rais (1404–1440)," 1.

83. Gribben, "Inquisition," 1; Gribben, "Confession," 1.

84. Gribben, "Inquisition," 1; Morrison and Goldberg, My *Life among the Serial Killers*, 56; Gribben, "Confession," 1.

85. Lane and Gregg, *The Encyclopedia of Serial Killers*, 138; Schechter, *The Serial Killer Files*, 87.

86. Everitt, *Human Monsters*, 7; Lane and Gregg, *The Encyclopedia of Serial Killers*, 139; Schechter, *The Serial Killer Files*, 88.

87. Ramsland, *The Human Predator*, 16; Lasswell, "Gilles de Rais," 3.

88. Everitt, *Human Monsters*, 8; Schechter, *The Serial Killer Files*, 88; Lane and Gregg, *The Encyclopedia of Serial Killers*, 138; Ramsland, *The Human Predator*, 16; Morrison and Goldberg, My *Life among the Serial Killers*, 56.

CHAPTER TEN: VLAD THE IMPALER

1. David Carroll, "This Man Belongs to Me: The Life and Deaths of Vlad the Impaler," *Tabula Rasa*, 2010, retrieved October 21, 2010, from http://www.tabula-rasa.info/DarkAges/VladTheImpaler.html, 8.

2. Harold Schechter, *The Serial Killer Files* (New York: Ballantine Books, 2003), 129.

3. David Everitt, *Human Monsters: An Illustrated Encyclopedia of the World's Most Vicious Murderers* (Chicago: Contemporary Books, 1993), 8–9.

4. Carroll, "This Man Belongs to Me," 6; Joseph Geringer, "Man More Than Myth," in "Vlad the Impaler," *Crime Library*, 2010, retrieved October 21, 2010, from http://www.trutv.com/library/crime/serial_killers/history/vlad/index, 1.

5. Schechter, *The Serial Killer Files*, 107; Carroll, "This Man Belongs to Me," 5.

6. Katherine Ramsland, *The Human Predator: A Historical Chronicle of Serial Murder and Forensic Investigation* (New York: Berkley Books, 2005), 18; Schechter, *The Serial Killer Files*, 132.

7. Geringer, "Man More Than Myth," 1; Joseph Geringer, "The Impaler," in "Vlad the Impaler," *Crime Library*, 2010, retrieved October 21, 2010, from http://www.trutv.com/library/crime/serial_killers/history/vlad/impaler, 1.

8. Ramsland, *The Human Predator*, 18; Geringer, "Man More Than Myth," 2; Eric Hickey, *Serial Killers and Their Victims* (Belmont, CA: Wadsworth, 1997), 32; Everitt, *Human Monsters*, 8.

9. Carroll, "This Man Belongs to Me," 2, 4; Will Bradbury, *Into the Unknown* (Pleasantville, NY: Reader's Digest Association, 1981), 100.

10. Geringer, "Man More Than Myth," 1; Schechter, *The Serial Killer Files*, 132; Everitt, *Human Monsters*, 8; Ramsland, *The Human Predator*, 18.

11. Bradbury, *Into the Unknown*, 100.

12. Carroll, "This Man Belongs to Me," 2; Bradbury, *Into the Unknown*, 100.

13. Carroll, "This Man Belongs to Me," 2; Teena Perry, "The True Dracula: Vlad the Impaler," *essortment*, 2002, retrieved October 21, 2010, from http://www.essortment.com/all/vladtheimpaler_rdhv.htm, 1; Everitt, *Human Monsters*, 9; Bradbury, *Into the Unknown*, 100.

14. Joseph Geringer, "Staggering the Turks," in "Vlad the Impaler," *Crime Library*, 2010, retrieved October 21, 2010, from http://www.trutv.com/library/crime/serial_killers/predators/vlad, 1; Perry, "The True Dracula," 1.

15. Perry, "The True Dracula," 1.

16. Joseph Geringer, "Gotterdamerung," in "Vlad the Impaler," *Crime Library*, 2010, retrieved October 21, 2010, from http://www.trutv.com/library/crime/serial_killers/predators/vlad, 1; Joseph Geringer, "Among the Ottomans," in "Vlad the Impaler," *Crime Library*, 2010, retrieved October 21, 2010, from http://www.trutv.com/library/crime/serial_killers/predators/vlad, 1; Carroll, "This Man Belongs to Me," 3, 7.

17. Carroll, "This Man Belongs to Me," 7; Geringer, "Among the Ottomans," 2; Perry, "The True Dracula," 1.

18. Geringer, "Among the Ottomans," 2; Perry, "The True Dracula," 1.

19. Geringer, "Among the Ottomans," 1; Carroll, "This Man Belongs to Me," 2, 8.

20. Bradbury, *Into the Unknown*, 100.

21. Geringer, "Among the Ottomans," 2; Colin Wilson and Donald Seaman, *The Serial Killers: The Psychology of Violence* (New York: Carol Publishing Group, 1992), 7; Schechter, *The Serial Killer Files*, 132; Ramsland, *The Human Predator*, 18; Hickey, *Serial Killers and Their Victims*, 32.

22. Carroll, "This Man Belongs to Me," 3–4.

23. Everitt, *Human Monsters*, 8–9.

24. Joseph Geringer, "A Brother's Treason," in "Vlad the Impaler," *Crime Library*, 2010, retrieved October 21, 2010, from http://www/trutv.com/library/crime/serial_killers/predators/vlad, 2.

25. Carroll, "This Man Belongs to Me," 3.

26. Geringer, "Among the Ottomans," 3; Geringer, "Staggering the Turks," 1.

27. Geringer, "A Brother's Treason," 2; Everitt, *Human Monsters*, 10–11.

28. Joseph Geringer, "Voivode," in "Vlad the Impaler," *Crime Library*, 2010, retrieved October 21, 2010, from http://www.trutv.com/library/crime/serial_killers/predators/vlad, 1.

29. Bradbury, *Into the Unknown*, 100; Perry, "The True Dracula," 1; Carroll, "This Man Belongs to Me," 7.

30. Bradbury, *Into the Unknown*, 100.

31. Geringer, "The Impaler," 2.

32. Geringer, "The Impaler," 2.

33. Everitt, *Human Monsters*, 8–9.

34. Geringer, "Voivode," 1; Everitt, *Human Monsters*, 9.

35. Geringer, "A Brother's Treason," 2; Everitt, *Human Monsters*, 10–11.

36. Everitt, *Human Monsters*, 9; Ramsland, *The Human Predator*, 18; Hickey, *Serial Killers and Their Victims*, 32; Bradbury, *Into the Unknown*, 100.

37. Hickey, *Serial Killers and Their Victims*, 32.

38. Ramsland, *The Human Predator*, 18; Perry, "The True Dracula," 2.

39. Hickey, *Serial Killers and Their Victims*, 32.

40. Carroll, "This Man Belongs to Me," 7.

41. Bradbury, *Into the Unknown*, 101; Carroll, "This Man Belongs to Me," 4.

42. Geringer, "Voivode," 2; Bradbury, *Into the Unknown*, 101.

43. Geringer, "The Impaler," 2; Everitt, *Human Monsters*, 10; Schechter, *The Serial Killer Files*, 133.

44. Geringer, "The Impaler," 1; Geringer, "Voivode," 2–3.

45. Geringer, "The Impaler," 1.

46. Carroll, "This Man Belongs to Me," 5; Geringer, "Staggering the Turks," 2.

47. Geringer, "The Impaler," 1; Schechter, *The Serial Killer Files*, 133.

48. Everitt, *Human Monsters*, 10.

49. Carroll, "This Man Belongs to Me," 5; Bradbury, *Into the Unknown*, 101.

50. Carroll, "This Man Belongs to Me," 6; Geringer, "The Impaler," 1.

51. Carroll, "This Man Belongs to Me," 6.

52. Geringer, "Among the Ottomans," 3; Carroll, "This Man Belongs to Me," 5.

53. Carroll, "This Man Belongs to Me," 5; Perry, "The True Dracula," 2.

54. Ramsland, *The Human Predator*, 18–19.

55. Geringer, "The Impaler," 1; Everitt, *Human Monsters*, 10; Carroll, "This Man Belongs to Me," 6.

56. Ramsland, *The Human Predator*, 18; Geringer, "The Impaler," 1; Everitt, *Human Monsters*, 10.

57. Bradbury, *Into the Unknown*, 101; Perry, "The True Dracula," 2.

58. Schechter, *The Serial Killer Files*, 133; Everitt, *Human Monsters*, 10; Geringer, "The Impaler," 1; Carroll, "This Man Belongs to Me," 7–8.

59. Carroll, "This Man Belongs to Me," 8–10; Schechter, *The Serial Killer Files*, 133; Geringer, "The Impaler," 2.

60. Geringer, "Staggering the Turks," 1; Schechter, *The Serial Killer Files*, 133.

61. Hickey, *Serial Killers and Their Victims*, 32; Perry, "The True Dracula," 2.

62. Geringer, "The Impaler," 1.

63. Perry, "The True Dracula," 1; Ramsland, *The Human Predator*, 18; Everitt, *Human Monsters*, 8–9.

64. Bradbury, *Into the Unknown*, 100; Schechter, *The Serial Killer Files*, 124, 132.

65. Hickey, *Serial Killers and Their Victims*, 32; Ramsland, *The Human Predator*, 18; Everitt, *Human Monsters*, 8–9.

66. Carroll, "This Man Belongs to Me," 3; Schechter, *The Serial Killer Files*, 133.

67. Carroll, "This Man Belongs to Me," 4.

68. Geringer, "Man More Than Myth," 1.

69. Everitt, *Human Monsters*, 10; Perry, "The True Dracula," 2; Geringer, "Gotterdamerung," 1.

70. Geringer, "Gotterdamerung," 1.

71. Perry, "The True Dracula," 2; Carroll, "This Man Belongs to Me," 8.

72. Geringer, "Gotterdamerung," 1.

73. Joseph Geringer, "Epilogue," In "Vlad the Impaler," Crime Library, 2010, retrieved October 21, 2010, from http://www.trutv.com/library/crime/serial_killers/history/vlad/epilogue.html, 1; Perry, "The True Dracula," 2; Carroll, "This Man Belongs to Me," 8; Geringer, "Gotterdamerung," 1.

74. Perry, "The True Dracula," 2.

CHAPTER ELEVEN: QUEEN NZINGA

1. *Encyclopedia of World Biography*, "Anna Nzinga Biography," 2005–2006, retrieved May 3, 2010, from http://www.bookrags.com/biography/anna-nzinga, 1; *Encyclopedia.com*, "Anna Nzinga," 2004, retrieved October 25, 2010, from http://www.encyclopedia.com/doc/1G2-3404708259.html, 1.

2. Joseph C. Miller, *Kings and Kinsmen: Early Mbundu States in Angola* (Oxford: Clarendon Press, 1976), 42; Lawrence W. Henderson, *Angola: Five Centuries of Conflict* (Ithaca, NY: Cornell University Press, 1979), 89.

3. *Black History Pages*, "Queen Nzinga (1583–1663)," 1996–2008, retrieved May 3, 2010, from http://blackhistorypages.net/pages/nzinga.php, 1; *Fact-Index.com*, "Ann Nzinga Mbande," 2010, retrieved October 25, 2010, from http://www.fact-index.com/a/an/ann_nzinga_mbande.html, 1.

4. David Birmingham, *The Portuguese Conquest of Angola* (London: Oxford University Press, 1965), 29–30.

5. Henderson, *Angola*, 89.

6. Carole Levin, Debra Barnett-Graves, Jo-Eldridge Carney, W. M. Spellman, Gwynne Kennedy, and Stephanie Witham, "Nzinga: Queen of Angola," in *Extraordinary Women of the Medieval and Renaissance World: A Bibliographical Dictionary* (Westport, CT: Praeger, 2000), 223; Adebayo O. Oyebade, *Culture and Customs of Angola* (Westport, CT: Greenwood Press, 2007), 21–22.

7. *Black History Pages*, "Queen Nzinga (1583–1663)," 1.

8. Katherine Ramsland, *The Human Predator: A Historical Chronicle of Serial Murder and Forensic Investigation* (New York: Berkley Books, 2005), ix.

9. Metropolitan Museum of Art, Heilbruner Timeline of Art History, "Ann Nzinga: Queen of Ndongo," 2010, retrieved October 25, 2010, from http://www.metmusem.org/toah/hd/pwmn_2/hd_pwmn_2.htm, 1; Miller, *Kings and Kinsmen*, 97.

10. *Encyclopedia of World Biography*, "Anna Nzinga Biography," 1.

11. *Encyclopedia of World Biography*, "Anna Nzinga Biography," 1.

12. *Black History Pages*, "Queen Nzinga (1583–1663)," 1.

13. *Fact-Index.com*, "Ann Nzinga Mbande," 1.

14. *Encyclopedia.com*, "Anna Nzinga," 1.

15. *Encyclopedia.com*, "Anna Nzinga," 1–2.

16. Birmingham, *The Portuguese Conquest of Angola*, 29; Oyebade, *Culture and Customs of Angola*, 21; Henderson, *Angola*, 89.

17. Henderson, *Angola*, 89–90.

18. Miller, *Kings and Kinsmen*, 220; *Encyclopedia.com*, "Anna Nzinga," 2.

19. *Encyclopedia.com*, "Anna Nzinga," 2.

20. *Encyclopedia of World Biography*, "Anna Nzinga Biography," 1.

21. Metropolitan Museum of Art, "Ann Nzinga," 1.

22. *Encyclopedia.com*, "Anna Nzinga," 1.

23. *Encyclopedia of World Biography*, "Anna Nzinga Biography," 1; *Encyclopedia.com*, "Anna Nzinga," 1.

24. *Encyclopedia.com*, "Anna Nzinga," 1; *Black History Pages*, "Queen Nzinga (1583–1663)," 1.

25. Metropolitan Museum of Art, "Ann Nzinga," 1; *Encyclopedia.com*, "Anna Nzinga," 2.

26. *Encyclopedia.com*, "Anna Nzinga," 2.

27. *Encyclopedia.com*, "Anna Nzinga," 1–2.

28. *Encyclopedia.com*, "Anna Nzinga," 2; Metropolitan Museum of Art, "Ann Nzinga," 1.

29. Birmingham, *The Portuguese Conquest of Angola*, 29–30; *Encyclopedia.com*, "Anna Nzinga," 2; Metropolitan Museum of Art, "Ann Nzinga," 1; *Black History Pages*, "Queen Nzinga (1583–1663)," 1.

30. *Encyclopedia.com*, "Anna Nzinga," 2.

31. Metropolitan Museum of Art, "Ann Nzinga," 1.

32. Metropolitan Museum of Art, "Ann Nzinga," 1.

33. Metropolitan Museum of Art, "Ann Nzinga," 1.

34. Metropolitan Museum of Art, "Ann Nzinga," 1.

35. *Encyclopedia.com*, "Anna Nzinga," 2; *Fact-Index.com*, "Ann Nzinga Mbande," 1.

36. *Fact-Index.com*, "Ann Nzinga Mbande," 1.

37. *Fact-Index.com.*, "Ann Nzinga Mbande," 1.

38. *Encyclopedia.com*, "Anna Nzinga," 1.

39. *Fact-Index.com*, "Ann Nzinga Mbande," 1.

40. Birmingham, *The Portuguese Conquest of Angola*, 30–31; Levin et al., "Nzinga," 226.

41. Birmingham, *The Portuguese Conquest of Angola*, 30–32; Levin et al., "Nzinga," 226.

42. Metropolitan Museum of Art, "Ann Nzinga," 1.

43. *Encyclopedia.com*, "Anna Nzinga," 1; Ramsland, *The Human Predator*, ix.

44. Oyebade, *Culture and Customs of Angola*, 21–22.

45. Ramsland, *The Human Predator*, ix.

46. *Encyclopedia.com*, "Anna Nzinga," 1.

47. Marquise de Sade, *Philosophy in the Boudior, or, the Immoral Mentors* (Paris, 1795), 49.

48. De Sade, *Philosophy in the Boudior*, 49.

49. Ramsland, *The Human Predator*, ix.

50. Henderson, *Angola*, 89; *Encyclopedia.com*, "Anna Nzinga," 1.

51. Miller, *Kings and Kinsmen*, 220; Levin et al., "Nzinga," 225.

52. Ramsland, *The Human Predator*, ix.

53. *Fact-Index.com*, "Ann Nzinga Mbande," 1.

54. *Black History Pages*, "Queen Nzinga (1583–1663)," 1.

55. Oyebade, *Culture and Customs of Angola*, 55; Metropolitan Museum of Art, "Ann Nzinga," 1.

56. *Encyclopedia.com*, "Anna Nzinga," 2.

57. Miller, *Kings and Kinsmen*, 209.

58. Henderson, *Angola*, 89.

59. Ramsland, *The Human Predator*, ix.

CHAPTER TWELVE: DOWAGER EMPRESS CIXI

1. Tony Sit, "The Life of Empress Cixi," *China in Focus*, 2001, 18; Thomas J. Gilroy, "Tz'u-hsi or Cixi: The Dowager Empress of China," November 9, 2004, retrieved May 3, 2010, from http://departments.kings.edu/womens_history/tzuhsi .html, 2.

2. Gilroy, "Tz'u-hsi or Cixi," 1-2.

3. Shelly Klein, *The Most Evil Women in History* (New York: Barnes & Noble Books, 2003), 60; Sit, "The Life of Empress Cixi," 2.

4. Sit, "The Life of Empress Cixi," 2-3; Gilroy, "Tz'u-hsi or Cixi," 2.

5. Klein, *The Most Evil Women in History*, 59.

6. Gilroy, "Tz'u-hsi or Cixi," 1.

7. Sit, "The Life of Empress Cixi," 2; Gilroy, "Tz'u-hsi or Cixi," 1.

8. Sit, "The Life of Empress Cixi," 1.

9. Gilroy, "Tz'u-hsi or Cixi," 1; *Columbia Encyclopedia*, "Tz'u Hsi," 2008, 6th ed., retrieved May 3, 2010, from http://www.encyclopedia.com/topic/Tzu_Hsi.aspx, 1.

10. *Biography*, "Tz'u-hsi," 2010, retrieved May 3, 2010, from http://www.answers .com/topic/empress-dowager-cixi, 1; *Chinapage.com*, "The Dowager Empress Cixi (Tzu Hsi)," n.d., retrieved May 3, 2010, from http://www.chinapage.com/biography/ cixi.html, 1.

11. *Biography*, "Tz'u-hsi," 1; *Columbia Encyclopedia*, "Tz'u Hsi," 1.

12. Gilroy, "Tz'u-hsi or Cixi," 1.

13. Klein, *The Most Evil Women in History*, 56; Sit, "The Life of Empress Cixi," 1.

14. Klein, *The Most Evil Women in History*, 56.

15. Sit, "The Life of Empress Cixi," 1.

16. Klein, *The Most Evil Women in History*, 56; Sit, "The Life of Empress Cixi," 1.

17. Gilroy, "Tz'u-hsi or Cixi," 1; Klein, *The Most Evil Women in History*, 60.

18. Klein, *The Most Evil Women in History*, 56; Sit, "The Life of Empress Cixi," 1; *Biography*, "Tz'u-hsi," 1.

19. Klein, *The Most Evil Women in History*, 63; Gilroy, "Tz'u-hsi or Cixi," 1; Sit, "The Life of Empress Cixi," 3.

20. Klein, *The Most Evil Women in History*, 61.

21. Klein, *The Most Evil Women in History*, 66; Sit, "The Life of Empress Cixi," 1.

22. Klein, *The Most Evil Women in History*, 69; Gilroy, "Tz'u-hsi or Cixi," 2.

23. Gilroy, "Tz'u-hsi or Cixi," 2; *Encyclopedia.com*, "Tzu Hsi," 2008, retrieved May 3, 2010, from http://www.encyclopedia.com/topic/Tzu_Hsi.aspx, 1.

24. *Biography*, "Tz'u-hsi," 1.

25. Klein, *The Most Evil Women in History*, 56; Sit, "The Life of Empress Cixi," 1–2; *Biography*, "Tz'u-hsi," 1.

26. Klein, *The Most Evil Women in History*, 58; Sit, "The Life of Empress Cixi," 1.

27. Sit, "The Life of Empress Cixi," 2.

28. Sit, "The Life of Empress Cixi," 2.

29. Sit, "The Life of Empress Cixi," 2; Klein, *The Most Evil Women in History*, 59; Gilroy, "Tz'u-hsi or Cixi," 1.

30. Klein, *The Most Evil Women in History*, 69; Gilroy, "Tz'u-hsi or Cixi," 2.

31. Klein, *The Most Evil Women in History*, 56.

32. Klein, *The Most Evil Women in History*, 61.

33. Klein, *The Most Evil Women in History*, 66.

34. Alison McLean, "110 Years Ago Sobby Boxers," *Smithsonian.com*, June 2010, 22.

35. Klein, *The Most Evil Women in History*, 59-60.

36. Sit, "The Life of Empress Cixi," 2.

37. Klein, *The Most Evil Women in History*, 64, 66; David Wallechinsky and Irving Wallace, "Famous Rulers in History: Empress Dowager of China Tzu Hsi Part 4," *The People's Almanac*, 1975–1981, retrieved May 3, 2010, from http://www.trivia-library.com/b/famous-rulers-in-history-empress, 1.

38. McLean, "110 Years Ago Sobby Boxers," 22.

39. Klein, *The Most Evil Women in History*, 68–69.

40. Gilroy, "Tz'u-hsi or Cixi," 2.

41. Klein, *The Most Evil Women in History*, 69.

42. Sit, "The Life of Empress Cixi," 1–2; Klein, *The Most Evil Women in History*, 69.

43. Klein, *The Most Evil Women in History*, 63.

44. Klein, *The Most Evil Women in History*, 60.

45. Klein, *The Most Evil Women in History*, 60.

46. Klein, *The Most Evil Women in History*, 69.

47. Klein, *The Most Evil Women in History*, 62–63.

48. Gilroy, "Tz'u-hsi or Cixi," 1.

49. McLean, "110 Years Ago Sobby Boxers," 22.

50. Klein, *The Most Evil Women in History*, 67.

51. Klein, *The Most Evil Women in History*, 60.

52. Klein, *The Most Evil Women in History*, 62.

53. Klein, *The Most Evil Women in History*, 59–60.

54. Klein, *The Most Evil Women in History*, 60.

55. Sit, "The Life of Empress Cixi," 2.

56. Sit, "The Life of Empress Cixi," 3.

57. Klein, *The Most Evil Women in History*, 63.

58. *Biography*, "Tz'u-hsi," 1.

59. Wallechinsky and Wallace, "Famous Rulers in History," 1.

CHAPTER THIRTEEN: LOCUSTA THE POISONER

1. Shelley Klein, *The Most Evil Women in History* (New York: Barnes & Noble Books, 2003), 52; Richard Glyn Jones, *The Mammoth Book of Women Who Kill* (New York: Carroll & Graf, 2002), 9.

2. L. Cilliers and F. P. Retief, "Poisons, Poisoning and the Drug Trade in Ancient Rome," *Akoterion* 45 (2000): 90.

3. Katherine Ramsland, "The Poisoners," in "Forensic Toxicology," *Crime Library*, 2008, retrieved February 11, 2009, from http://www.trutv.com/library/crime/criminal_mind/forensics/toxicology/5.html?sect=21, 1; Michael Newton, *The Encyclopedia of Serial Killers* (New York: Checkmark Books, 2000), 140; Katherine Ramsland, *The Human Predator: A Historical Chronicle of Serial Murder and Forensic Investigation* (New York: Berkley Books, 2005), 4.

4. Ramsland, "The Poisoners," 1; David Wallechinsky and Irving Wallace, "Human Disasters: Ancient Roman Poisoner Locusta Part I," *The People's Almanac*, in *TriviaLibrary.com*, 1975–1981, retrieved February 11, 2009, from http://www.trivia-library.com/b/human-disasters-ancient-roman-poisoner-locusta-part, 1; Cilliers and Retief, "Poisons, Poisoning and the Drug Trade in Ancient Rome," 90.

5. Vicki Leon, *Outrageous Women of Ancient Times* (New York: Wiley, 1998), 15.

6. Leeann Perry, "A Summarized History of Forensic Science," *Casebook: Jack the Ripper*, 2009, retrieved February 11, 2009, from http://www.casebook.org/dissertations/ripperoo-forensic.html, 1.

7. Newton, *The Encyclopedia of Serial Killers*, 140.

8. *Education World*, "Meet History's Most Outrageous Women!," 2009, retrieved February 11, 2009, from http://education-world.com_books/books036.shtml, 1.

9. Ann Wamack, "Locusta of Gaul, Roman 'Herbalist' and Professional Poisoner," *History'sWomen.com*, 2009, retrieved February 11, 2009, from http://www.historyswomen.com/moregreatwomen/Locusta.html, 1.

10. Ramsland, *The Human Predator*, 4.

11. Leon, *Outrageous Women of Ancient Times*, 14; Wamack, "Locusta of Gaul, Roman 'Herbalist' and Professional Poisoner," 1; Ramsland, *The Human Predator*, 4.

12. David Wallechinsky and Irving Wallace, "About the Ancient Roman Poisoner Locusta: Biography and History of the Woman Responsible for Numerous Murders, Including That of Emperor Claudius," Part II, 1975–1981, *Trivia-Library.com*, 2010,

retrieved February 11, 2009, from http://www.trivia-library.com/b/human-disasters
-ancient-roman-poisoner-locusta-part, 1.

13. Cilliers and Retief, "Poisons, Poisoning and the Drug Trade in Ancient Rome," 90.

14. Ramsland, *The Human Predator*, 4.

15. Ramsland, *The Human Predator*, 5; Wamack, "Locusta of Gaul, Roman 'Herbalist' and Professional Poisoner," 1.

16. Cilliers and Retief, "Poisons, Poisoning and the Drug Trade in Ancient Rome," 90.

17. Wamack, "Locusta of Gaul, Roman 'Herbalist' and Professional Poisoner," 2; Ramsland, *The Human Predator*, 5; Leon, *Outrageous Women of Ancient Times*, 14.

18. Ramsland, *The Human Predator*, 4; Wamack, "Locusta of Gaul, Roman 'Herbalist' and Professional Poisoner," 2.

19. Leon, *Outrageous Women of Ancient Times*, 15; Wamack, "Locusta of Gaul, Roman 'Herbalist' and Professional Poisoner," 1.

20. Cilliers and Retief, "Poisons, Poisoning and the Drug Trade in Ancient Rome," 9.

21. Perry, "A Summarized History of Forensic Science," 1.

22. *Education World*, "Meet History's Most Outrageous Women!," 1.

23. Ramsland, *The Human Predator*, 5; Wamack, "Locusta of Gaul, Roman 'Herbalist' and Professional Poisoner," 2.

24. Cilliers and Retief, "Poisons, Poisoning and the Drug Trade in Ancient Rome," 90; Wallechinsky and Wallace, "About the Ancient Roman Poisoner Locusta," 1.

25. Wallechinsky and Wallace, "About the Ancient Roman Poisoner Locusta," 1.

26. Ramsland, *The Human Predator*, 5.

27. Wallechinsky and Wallace, "About the Ancient Roman Poisoner Locusta," 1.

28. Peter Vronsky, *Female Serial Killers: How and Why Women Become Monsters* (New York: Berkley Books, 2007), 75; Ramsland, *The Human Predator*, 5; Ramsland, "The Poisoners," 1.

29. Harold Schechter, *The Serial Killer Files* (New York: Ballantine Books, 2003), 130; Wallechinsky and Wallace, "About the Ancient Roman Poisoner Locusta," 1; Leon, *Outrageous Women of Ancient Times*, 16; Wamack, "Locusta of Gaul, Roman 'Herbalist' and Professional Poisoner," 1.

30. Ramsland, *The Human Predator*, 4.

31. Leon, *Outrageous Women of Ancient Times*, 16; Wamack, "Locusta of Gaul, Roman 'Herbalist' and Professional Poisoner," 1.

32. Wamack, "Locusta of Gaul, Roman 'Herbalist' and Professional Poisoner," 1.

33. Ramsland, *The Human Predator*, 5.

34. Ramsland, *The Human Predator*, 5; Leon, *Outrageous Women of Ancient Times*, 17.

35. Wamack, "Locusta of Gaul, Roman 'Herbalist' and Professional Poisoner," 2; Jones, *The Mammoth Book of Women Who Kill*, 11–12.

36. Leon, *Outrageous Women of Ancient Times*, 12; Wamack, "Locusta of Gaul, Roman 'Herbalist' and Professional Poisoner," 2.

37. Leon, *Outrageous Women of Ancient Times*, 12; Wallechinsky and Wallace, "About the Ancient Roman Poisoner Locusta," 1.

38. Leon, *Outrageous Women of Ancient Times*, 12; Wallechinsky and Wallace, "About the Ancient Roman Poisoner Locusta," 1.

39. Leon, *Outrageous Women of Ancient Times*, 12.

40. Wallechinsky and Wallace, "About the Ancient Roman Poisoner Locusta," 1.

41. Leon, *Outrageous Women of Ancient Times*, 12; Wallechinsky and Wallace, "About the Ancient Roman Poisoner Locusta," 1.

42. Newton, *The Encyclopedia of Serial Killers*, 140.

43. Ramsland, *The Human Predator*, 4.

44. Schechter, *The Serial Killer Files*, 130.

45. Ramsland, *The Human Predator*, 4; Newton, *The Encyclopedia of Serial Killers*, 140.

46. Klein, *The Most Evil Women in History*, 53; Wamack, "Locusta of Gaul, Roman 'Herbalist' and Professional Poisoner," 1.

47. Schechter, *The Serial Killer Files*, 130; Ramsland, *The Human Predator*, 5.

48. Newton, *The Encyclopedia of Serial Killers*, 140; Ramsland, *The Human Predator*, 4.

49. Leon, *Outrageous Women of Ancient Times*, 14; Ramsland, *The Human Predator*, 4.

50. Ramsland, "The Poisoners," 1.

51. Perry, "A Summarized History of Forensic Science," 1.

52. Perry, "A Summarized History of Forensic Science," 1.

53. Jones, *The Mammoth Book of Women Who Kill*, 9; Newton, *The Encyclopedia of Serial Killers*, 140; Wamack, "Locusta of Gaul, Roman 'Herbalist' and Professional Poisoner," 1.

54. Leon, *Outrageous Women of Ancient Times*, 14.

55. Ramsland, *The Human Predator*, 4.

56. Leon, *Outrageous Women of Ancient Times*, 14.

57. Schechter, *The Serial Killer Files*, 130; Newton, *The Encyclopedia of Serial Killers*, 140; Wallechinsky and Wallace, "About the Ancient Roman Poisoner Locusta," 1.

58. Jones, *The Mammoth Book of Women Who Kill*, 9; Klein, *The Most Evil Women in History*, 53.

59. Wamack, "Locusta of Gaul, Roman 'Herbalist' and Professional Poisoner," 2; Ramsland, *The Human Predator*, 4.

60. Leon, *Outrageous Women of Ancient Times*, 14; Wamack, "Locusta of Gaul, Roman 'Herbalist' and Professional Poisoner," 2.

61. Ramsland, *The Human Predator*, 5–6; Wamack, "Locusta of Gaul, Roman 'Herbalist' and Professional Poisoner," 2; Leon, *Outrageous Women of Ancient Times*, 19.

62. Wallechinsky and Wallace, "About the Ancient Roman Poisoner Locusta," 1–2.

63. Newton, *The Encyclopedia of Serial Killers*, 140.

64. Newton, *The Encyclopedia of Serial Killers*, 140.

65. Newton, *The Encyclopedia of Serial Killers*, 140; Ramsland, *The Human Predator*, 5–6.

66. Perry, "A Summarized History of Forensic Science," 1; Newton, *The Encyclopedia of Serial Killers*, 140.

CHAPTER FOURTEEN: LA TOFANIA

1. Richard Glyn Jones, *The Mammoth Book of Women Who Kill* (New York: Carroll & Graf, 2002), 413; D. M. Gibson, "The Killer That Cures," *Health and Homeopathy*, Spring 2002, 2; Montague Summers, *Witchcraft and Black Magic* (London: Rider & Co., 1946), 202.

2. Harold Schechter, *The Serial Killer Files* (New York: Ballantine Books, 2003), 137.

3. Kerry Seagrave, *Women Serial and Mass Murderers: A Worldwide Reference, 1580 through 1990* (Jefferson, NC: McFarland, 1992), 282.

4. Jones, *The Mammoth Book of Women Who Kill*, 414.

5. Seagrave, *Women Serial and Mass Murderers*, 282; Katherine Ramsland, *The Human Predator: A Historical Chronicle of Serial Murder and Forensic Investigation* (New York: Berkley Books, 2005), 32.

6. Pompa Bannerjee, "Hard to Swallow: Women Poisoners and Hindu Widowburning," *Continuity and Change* 15, no. 2 (2000): 187–207.

7. Theodoric Romeyn Beck and William Dunlop, *Elements of Medical Jurisprudence* (Dublin: John Anderson Medical Bookseller, 1825), 362.

8. BBC, "Infamous Historical Poisoners," July 15, 2005, retrieved May 22, 2010, from http://www.bbc.co.uk/dna/h2g2/A4197585, 1.

9. J. W. Wainwright, "Secret Poisons and Their Uses," *Medical Record* 64 (August 22, 1903): 287.

10. Seagrave, *Women Serial and Mass Murderers*, 282.

11. "Poisoning in Italy," *London Magazine* 8 (1902): 548.

12. William Chambers and Robert Chambers, *Chamber's Edinburgh Journal* 1 (1883): 416.

13. Wainwright, "Secret Poisons"Secret Poisons and Their Uses," 288.

14. Wainwright, "Secret Poisons and Their Uses," 288.

15. Bannerjee, "Hard to Swallow," 187–207; University of Calcutta, *Calcutta Review* 88–89 (1889): 86.

16. Peter Vronsky, *Female Serial Killers: How and Why Women Become Monsters* (New York: Berkley Books, 2007), 93; Seagrave, *Women Serial and Mass Murderers*, 282; Wainwright, "Secret Poisons and Their Uses," 287.

17. Jones, *The Mammoth Book of Women Who Kill*, 413.

18. Seagrave, *Women Serial and Mass Murderers*, 282.

19. Chambers and Chambers, *Edinburgh Journal*, 41; Schechter, *The Serial Killer Files*, 137; Jones, *The Mammoth Book of Women Who Kill*, 414.

20. Schechter, *The Serial Killer Files*, 137.

21. Jones, *The Mammoth Book of Women Who Kill*, 413.

22. Seagrave, *Women Serial and Mass Murderers*, 283.

23. "Slow and Secret Poisoning," *The Cincinnati Lancet and Clinic* 55 (1835): 76.

24. BBC, "Infamous Historical Poisoners," 2; "Slow and Secret Poisoning," 76; University of Calcutta, *Calcutta Review*, 86.

25. Wainwright, "Secret Poisons and Their Uses," 287.

26. Jones, *The Mammoth Book of Women Who Kill*, 414.

27. Vronsky, *Female Serial Killers*, 93–94.

28. BBC, "Infamous Historical Poisoners," 1; Jones, *The Mammoth Book of Women Who Kill*, 41; Seagrave, *Women Serial and Mass Murderers*, 282.

29. BBC, "Infamous Historical Poisoners," 1.

30. Vronsky, *Female Serial Killers*, 94.

31. Ramsland, *The Human Predator*, 32; Gibson, "The Killer That Cures," 2.

32. Chambers and Chambers, *Edinburgh Journal*, 416.

33. "Slow and Secret Poisoning," 76; Wainwright, "Secret Poisons and Their Uses," 278; Jones, *The Mammoth Book of Women Who Kill*, 414.

34. Beck and Dunlop, *Elements of Medical Jurisprudence*, 362; "Slow and Secret Poisoning," 76; Chambers and Chambers, *Edinburgh Journal*, 416.

35. Jones, *The Mammoth Book of Women Who Kill*, 414.

36. Jones, *The Mammoth Book of Women Who Kill*, 415–16.

37. Gibson, "The Killer That Cures," 2; Seagrave, *Women Serial and Mass Murderers*, 282.

38. Ramsland, *The Human Predator*, 32; Schechter, *The Serial Killer Files*, 137.

39. Seagrave, *Women Serial and Mass Murderers*, 283.

40. Vronsky, *Female Serial Killers*, 94; Seagrave, *Women Serial and Mass Murderers*, 282.

41. Jones, *The Mammoth Book of Women Who Kill*, 414.

42. Jones, *The Mammoth Book of Women Who Kill*, 414; Vronsky, *Female Serial Killers*, 93; Ramsland, *The Human Predator*, 32; BBC, "Infamous Historical Poisoners," 2; Schechter, *The Serial Killer Files*, 137; and Seagrave, *Women Serial and Mass Murderers*, 283.

43. Bannerjee, "Hard to Swallow," 187–207.

44. BBC, "Infamous Historical Poisoners," 2; Gibson, "The Killer That Cures," 2; Jones, *The Mammoth Book of Women Who Kill*, 413; Vronsky, *Female Serial Killers*, 93; Seagrave, *Women Serial and Mass Murderers*, 282.

45. Gibson, "The Killer That Cures," 2; Seagrave, *Women Serial and Mass Murderers*, 282.

46. Gibson, "The Killer That Cures," 2.

47. Schechter, *The Serial Killer Files*, 137.

48. Jones, *The Mammoth Book of Women Who Kill*, 414.

49. "Slow and Secret Poisoning," 76; University of Calcutta, *Calcutta Review*, 86; Gibson, "The Killer That Cures," 2; BBC, "Infamous Historical Poisoners," 2; Seagrave, *Women Serial and Mass Murderers*, 282.

50. Ramsland, *The Human Predator*, 32.

51. Seagrave, *Women Serial and Mass Murderers*, 282; Gibson, "The Killer That Cures," 2.

52. Ramsland, *The Human Predator*, 32; Vronsky, *Female Serial Killers*, 93–94; Schechter, *The Serial Killer Files*, 137.

53. Schechter, *The Serial Killer Files*, 137.

54. Wainwright, "Secret Poisons and Their Uses," 287.

55. Jones, *The Mammoth Book of Women Who Kill*, 413; Schechter, *The Serial Killer Files*, 137; University of Calcutta, *Calcutta Review*, 87.

56. Seagrave, *Women Serial and Mass Murderers*, 282; Gibson, "The Killer That Cures," 2.

57. Seagrave, *Women Serial and Mass Murderers*, 283; BBC, "Infamous Historical Poisoners," 2.

58. Jones, *The Mammoth Book of Women Who Kill*, 414; BBC, "Infamous Historical Poisoners," 2.

59. Seagrave, *Women Serial and Mass Murderers*, 283; Schechter, *The Serial Killer Files*, 137.

60. BBC, "Infamous Historical Poisoners," 2; Vronsky, *Female Serial Killers*, 94; Schechter, *The Serial Killer Files*, 137; and Seagrave, *Women Serial and Mass Murderers*, 283.

61. Jones, *The Mammoth Book of Women Who Kill*, 414.

62. Jones, *The Mammoth Book of Women Who Kill*, 415; Seagrave, *Women Serial and Mass Murderers*, 283; BBC, "Infamous Historical Poisoners," 1; Vronsky, *Female Serial Killers*, 94.

63. Seagrave, *Women Serial and Mass Murderers*, 283.

64. Jones, *The Mammoth Book of Women Who Kill*, 414; Seagrave, *Women Serial and Mass Murderers*, 283.

65. BBC, "Infamous Historical Poisoners," 2; Ramsland, *The Human Predator*, 32; Vronsky, *Female Serial Killers*, 94; Jones, *The Mammoth Book of Women Who Kill*, 415.

66. Seagrave, *Women Serial and Mass Murderers*, 283.

67. Schechter, *The Serial Killer Files*, 137.

68. Chambers and Chambers, *Edinburgh Journal*, 416.

69. Vronsky, *Female Serial Killers*, 94; BBC, "Infamous Historical Poisoners," 2; Jones, *The Mammoth Book of Women Who Kill*, 415; Seagrave; *Women Serial and Mass Murderers*, 283; Schechter, *The Serial Killer Files*, 137.

CHAPTER FIFTEEN: ANDREAS BICHEL

1. William Westall, "A Precedent for the Whitechapel Murder," *Pall Mall Gazette*, September 7, 1888, 1; Katherine Ramsland, *The Human Predator: A Historical Chronicle of Serial Murder and Forensic Investigation* (New York: Berkley Books, 2005), 39.

2. Ramsland, *The Human Predator*, 39.

3. L. T. Woodward, *Sadism: A Documented Study of the Strange Ecstasies That Some Human Beings Find in the Infliction of Pain: Those Sexy Vintage Sleaze Books: A Blog about Vintage Soft Core Paperbacks* (New York: A Lancer Special), 74– 835; David Everitt, *Human Monsters: An Illustrated Encyclopedia of the World's Most Vicious Murderers* (Chicago: Contemporary Books, 1993), 23.

4. *Washington Post*, "Criminals Who Revel in Torture Are Fit Subjects for the Surgeon," March 24, 1907, 1.

5. Everitt, *Human Monsters*, 23.

6. Ramsland, *The Human Predator*, 39.

7. Richard Krafft-Ebing, *Psychopathia Sexualis, with Especial Reference to the Antipathic Sexual Instinct: A Medico-Forensic Study* (London: Stationer's Hall, 1886), 88.

8. Everitt, *Human Monsters*, 21.

9. Paul Johann Anselm Feuerbach, *Andreas Bichel, der Madchenschlachter* (Giessen: Merk, 1811), 3–30; Westall, "A Precedent for the Whitechapel Murder," 1.

10. Everitt, *Human Monsters*, 21; Westall, "A Precedent for the Whitechapel Murder," 1.

11. Westall, "A Precedent for the Whitechapel Murder," 1.

12. Everitt, *Human Monsters*, 21; Westall, "A Precedent for the Whitechapel Murder," 1.

13. Everitt, *Human Monsters*, 21.

14. Westall, "A Precedent for the Whitechapel Murder," 1.

15. Feuerbach, *Andreas Bichel, der Madchenschlachter*, 3–30.

16. Dan Norder, Wolf Vanderlinden, and Paul Begg, *Ripper Notes: Madmen, Myths and Magic*, October, 2004, 17.

17. Wade C. Myers, David S. Husted, Mark E. Safarik, and Mary Ellen O'Toole, "The Motivations behind Serial Sexual Homicide: Is It Sex, Power, Control or Anger?," *Journal of Forensic Sciences* 51, no, 4 (July 2006): 900–907.

18. Peter Vronsky, *Serial Killers: The Method and the Madness* (New York: Berkley Books, 2004), 57.

19. Eric Hickey, *Serial Murderers and Their Victims* (Belmont, CA: Wadsworth, 1997), 248.

20. Everitt, *Human Monsters*, 21.

21. Amanda Howard, "Sex or No Sex: Was Jack the Ripper a Sexual Serial Killer?," 2010, retrieved November 5, 2010, from http://www.amandahoward .com.au/sex_or_no_sex.htm, 1.

22. Amanda Howard, "Jack the Ripper: Not the First," March 29, 2009, retrieved November 28, 2009, from http://www.amandahoward.com.au/not_the _first.htm, 2.

23. Myers et al., "The Motivations behind Serial Sexual Homicide," 900–907.

24. *Evening News*, "A Theory of the Whitechapel Murders," October 15, 1888, 1; Howard, "Jack the Ripper," 2; Norder et al., *Ripper Notes*, 17.

25. Westall, "A Precedent for the Whitechapel Murder," 1; Howard, "Sex or No Sex," 1.

26. Howard, "Sex or No Sex," 1; Howard, "Jack the Ripper," 2.

27. *Evening News*, "A Theory of the Whitechapel Murders," 1.

28. Westall, "A Precedent for the Whitechapel Murder," 1.

29. Myers et al., "The Motivations behind Serial Sexual Homicide,"900–907; *Evening News*, "A Theory of the Whitechapel Murders," 1.

30. Howard, "Jack the Ripper," 2; Howard, "Sex or No Sex," 1.

31. Westall, "A Precedent for the Whitechapel Murder," 1.

32. Sabine Baring-Gould, *The Book of Werewolves* (London: Smith, Elder & Co., 1865), 134; Vronsky, *Serial Killers*, 57; Westall, "A Precedent for the White-chapel Murder," 1; Howard, "Sex or No Sex," 1.

33. Baring-Gould, *The Book of Werewolves*, 134.

34. Westall, "A Precedent for the Whitechapel Murder," 1.

35. Baring-Gould, *The Book of Werewolves*, 134.

36. Woodward, *Sadism*, 1; *Evening News*, "A Theory of the Whitechapel Murders," 1; and *Washington Post*, "Criminals Who Revel in Torture Are Fit Subjects for the Surgeon," 1.

37. Everitt, *Human Monsters*, 23; Hickey, *Serial Murderers and Their Victims*, 248.

38. Everitt, *Human Monsters*, 22.

39. Myers et al., "The Motivations behind Serial Sexual Homicide,"900-907; Norder et al., *Ripper Notes*, 17; Howard, "Sex or No Sex," 1.

40. Westall, "A Precedent for the Whitechapel Murder," 1; Ramsland, *The Human Predator*, 39; Hickey, *Serial Murderers and Their Victims*, 248.

41. Everitt, *Human Monsters*, 22; Westall, "A Precedent for the Whitechapel Murder," 1; Ramsland, *The Human Predator*, 39.

42. Ramsland, *The Human Predator*, 39; Everitt, *Human Monsters*, 22.

43. Westall, "A Precedent for the Whitechapel Murder," 1.

44. Westall, "A Precedent for the Whitechapel Murder," 1.

45. Baring-Gould, *The Book of Werewolves*, 134; Everitt, *Human Monsters*, 22.

46. Everitt, *Human Monsters*, 22; Westall, "A Precedent for the Whitechapel Murder," 1.

47. Norder et al., *Ripper Notes*, 17.

48. Howard, "Sex or No Sex," 1.

49. Westall, "A Precedent for the Whitechapel Murder," 1.

50. Vronsky, *Serial Killers*, 57; Krafft-Ebing, *Psychopathia Sexualis*, 88; Westall, "A Precedent for the Whitechapel Murder," 1.

51. Peter Becker and Richard F. Wetzell, *International Criminals and Their Scientists: The History of Criminology* (London: Cambridge University Press, 2006), 125; Baring-Gould, *The Book of Werewolves*, 13.

52. Ramsland, *The Human Predator*, 39; Everitt, *Human Monsters*, 23; Westall, "A Precedent for the Whitechapel Murder," 1.

53. Becker and Wetzell, *International Criminals and Their Scientists*, 125; Westall, "A Precedent for the Whitechapel Murder," 1.

54. Becker and Wetzell, *International Criminals and Their Scientists*, 125; Westall, "A Precedent for the Whitechapel Murder," 1.

55. Ramsland, *The Human Predator*, 39; Westall, "A Precedent for the Whitechapel Murder," 1.

56. Westall, "A Precedent for the Whitechapel Murder," 1.

57. Ramsland, *The Human Predator*, 39.

58. Everitt, *Human Monsters*, 22–23.

59. Everitt, *Human Monsters*, 23.

60. Everitt, *Human Monsters*, 23; Westall, "A Precedent for the Whitechapel Murder," 1.

61. Everitt, *Human Monsters*, 23; Westall, "A Precedent for the Whitechapel Murder," 1.

62. Westall, "A Precedent for the Whitechapel Murder," 1; Vronsky, *Serial Killers*, 57; *Washington Post*, "Criminals Who Revel in Torture Are Fit Subjects for the Surgeon," 1.

63. Ramsland, *The Human Predator*, 39.

64. Everitt, *Human Monsters*, 23.

65. Ramsland, *The Human Predator*, 39; Westall, "A Precedent for the Whitechapel Murder," 1.

66. Baring-Gould, *The Book of Werewolves*, 134; Krafft-Ebing, *Psychopathia Sexualis*, 88.

67. Ramsland, *The Human Predator*, 39; Everitt, *Human Monsters*, 23.

68. Everitt, *Human Monsters*, 24.

69. Westall, "A Precedent for the Whitechapel Murder," 1.

BIBLIOGRAPHY

BOOKS

Baring-Gould, Sabine. *The Book of Werewolves*. London: Smith, Elder & Co., 1865.

Caputi, Jane. *The Age of Sex Crime*. Bowling Green, KY: Bowling Green State University Press, 1987.

Cawthorne, Nigel. *Black Magic Killers: Real-Life Accounts of Satanic Murderers*. London: Magpie Books, 2008.

Demos, John. *The Enemy Within: 200 Years of Witch Hunting*. New York: Viking Press, 2008.

Everitt, David. *Human Monsters: An Illustrated Encyclopedia of the World's Most Vicious Murderers*. Chicago: Contemporary Books, 1993.

Gibson, Dirk C. *Serial Killing for Profit: Multiple Murder for Money*. Santa Barbara, CA: Praeger, 2009.

Jones, Richard Glyn. *The Mammoth Book of Women Who Kill*. New York: Carroll & Graf, 2002.

Krafft-Ebing, Richard. *Psychopathia Sexualis, with Especial Reference to the Antipathic Sexual Instinct: A Medico-Forensic Study*. London: Stationer's Hall, 1886.

Lane, Brian, and Wilfred Gregg. *The Encyclopedia of Serial Killers*. New York: Berkley Books, 1995.

Leon, Vicki. *Outrageous Women of Ancient Times*. New York: John Wiley & Sons, 1998.

Meltzer, Milton. *Witches and Witch-Hunts: A History of Persecution*. New York: Blue Sky Press, 2006.

Morrison, Helen, and Harold Goldberg. *My Life among the Serial Killers*. New York: William Morrow, 2004.

Newton, Michael. *Hunting Humans: An Encyclopedia of Modern Serial Killers*. New York: Avon Books, 1990.

Newton, Michael. *The Encyclopedia of Serial Killers*. New York: Checkmark Books, 2000.

Odell, Robin, and Wilfred Gregg. *Murderers' Row: An International Murderers' Who's Who*. London: Sutton Publishing, 2006.

Ramsland, Katherine. *The Human Predator: A Historical Chronicle of Serial Murder and Forensic Investigation*. New York: Berkley Books, 2005.

Robbins, Rossell. *The Encyclopedia of Witchcraft and Demonology*. New York: Crown Publishers, 1959.

Schechter, Harold. *The Serial Killer Files*. New York: Ballantine Books, 2003

Seagrave, Kerry. *Women Serial and Mass Murderers: A Worldwide Reference, 1580 through 1990*. Jefferson, NC: McFarland, 1992.

Sidky, Homayun. *Witchcraft, Lycanthropy, Drugs and Disease*. Eugene, OR: Wipf & Stock, 1997.

Vronsky, Peter. *Serial Killers: The Method and Madness of Monsters*. New York: Berkley Books, 2004.

Wilson, Colin, and Donald Seaman. *Serial Killers: A Study in the Psychology of Violence*. New York: Carol Publishing Group, 1992.

SCHOLARLY PERIODICALS

Bannerjee, Pompa. "Hard to Swallow: Women Poisoners and Hindu Widowburning," *Continuity and Change* 15, no. 2 (2000).

Canter, David, Christopher Missen, and Samantha Hodge. "Are Serial Killers Special? A Case for Special Agents." *Policing Today* 2, no. 1 (April 1996).

Carroll, David. "This Man Belongs to Me: The Life and Deaths of Vlad the Impaler." *Tabula Rasa* (2010). Retrieved October 21, 2010, from http://www.tabula-rasa.info/DarkAges/VladTheImpaler.html.

Cilliers, L., and F. P. Retief. "Poisons, Poisoning and the Drug Trade in Ancient Rome." *Akoterion* 45 (2000).

McLean, Allison. "110 Years Ago Sobby Boxers." *Smithsonian.com*. (June 2010).

Myers, Wade C., David S. Husted, Mark E. Safarik, and Mary O'Toole. "The Motivations behind Serial Sexual Homicide: Is It Sex, Power, Control or Anger?" *Journal of Forensic Sciences* 51, no. 4 (July 2006).

Smith, Timothy B. "Assistance and Repression: Rural Exodus, Vagabondage and Social Crisis in France, 1880–1914." *Journal of Social History* (Summer 1999).

Stone, Michael H. "Serial Sexual Homicide: Biological, Psychological, and Sociological Aspects." *Journal of Personality Disorders* 15, no. 1 (February 2001).

Wainwright, J. W. "Secret Poisons and Their Uses." *Medical Record* 64 (August 22, 1903).

POPULAR PERIODICALS

Fiske, John. "Werewolves & Swan-Maidens: The Mediaeval Belief in Werewolves is Especially Adapted to Illustrate the Complicated Manner in which Divers Mythical Conceptions & Misunderstood Natural Occurrences Will Combine to Generate a Long-Enduring Superstition." *Atlantic Monthly* (August 1871).

"French 'Ripper' Guillotined. Joseph Vacher, Who Murdered More Than a Score of Persons, Executed at Bourg-en-Bresse." *New York Times* (January 1, 1899).

"The Mystery of Whitechapel, Him or Her? Dark Conjectures." *El Universal* (November 5, 1889). Retrieved May 22, 2010, from http://www.casebook.org/ forum/messages/4927/7365.html.

INTERNET RESOURCES

Black History Pages. "Queen Nzinga (1583–1663)" (1996–2008). Retrieved May 3, 2010, from http://blackhistorypages.net/pages/nzinga.php.

British Broadcasting Corporation. "Infamous Historical Poisoners" (July 15, 2005). Retrieved May 22, 2010, from http://www.bbc.co.uk/dna/h2g2/A419785.

Brittanica Online Encyclopedia. "Gilles de Rais" (2010). Retrieved October 15, 2010, from http://www.brittanica.com/EBchecked/topic/489979/Gilles-de-Rais.

Chinapage.com. "The Dowager Empress Cixi (Tzu Hsi)" (N.d.). Retrieved May 3, 2010, from http://www.chinapage.com/biography/cixi.html.

Elizabethan Era. "Elizabeth Bathory" (2009). Retrieved November 28, 2009, from http://www.elizabethan-era.org.uk/elizabethan-bathory.html.

Encyclopedia of World Biography. "Anna Nzinga Biography" (2005–2006). Retrieved May 3, 2010, from http://www.bookrags.com/biography/anna-nzinga.

Encyclopedia.com. "Anna Nzinga" (2004). Retrieved October 25, 2010, from http:// www.encyclopedia.com/doc/1G2-3404708259.html.

ExecutedToday.com. "1898: Joseph Vacher" (2010). Retrieved May 21, 2010, from http://www.executedtoday.com/2007/12/31/1898-joseph-vacher.

ExecutedToday.com. "1589: Peter Stubbe, Sybil Stubbe and Katharina Trump" (October 31, 2007). Retrieved May 20, 2010, from http://www.executedtoday.com/ 2007/10/31/1589-peter-stubbe-sybil-stubbe-katharina.

Gambit, Joseph. "A Philosophical Exploration: Are Dragons Real?" *Ezine Articles* (January 15, 2009). Retrieved December 1, 2009, from http://ezine articles.com/?A-Philosophical-Exploration—Are.

Geringer, Joseph. "Man More Than Myth." In "Vlad the Impaler." *Crime Library* (201)0. Retrieved October 21, 2010, from http://www.trutv.com/library/ crime/serial_killers/history/vlad/index.

Gilroy, Thomas J. "Tz'u-hsi or Cixi: The Dowager Empress of China" (November 9, 2004). Retrieved May 3, 2010, from http://departments.kings.edu/womens _history/tzuhsi.html.

Gribben, Mark. "Black Magic." In "Gilles De Rais." *Crime Library* (2010). Retrieved October 15, 2010, from http://www.trutv.com/library/crime/serial_killers/ predators/rais/ma.

Howard, Amanda. "Jack the Ripper: Not the First" (March 29, 2009). Retrieved November 28, 2009, from http://www.amandahoward.com.au/not_the _first.htm.

Metropolitan Museum of Art. Heilbruner Timeline of Art History. "Ann Nzinga: Queen of Ndongo" (2010). Retrieved October 25, 2010, from http://www .metmusem.org/toah/hd/pwmn_2/hd_pwmn_2.htm.

Noe, Denise. "Elizabeth Bathory, 'The Blood Countess'" (2010). Retrieved November 28, 2009, from http://www.francesfarmersrevenge.com/stuff/serialkillers/ bathory.htm.

Owens, Kevin. "Dragons across Cultures." *Dragonika* (2000–2009). Retrieved December 1, 2009, from http://www.dragonika.com/culture.php.

Ramsland, Katherine. "The Poisoners." In "Forensic Toxicology." *Crime Library* (2008). Retrieved February 11, 2009, from http://wwwtrutv.com/library/crime/criminal_mind/forensics/toxicology/5.html?sect=21.

Ramsland, Katherine. "For the Record." In "Lady of Blood: Countess Bathory." *Crime Library* (2009). Retrieved November 28, 2009, from http://www.trutv.com/library/crime/serial_killers/predators/bathory.

The Rise of Satanism in the Middle Ages Forum. "Catherine Montvoison" (2008). Retrieved May 22, 2010, from http://www.unexplainedstuff.com/Religious-Phenomenon/The-Rise-of-Satanism.

Rodriguez, David. "Erzebet Bathory" (April 5, 2009). Retrieved November 28, 2009, from http://www.departments.kings.edu/womens_history/erzebet.html.

Sleman, Tom. "Werewolves." *BBC* (December 2, 2009). Retrieved November 15, 2010, from http://www.bbc.co.uk/wales/northeast/guides/weird/mythsand legends.

Toxipedia. "Catherine Deshayes Monvoison" (N.d.). Retrieved May 22, 2010, from http://toxipedia.org/display/toxipedia/Catherine+Deshayes+Monvoison.

Wamack, Anne. "Locusta of Gaul, Roman 'Herbalist' and Professional Poisoner." *History'sWomen.com* (2009). Retrieved February 11, 2009, from http://www.historyswomen.com/moregreatwomen/Locusta.html.

INDEX

ABOUT THE AUTHOR

DIRK C. GIBSON is an associate professor of communication and journalism at the University of New Mexico. Recent related publications include *Serial Killing for Profit* (2009), *Serial Murder and Media Circuses* (2006), and *Clues from Killers: Serial Murder and Crime Scene Messages* (2004), all published by Praeger.